X.media.publishing

Springer
Berlin
Heidelberg
New York
Hong Kong
London
Milan
Paris
Tokyo

Ralf Steinmetz   Klara Nahrstedt

Multimedia Applications

With 77 Figures

 Springer

Ralf Steinmetz
Technische Universität Darmstadt
KOM
Merckstr. 25
64238 Darmstadt, Germany
ralf.steinmetz@kom.tu-darmstadt.de

Klara Nahrstedt
University of Illinois
Department of Computer Science
1304 West Springfield Avenue
Urbana, IL 61801
klara@cs.uiuc.edu

ISSN 1612-1449

ISBN 3-540-40849-5 Springer-Verlag Berlin Heidelberg New York

Library of Congress Cataloging-in-Publication-Data applied for

Bibliographic information published by Die Deutsche Bibliothek
Die Deutsche Bibliothek lists this publication in the Deutsche
Nationalbibliografie; detailed bibliographic data is available in the
Internet at <http://dnb.ddb.de>.

Springer-Verlag is a part of Springer Science+Business Media
springeronline.com

© Springer-Verlag Berlin Heidelberg 2004
Printed in Germany

Cover design: KünkelLopka, Heidelberg
Typesetting: Camera-ready by the authors
Printed on acid-free paper   33/3142GF – 543210

Preface

Multimedia Applications and Systems are an increasingly common part of our everyday lives—emerging mobile terminals which can display pictures and video data, DVD players in the home, downloadable games, streaming in the Internet, radio stations on the World Wide Web—are just a few examples. These applications and systems are becoming an integral part of our heterogeneous computing and communication environment. Over the last decade, we have experienced an explosive growth of multimedia computing, communication, and applications (World Wide Web, conferencing, digital entertainment, etc.) which provide not just text and images but also video, audio, and other continuous media. In the future, all computers and networks will contain multimedia devices. They will also require appropriate processing and communication support to provide seamless and ubiquitous services for the relevant multimedia applications.

This book is one of three closely related volumes which aim to cover the whole area of multimedia technology and its applications: The first volume (*Ralf Steinmetz, Klara Nahrstedt, "Multimedia Fundamentals Volume 1: Media Coding and Content Processing", Prentice-Hall, 2002*) deals mainly with the fundamentals of media per se, and covers media-specific considerations such as individual media characteristics, media processing, and optical storage, content analysis, and processing. It includes coding, compression, and a detailed discussion of optical storage. The second volume (*Ralf Steinmetz, Klara Nahrstedt, "Multimedia Systems", Springer-Verlag, 2004*) focusses on issues intrinsic to systems: basic characteristics of multimedia operating systems, multimedia networking and communication, and multimedia middleware systems. Taken together, our three books are intended to be the standard reference books on "multimedia fundamentals".

Do the volumes published to date contain information which readers might need to make the most out of reading this book?

The present book can be read (and understood) without detailed knowledge of media coding and content processing. However, a basic grasp of the notion of compression would certainly be useful (but is not necessary). With respect to multimedia system issues, some knowledge about the concept of quality of service, as well as about basic system issues, would be extremely helpful. To some extent, such knowledge is required in order to understand many specific issues of multimedia applications, such as synchronization, group communications, databases, and programming.

In this book, we emphasize the field of multimedia applications, together with some services. Chapters 2 to 5 relate to more generic service issues: In Chapter 2 we present issues related to generic multimedia database management systems. Chapter 3 describes programming issues at different levels of abstraction. It also covers some object-based and object-oriented approaches, such as DSM-CC and DAVIC. Chapter 4 concentrates on security issues, with the focus on watermarking. Chapter 5 goes into some detail about documents and hypertext. Chapters 6 through 9 cover more dedicated, application-related issues. Chapter 6 outlines details of media design, while Chapter 7 deals with general user-interface topics. In Chapter 8, we present some issues relevant for multimedia learning, and Chapter 9 covers various possible applications and presents a detailed case study.

Overall, the book covers a wide scope, due to its intended purpose of serving as a reference. It evolved from the third edition of our book on multimedia technology, published in German in 2000 [Ste00]. (Figures from this book have been reused with the permission of Springer-Verlag). However, several sections of the English text depart from the corresponding material in the German edition. The present volume can be used by computer professionals who are interested in multimedia systems, or by instructors as a textbook for introductory multimedia courses in computer science and related disciplines.

To help instructors use this book, additional material is available on our Web site: `http://www.kom.tu-darmstadt.de/mm-book/`. Please enter `mm_book` and `mm_docs` for user name and password, respectively.

Many people have helped us to prepare this book: R. Ackermann, M. Bräuer, D. Dimitriu, J. Dittmann, A. El Saddik, M. Farber, S. Fischer, J. Geißler, N. Georganas, C. Griwodz, T. Hollmer, T. Kamps, T. Kunkelmann, A. Mauthe, A. Meissner, K. Reichenberger, J. Schmitt, K. Schork-Jakobi, C. Seeberg, A. Steinacker, N. Streitz, P. Tandler, H. Thimm, D. Tietze, M. Wessner, L. Wolf. Thank you!

However, we would especially like to thank Ivica Rimac for his outstanding dedication to this project.

Last but not least, we would like to thank our families for their support, love, and patience.

Ralf Steinmetz
Darmstadt, Germany
www.kom.tu-darmstadt.de

Klara Nahrstedt
Urbana, IL, USA
cairo.cs.uiuc.edu

Contents

CHAPTER 1

Introduction

Multimedia is probably one of the most overused terms of the 90s (for example, see [Sch97]). The field is at the crossroads of several major industries: computing, telecommunications, publishing, consumer audio-video electronics, and television/movie/broadcasting. Multimedia not only brings new industrial players to the game, but adds a new dimension to the potential market. For example, while computer networking was essentially targeting a professional market, multimedia embraces both the commercial and the consumer segments. Thus, the telecommunications market involved is not only that of professional or industrial networks—such as medium- or high-speed leased circuits or corporate data networks—but also includes standard telephony or low-speed ISDN and DSL. Similarly, not only the segment of professional audio-video is concerned, but also the consumer audio-video market, and the associated TV, movie, and broadcasting sectors.

As a result, it is no surprise when discussing and establishing multimedia as a discipline to find difficulties in avoiding fuzziness in scope, multiplicity of definitions, and non-stabilized terminology. When most people refer to multimedia, they generally mean the combination of two or more continuous media, that is, media that have to be played during some well-defined time interval, usually with some user interaction. In practice, the two media are normally audio and video, that is, sound plus moving pictures.

One of the first and best known institutes that has studied multimedia is the Massachusetts Institute of Technology (MIT) Media Lab in Boston, Massachusetts. They have been conducting research work in a wide variety of innovative applications, including personalized newspapers, life-sized holograms, or telephones that chat with callers [Bra87]. Today, many universities, large-scale research institutes, and industrial organizations work on multimedia projects.

From the user's perspective, "multimedia" means that information can be represented in the form of audio signals or moving pictures. For example, movement sequences in sports events [Per97] or an ornithological lexicon can be illustrated much better with multimedia compared to text and still images only, because it can represent the topics in a more natural way.

Integrating all of these media in a computer allows the use of existing computing power to represent information interactively. Then this data can be transmitted over computer networks. The results have implications in the areas of information distribution and cooperative work. Multimedia enables a wide range of new applications, many of which are still in the experimental phase. Please remember that the World Wide Web (WWW) took its current form only at the beginning of the 90s. On the other hand, social implications inherent in global communication should not be overlooked. When analyzing such a broad field as multimedia from a scientific angle, it is difficult to avoid reflections on the effects of these new technologies on society as a whole. However, the sociological implications of multimedia are not the subject of this book. We are essentially interested in the technical aspects of multimedia.

1.1 Interdisciplinary Aspects of Multimedia

If we look at applications and technologies, there is a strong interest in existing multimedia systems and their constant enhancement. The process of change that takes place in the background in various industrial sectors should not be underestimated:

- The telecommunications industry used to be interested primarily in telephony. Today, telephone networks evolve increasingly into digital networks that are very similar to computer networks. Switching systems used to be made up of mechanical rotary switches. Today, they are computers. Conventional telephones have been evolving into computers, or they even exist as pure software in the form of "IP telephony."

- The consumer electronics industry—with its "brown ware"—contributed considerably to bringing down the price of video technology that is used in computers. Optical storage technology, for example, emerged from the success of CD players. Today, many manufacturers produce CD drives for computers and hi-fi equipment or television sets and computer screens.

- The TV and radio broadcasting sector has been a pioneer in professional audio-video technology. Professional systems for digital cutting of TV movies are commercially available today. Some of these systems are simple standard computers equipped with special add-on boards. Broadcasters now transmit their information over cables so it is only natural that they will continue to become information vendors over computer networks in the future.

- Most publishing companies offer publications in electronic form. In addition, many are closely related to movie companies. These two industries have become increasingly active as vendors of multimedia information.

This short list shows that various industries merge to form interdisciplinary vendors of multimedia information.

Many hardware and software components in computers have to be properly modified, expanded, or replaced to support multimedia applications. Considering that the performance of processors increases constantly, storage media have sufficient capacities, and communication systems offer increasingly better quality, the overall functionality shifts more and more from hardware to software. From a technical viewpoint, the time restrictions in data processing imposed on all components represent one of the most important challenges. Real-time systems are expected to work within well-defined time limits to form fault-tolerant systems, while conventional data processing attempts to do its job as fast as possible.

For multimedia applications, fault tolerance and speed are the most critical aspects because they use both conventional media and audio-video media. The conventional data (e.g., control information, metadata) must be delivered in a reliable fashion in order to assist audio-video data. The data of both media classes needs to get from the source to the destination as fast as possible, i.e., within a well-defined time limit. However, in contrast to real-time systems and conventional data processing, the elements of a multimedia application are not independent from one another. In other words, they must be integrated and synchronized. This means that in addition to being an integrated system, composed of various components from both data types, there has to be some form of synchronization between these media.

Our goal is to present the multimedia application and systems from an integrated and global perspective. However, as outlined above, multimedia applications and systems include many areas, hence we have decided to split the content about multimedia system fundamentals into three books. The first book deals with media coding and content processing (*Ralf Steinmetz, Klara Nahrstedt, "Media Coding and Content Processing", Prentice Hall 2002*). The second book describes media processing and communication (*Ralf Steinmetz, Klara Nahrstedt, "Multimedia Systems", Springer Verlag 2004*). The third book presents topics such as multimedia documents, security, and various applications (*Ralf Steinmetz, Klara Nahrstedt, "Multimedia Applications and Security", Springer Verlag 2004*).

1.2 Contents of This Book

This book is on *Multimedia Aplications*, presenting fundamental information and properties of multimedia document handling, multimedia security, and various aspects of multimedia applications. The primary objective is to provide a comprehensive panorama of multimedia technologies, and their integration. Understanding of the close relationship among the wide range of disciplines and components that make up a multimedia system is a prerequesite for the successful building of multimedia systems and their applications.

The book is structured as a *reference book*, so that it allows fast familiarization with all issues concerned. However, it can be also used in educational process as an introductory book for a multimedia systems class in computer science and related disciplines. Solid introductory background on concepts in media coding as well as basic system and service issues would be very helpful.

1.3 Organization of This Book

As mentioned above, this book as an integral part of a comprehensive overview and practical view on multimedia technologies. Figure 1-1 shows the global view of the most important multimedia fields spanning across the three volumes. The overall organization attempts to explain the largest dependencies between the components involved in terms of space and time. We distinguish between:

- *Basics*: One of the most important aspects is a media-specific consideration, in addition to the computer architecture for multimedia systems.
- *Systems*: This group of multimedia fields relates system areas such as processing, storage, and communication, and their relevant interfaces.
- *Services*: The multimedia fields such as content analysis, document handling, security and others represent important multimedia functions that rely and are implemented on the basis of system components.
- *Applications*: The group of multimedia fields such as design, learning and user interfaces studies the type and design of applications and the interface between users and multimedia applications and systems.

In this book, we emphasize the field of multimedia applications, and some service and system aspects (see Figure 1-1). Thus, the book first covers generic multimedia database management systems, programming issues, security aspects, and document handling. The book then deals with more dedicated, application-related issues: media design, general user-interface topics, and multimedia learning. Finally, we discuss various possible applications and present a case study.

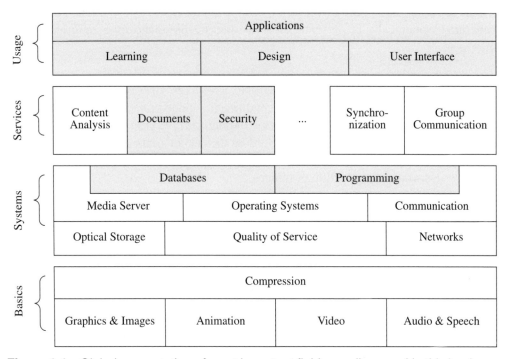

Figure 1-1 Global presentation of most important fields, as discussed in this book.

1.3.1   Systems and Services for Multimedia Applications

The first topic of this book are multimedia database management systems (MMDBMS), which are very important for the efficient handling of multimedia data and are intended to appropriately support multimedia applications.

While MMDBMSs allow for the management of a large amount of multimedia data, there are several possibilities how the data can be represented and accessed by the developers of multimedia applications. Therefore, we address programming issues at different levels of abstraction, covering some object-based and object-oriented approaches.

More and more current multimedia applications are executed on several computers within cooperative tasks in networked environments. The trend towards networking, particularly for communication over public networks, increases the risk of damage caused by intruders or malicious users. The acceptance of new information technology systems depends largely on the security offered by the distributed application. Consequently, the book covers topics related to technical data protection and data security, which are becoming increasingly important. Thereby, the focus is on digital watermarking of different media types.

The subsequent chapter is dedicated to the handling of multimedia documents, which are usually composed of a set of various media types. These documents can be generated dynamically at presentation time, and are presented by a multimedia user interface.

1.3.2   Multimedia Applications

The design of commercially successful multimedia applications, which use the possibilities offered by new media, involves new requirements to graphics design. Thus, one chapter of the book deals with issues regarding the design goals to be achieved by each medium, and the available design tools. In particular, we concentrate on typography and layout issues, and the production of images.

Subsequently, the book introduces a series of general aspects for the design of multimedia interfaces in general, and graphical user interfaces (GUIs) in particular. An important property of such an interface is the use of graphical or typographic means to present data and operations, since visualization and graphical interaction form the two sides of a GUI. Based on an example, conflicts in the design of user-friendly user interfaces are explained, whereby various principles and their benefits and drawbacks will be described.

The introduced design and user interface principles are supposed to help in the development of more appealing and user-friendly applications, such as for the purpose of multimedia learning. The latter application area has gained increasing interest by schools and companies recognizing the potential pedagogic and didactic benefit of multimedia learning environments, which allow for a wide spectrum of representation forms. Hence, the book covers learning theories, learning systems, and eLearning standards.

Applications are of central significance for users of multimedia systems wanting to interact with multimedia data. In the case of multimedia learning, e.g., the user might be a teacher who wants to create a presentation combining audio, video, and animation. There is a large number of existing applications for creating, modifying, viewing, and interacting with multimedia data. This book introduces a representative set of this wealth and variety of multimedia applications, and presents a case study.

1.4   Further Reading About Multimedia

There is an extensive literature on all aspects of multimedia systems. Some journals frequently publish multimedia systems and networking research results such as *IEEE Multimedia, IEEE Transactions on Multimedia, ACM/Springer Multimedia Systems Journal*, and *Kluwer Multimedia Tools and Applications Journal*. Many other journals have special issues on this subject such as the *IEEE Journal on Selected Areas on Communication, Elsevier Computer Communication Journal*, and others.

In addition to a large number of system and networking national and international conferences and workshops, that have special tracks or sessions on multimedia system research, there are several international conference focussed on multimedia systems only, in particular: *ACM Multimedia Conference* (the first conference took place in Anaheim, California, August 1993), *IEEE International Conference on Multimedia and Expo* (the first conference was held in May 1994), *SPIE Multimedia Computing and Networking* (MMCN), *ACM Network and Operating System Support for Digital Audio and Video* (NOSSDAV), and *International Workshop on Multimedia Interactive Protocols and Systems* (MIPS, former IDMS).

Database Systems

T he database technology was originally developed for large volumes of heavily structured (alphanumeric) data with requirements that differ from multimedia applications. For this reason, the traditional database systems are currently being expanded by multimedia-specific components and language primitives, allowing *multimedia database management systems* (*MMDBMSs*) to efficiently handle multimedia data and appropriately support multimedia applications. In particular, this concerns expansions to allow the interpretation of media data contents for processing and output, and to include the specific properties of media data, such as large data volumes, synchronization, and real-time processing conditions.

2.1 Multimedia Database Management Systems

Multimedia applications address the management file interfaces generally through abstractions on various levels. Consider the following three applications: A hypertext applications is able to handle nodes and edges; an audio editor can read, write and process audio sections; and an audio-video distribution service can distribute stored video information.

At first sight, these three applications seem to have little in common. However, the functions of all three examples can be executed uniformly within an MMDBMS, because the abstraction of the details of the storage access and storage management are generally the main tasks of a database management system (DBMS). In addition to data abstraction, a DBMS provides other properties:

• *Data persistence*: Data can survive programs, processes, and technologies. For example, insurance companies have to store data over several decades in their databases. During this time, computer technology continues to develop and, together with this development, operating systems and other programs change. For this reason, a DBMS should be able to process data, even when the environment has changed.

- *Consistent view of the data*: Particularly in concurrent multi-user operation, it is important to provide a consistent view of the data during concurrent database queries at specific points in time. This property is ensured by protocols for time synchronization.

- *Data security*: The security and integrity of data in case of an error is one of the most important conditions for a DBMS. This property is achieved by use of the transaction concept.

- *Database query and output*: Databases store different information (entries), which can be retrieved at any given time by database queries. Database queries are formulated by use of query languages, such as SQL. In addition, each entry in a database includes some status information (e.g., that the entry was changed). This information has to be reproduced exactly to ensure that the correct information about that entry is supplied.

The fundamental difference between conventional data and multimedia data also reflects the type of database management system required. A conventional relational DBMS serves to process data structured with regard to a data model. This data model determines the operations we can use. For example, a formally exactly defined language (SQL), which is structured strictly mathematically (relational algebra), describes the possible operations we can use for the definition and manipulation of the data in a conventional RDBMS. This is different with an MMDBMS: Depending on the types of operations the MMDBMS supports, various data models are required.

Often, the role of an MMDBMS is considered to be that of a repository for multimedia data with conventional database technology, without the support of particular media processing options. Such a repository would contain only references to the unprocessed media data and a few pieces of administrative information about these media data. The actual processing of media data would then mainly be handled by the devices themselves and by other components of the system domain.

Another opinion about the role of MMDBMSs is based on a different view, which also strongly reflects the development in the field of multimedia data management: MMDBMSs support the management of multimedia data in a particular way, by using the fundamental and proven properties of conventional DBMSs. In addition to the conventional database services mentioned above, the different properties of information representation with digital media lead to a series of problems which have to solved by an MMDBMS:

- To ensure well-performing and effective management of media data, it is necessary to interpret, at least in part, the internal structure and the contents of the data. This holds true both for the internal processing (on a physical level) and for the data modeling (on a logical level). For example, the physical level utilizes the sequence of continuous data for storage and buffer management, while the logical level uses the contents of media data to support queries.
- MMDBMSs have to support the representation of different types of media contents. This functionality is also called *playout management* [TK96c]. *Perception* is a time-dependent process, so that media data are represented in a time-dependent and time-independent way by their very nature. In contrast to conventional database systems, this situation requires a functional expansion which considers both the time-dependency and the interactivity of a media presentation.
- In addition, the characteristic properties of multimedia data require a series of particularities for data processing on the technical side, which are essentially different from those required for conventional database systems. Media data are extensive and their processing is time-consuming. It is necessary to be able to handle continuous media data streams and to support both synchronization and interaction.

The rest of this chapter is constructed as follows: Section 2.2 describes the multimedia-specific features an MMDBMS should provide. Section 2.3 discusses different aspects of data modeling for MMDBMSs. Section 2.4 focuses on the principles of MMDBMS implementation, and Section 2.5 provides a summary of this chapter.

2.2 Multimedia-specific Properties of an MMDBMS

The previous section presented a summary of the conventional properties provided by the most commonly used DBMSs. More specifically, there are certain aspects of multimedia applications based on these properties. Nevertheless, multimedia-specific expansions and refinements can provide more comprehensive and better support for multimedia applications. This has been proven by various DBMS research projects (e.g., the projects described in [Nar96], [Che95], [MS96], [WK87], [Mas87], [MR97], and [GELP99]).

2.2.1 Data Types in Multimedia Databases

MMDBMSs require multimedia-specific language primitives to model database designs [AK94]. In addition, they should be available to support queries to multimedia database contents [GRG95] [LÖSO97] [ÖHK96]. In particular, MMDBMSs have to provide new data types for video [LR95], images, text, and digital animation [VB96]. These new data types have to support the operations of the corresponding media type, and they should hide the details of storage management structures from the user.

2.2.2   Information Retrieval and Multimedia Queries

In general, the methods developed in the field of information retrieval [ME97] [VVVV96] with respect to multimedia data are better suited to multimedia applications than the traditional query options provided by DBMSs. One reason is that the user often has to search a conventional database when he or she wants to retrieve information from a multimedia database (because the contents of the media data instruct the user to do so, e.g., objects in an image [AC97] [GWJ91]). In addition, matches in a search result in an MMDBMS are normally not exact matches. When comparing two multimedia data units, we can use similarities in a meaningful way. This means that MMDBMSs should implement methods for fuzzy queries, in addition to the conventional query features. This includes a *query-by-example* method, which is particularly useful for image and video databases.

2.2.3   Name-preserving Data Management

Relationships between the data of one medium or of various media have to be observed according to the defined specification. The MDBMS manages these relationships and can use them for queries and data output. This means, for example, that *navigation* through a document is supported and the relationships between individual parts of a document are properly managed. We distinguish between various relationships [Mey91]:

- An *attribute relationship* marks various descriptions, e.g., representations of the same object. For example, an ornithological lexicon would include the calls of each bird as an audio signal, a bird's flight as a motion picture sequence, various images, and a descriptive text. From the view of a relational database, a *tuple* is assigned to each bird, which includes the set of representations in the form of attributes.
- A *component relationship* includes all the individual items which belong to one data object. A car spare parts catalog and a document would be examples for such a relationship.
- A *substitute relationship* defines various types of presentations of the same piece of information. For example, a formula in relation to specific data can be represented as a table, a graph, or an animation.
- A *synchronization relationship* describes the temporal relationship between the data units. Lip synchronization between audio and video is one example.

2.2.4   Representation of Multimedia Data

An MMDBMS offers a representation mechanism for composite media elements which can be used for many multimedia applications [KdVB97] [RK95] [CHT86] and as a service to manage the playback process [TK96b] [TK96a]. This mechanism is based on a generic representation engine and represents synchronized composite multimedia data units of the user's request [LG90]. This service allows an MMDBMS to clearly differentiate between the representation and the processing, including storage [SMW95].

2.2.5 Management and Output of Continuous Data

Continuous data differ from discrete data in several respects. The main differences relate to the data quantity and the time dependence. For this reason, continuous data cannot be handled like discrete data, so that special mechanisms have to be developed to manage continuous data. MMDBMSs contain such mechanisms and use operating system functions, particularly for storage [RM93] [VR96] [MNO'96], intermediate storage in a buffer [RM93] [VR96] [MNO+96] [HGP98], transfer [LG92], and representation [RS92] of continuous data.

2.3 Data Modeling in MMDBMSs

We can distinguish between three main aspects with regard to the modeling of multimedia data: The modeling of temporal and spatial properties of media data, the use of documents to describe the media composition, and the role of meta data in providing additional information about the contents of media data.

2.3.1 Media and Documents

Media data are perceived either by humans or by tools used to handle, evaluate, and process media data. In many cases, media data are generated artificially, or combined by use of a specification. Such specifications of synthetic media data are called *documents* (for a detailed description, see Chapter 5). Although documents are managed in MMDBMSs similarly to media data with regard to databases, the terms "media data" and "documents" have to be clearly distinguished. We will discuss the respective properties required for data modeling in MMDBMSs below.

- *Media*: On the logical level, media data are always composed of measuring values for a given area in a discrete multidimensional space. The encoding of the actual information content of the media data is done on a sub-symbolic level. For this reason, the actual information content is represented in an implicit and (often) redundant way.

  On the physical level, the unprocessed media data are represented in a media type specific format as a binary sequence. This representation format often includes compression and pre-processing steps. Transformations between different representations of the same media and between media types are possible.

- *Documents*: Documents describe media data by means of a formal language, which can be processed by a computer. The specification of such data compositions by documents can include media data as a reference or as a value. For each document type, there is a transformation method to convert the documents for a representation or an additional processing step. This conversion does not necessarily have to be trivial or unique.

Text documents are one example of a specific document type. The LSGM language (see Chapter 5), which has become increasingly popular during the past years, is one good example. Another type is multimedia documents, for which languages like HTML or HyTime are used.

Documents play two distinctive roles within MMDBMSs. First, document data are handled in a binary representation by the DBMS, like unprocessed media data. For efficiency reasons, often only a partial interpretation of the internal structure of the documents is performed. Second, document types are based on the same abstraction used for the structural formula of media data, which we will discuss below.

2.3.2   Modeling the Structure and Behavior of Media Data

Structural models for multimedia data provide a framework for the *structural representation*, *interpretation*, and *processing* of media data. Such models are (ideally) characterized by the following properties:

- Structural models supply a *structural representation* of multimedia data units (Logical Data Units, *LDUs*), including properties and relationships to other multimedia data units. This representation can be derived automatically for existing multimedia data units from the corresponding unprocessed media data. Specific operations can be used to create the representation, to access, and to update it.
- Structural models supply an *identification mechanism*, allowing the automatic identification of multimedia data units as parts of unprocessed media data, and another identification mechanism for composite multimedia data units.
- Structural models supply a *materialization mechanism* for the creation of new, unprocessed media data. The materialization is done by processing the structural representation of multimedia data units.

Other data related to multimedia data units are the so-called *meta data* (see below). Structural models for multimedia data correspond to data models of conventional database systems. In conventional database systems, these data models are the properties of the *data definition language* (*DDL*) and the *data manipulation language* (*DML*).

The most important types of structural models for multimedia data are *space-time models*, because they provide the basis for modeling multimedia data. Whereas the spatial modeling of data has a long tradition in the field of image databases [CJT96] and graphical databases, the temporal modeling of data has evolved only in recent years in the context of MMDBMSs for continuous media data.

Temporal Data Models Objects can be identified in temporal models by basic time units, which can be either time intervals or points of time. *Qualitative relationships* between temporal media objects are described in temporal algebras [CC96]. Qualitative relations permit the definition of conditions for temporal media objects and the formulation of search conditions for temporal media objects. There are three basic relations for times ($<$, $=$, $>$) and 13 basic relations for time intervals (see Figure 2-1).

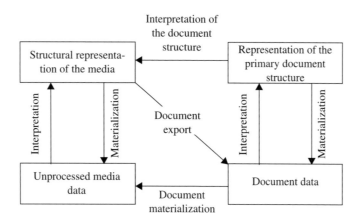

Figure 2-1 Relationships between media, documents, and structural models.

Spatial Data Models Data modeling for spatial data is well established in the fields of computer graphics, image database systems, and geographic information systems. The basic means to identify objects within media data are generalizations of intervals on several dimensions, such as rectangles and multidimensional bodies. Complex manipulation units are, for example, areas consisting of an arbitrary quantity of rectangles or multidimensional bodies. Regions can be represented effectively by use of space-filling curves (e.g., Hilbert curves or Peano curves [ACF⁺96]). Complex objects in spatial data are then approximated by some basic units, the so-called minimal bounding rectangles or regions.

Spatial relationships between media objects expand the temporal relationships. [LÖD96] identifies 12 directional relationships and five topological relationships for minimal bounding rectangles in a two-dimensional space. The five topological relationships can also be applied to regions, and they have been used in implantations of the QBISM system [ACF⁺96].

The composition of new, spatial media objects in a two- or three-dimensional space is a core issue in computer graphics. As was the case for the temporal model, we can distinguish models which permit an arrangement of the spatial composition by using absolute coordinates, or by relative positioning, e.g., by using distances and angles. In addition, more advanced models also allow the hierarchical composition of spatial media objects. One good example of this type of model is the data model used by VRML [CB97]. To model video data, spatial and temporal aspects are combined to describe media units in space and time, e.g., to handle movements of objects.

Active Multimedia Objects   Some of the models discussed here for composition of temporal media do not only handle the structure, but also the behavior of the media data. In this sense, they play a two-fold role. For example, an algebraic video expression can be interpreted as a structural composition of temporal media objects, resulting in a new temporal media object. Although this represents a structural perspective, this description can concurrently be interpreted as a *process description*. The described process is a representation of media, composed of different media objects. Due to their duality, temporal models play a special role in multimedia data modeling, compared to spatial data. In general, a representation contains interaction options for the user, in addition to the media representation processes.

2.3.3   Document Modeling

Document languages such as SGML [Org86] or MHEG [MHE93] play a significant role in the management of multimedia data. One aspect is that many structural models for multimedia objects have emerged from document languages. Originally, these languages had been designated for data exchange or multimedia data processing, e.g., in the publishing field. A second aspect is the management of the document data itself. We will discuss this second aspect below.

Within the logical structure of a document, we can distinguish between two components. The *primary structure* of a document corresponds to the hierarchical structurization of the parts of that document. This hierarchical structurization is determined by the grammar structure of the document language. Parsing techniques can be applied to documents to extract this structure and represent it explicitly in a structured data model. An explicit representation and storage of the primary document structure can be useful for the following reasons:

- It supports the effective and consistent updating of existing documents according to the grammar of the document language.
- In many cases, the document models are used for the representation of meta data (see Section 2.3.2), where the document model normally serves as a semi-structured data model [Abi97]. This means that we can access this information and its processing processes by using the primary document structure.
- For specific media types, the primary document structure corresponds to the logical structure of the media data. This applies particularly to text documents, which can be used to describe both the hierarchical and sequential composition of the text directly by use of the syntax tree.

Examples in which the primary structure of a document is modeled explicitly in an MMDBMS are discussed in [BAK97], [BAN95], [BANY97], [ÖIS⁺97], and [Abi97].

The *secondary structure* of a document refers to information about the media data, which can be extracted solely from an interpretation of the contents, going beyond a syntactic analysis. In particular, this includes the structure and behavior, i.e., the temporal and spatial relationships, and information about active media representation. Typical examples of these characteristics are *links* in hypertext documents and space-time compositions. Within the SGML document language, for example, there are corresponding language constructs provided by the HyTime standard [Org92]. The structural characteristics in the secondary structure of the documents are mapped to the structural representation of media objects, as discussed in Section 2.3.2. Examples of explicit representations of the secondary structure of documents are discussed in [ÖIS⁺97] [BA94].

Figure 2-1 illustrates the various relationships between the media data, the documents, and the structural data models discussed so far. In addition, this figure shows that documents can be created from a structural media representation. This export of documents is often used to exchange data between media-specific processing tools.

2.3.4 Meta Data

In a set of structured media objects, which are modeled in one of the data models discussed in Section 2.3.2, the meta data can be any type of data related to the structural media objects.

In contrast to structural media objects, which allow media data to be processed, meta data are used for management, processing, retrieval, and representation of media data. Meta data can be present in structural form, but they can also include media data. In general, media data can be assigned either directly to media objects or indirectly to their meta data. Although the term "meta data" also plays an important role in conventional databases, it is much more important in the context of multimedia data management for a number of reasons:

- To search media data, mechanisms for structural access are of limited use. A contents-based search requires information about the contents of the media beyond the sheer structural properties.
- Multimedia data are processed not only in DBMSs, but also in a number of accompanying applications. These applications need meta data about the stored media data to enable correct processing.
- An inherent property of the perception of media is the redundancy in the non-explicit information representation. This means that some quality limitation of the media data may be acceptable. To what extent such a quality limitation is acceptable is described in a specific type of meta data, the so-called quality of service (QoS) parameters.

There are many properties characterizing meta data (see [BR94], [Böh97], and [KKS96]). The following criteria can be considered to classify meta data from the contents view, which is of particular relevance for information queries:

- *Contents dependence*: Refers to the property that the meta data depend functionally on the contents of the media data (which is also often called *media-controlled meta data*).

- *Applications dependence*: Certain types of meta data are applicable either only to specific applications, or they use application-specific models (also often called *application-controlled meta data*).

Technical considerations lead to the following criteria for meta data:

- *Automatic calculation*: Meta data can be either calculated automatically, or they are generated manually or semi-automatically.

- *Global/local properties*: Meta data assigned to a specific media object can be described with a global property of the media object, or they refer to the property of a sub-object of that media object [KKS96].

Meta data that depend on an application are often not directly bound to media objects, but defined indirectly as a function of their characteristics. This means that they are automatically derived from the media data, and are independent of the application and dependent on the contents. Meta data that depend on the application are then used to evaluate the media data.

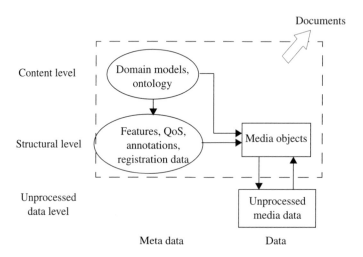

Figure 2-2   Abstraction levels for media data and meta data.

Figure 2-2 shows a number of different relationships between meta data and media data. The differentiation between a structural and a contents level corresponds to the model proposed for search activities, e.g., the *Hermes reference model* [Con] or the VIMSYS model [GWJ91]. This figure also shows that documents generally not only include the structural characteristics of the media objects, but also the relevant meta data.

2.4 MMDBMS Implementation

MMDBMSs are distributed multimedia systems for which no official standards have been proposed yet (not even for their components). However, most MMDBMS implementations, e.g., the AMOS system of GMD-IPSI [RKN96], the Universal Server of Informix [Gro96], and the MMDBMS developed at the University of Alberta [ÖIS+97] use the following complementary components, which will be described in detail below:

- A *platform for the management of structurized data*, provided by the existing database technology.
- A *dedicated media server*, allowing efficient management of the storage and buffers for media objects of any type, particularly for continuous media objects.
- *Multimedia application components*, providing a special mechanism for multimedia data output. The distribution is hidden.

These components, and optionally other multimedia-specific services, which provide an operating system and a high-speed network, have to be connected so that the multimedia data can be handled efficiently. One important factor for efficient handling of multimedia data is the number of media object duplicates that have to be maintained in the MMDBMS to meet application requirements.

Most of the currently available implementations of MMDBMSs use a best-effort architecture, which does not allocate resources [SN95]. In contrast, guaranties meeting the QoS requirements of the user [NS95] [VKBG95] can be given by further developing the mechanism generally available in real-time systems and particularly in distributed multimedia platforms [SN95] [RDF97].

Various architectures for the implementation can also differ in the mechanism used to output data (see Volume 2, Chapter 4 on media server). In *client-pull architectures*, the data output is global and controlled by the client. In these architectures, the client permanently calls data and outputs it in consecutive requests based on the network. This means that a client sends, explicitly and iteratively, requests based on a special output protocol, which make the server transmit the next data units.

In *server-push architectures*, the clients do not normally send explicit requests; instead, they inform the server only about user interventions to be considered in the data output [RVT96].

To achieve efficient data output in MMDBMSs, an appropriate solution appears to be to connect the physical unit that stores the mass of multimedia data directly to the network (i.e., to the network interface). This means that data output to the buffer for special objects of the DBMS is stopped, which would otherwise (unnecessarily) reduce the output throughput [TKW+96]. One example of this approach is the Oracle video server [LOP94].

2.4.1 Platform for Structural Data Management

The platform used to manage structural data has to implement the structural data models for temporal and spatial models, the modeling of the active media objects and the modeling of the structured documents. It has to support the management of meta data in connection with the media data and the application-specific alphanumeric data. In this context, "managing structural data" means, in general, the data management of exactly these structural alphanumeric data and references to objects.

Obviously, we could manage the structural data by using existing database technology. With this approach, the management of structural data would benefit from the efficiency of the typical database services, the support of queries by means of access mechanisms, and their optimization, and the possibility of operations which, based on corresponding control mechanisms, would allow concurrent multi-user operation.

There are two basic options to implement a new data model. We could either design a new database language, or expand an existing data model by adding new structures. The first approach involves modification of an existing language and embedding of the code for the implementation into a database system. The second approach involves the design of special structures suitable for multimedia data management; then they are added to an expandable DBMS. The extent a particular database system can provide special processing support depends mainly on the interfaces provided by the expandable DBMS for functional expansions.

The main benefit of the first approach is higher data type security in the modified database language. This arises because the limiting marginal conditions of the model are rather implicit, and an effective and more direct implementation is possible. Examples for this approach are found in experimental systems, mostly with specialized query languages (e.g., MOQL [LÖSO97]). However, the more direct approach means higher implementation costs, because little reuse is made of existing technology, and it is inflexible with respect to changing requirements. These observations favor the second approach. For industrial application systems, where implementation costs have to be considered, there are always good reasons to reuse the technologies which have been developed over many years, in particular in the field of RDBMSs.

Considering that there is no consensus about a universal or general data model for optimum support of multimedia applications, or that this is not even possible, the underlying data model has to be open for expansions. Conventional data management is based on the structured data types, which are managed, e.g., data in table form in relational databases. This determines in a unique way the types of operations required to process the data, and the system design appropriate for effective support. The situation is different for the management of multimedia data. The design of an MMDBMS is not determined by the structured data themselves, but primarily by the media data and their processing requirements.

The *applications* determine the type of operations required, i.e., how the media data are to be structurally interpreted in order to be able to effectively benefit from these data. The *requirements* determine the data structures used to support the effective implementation of these operations. This explains why it is so difficult to develop a universal model for multimedia data. For this reason, most commercial and research-oriented implementations of MMDBMSs use object-oriented or object-relational database technologies in one way or another. Note that this approach still suffers from the fact that the expansion of internal processing options is normally limited to expansions with new access structures and simple adaptations of the query optimization component. Examples of concrete system implementations based on this approach are the prototype of AMOS [RKN96], the STORM system [Adi96], the DISIMA database [OÖL+95], the QBISM medical database [ACF+96], and the VIMSYS image search system [GWJ91]. Also, most of the databases available on the market today offer expansions to manage media data, e.g., the VIRAGE system, which is based on Informix and Oracle, and IUS DataBlades, and expansions for IBM DB2.

2.4.2 Media Servers

Conventional file systems and storage servers are normally designed to handle the storage and call of conventional data, which do not have strict access rate requirements (see Volume 2, Chapter 4 on media servers). Such systems store and call continuous data, similar to conventional data. Accordingly, they do not offer any guaranties for storage and retrieval rates for continuous media data. If data are additionally moved to disk, and pages in the buffer cache are exchanged, and data are pre-fetched in the buffer cache, then these systems do not make full use of the sequential structure to access continuous data. Media servers are designed explicitly to handle media data with respect to these aspects, in particular continuous data. This means that they represent an important component for MMDBMSs, enhancing the conventional database technology. In an MMDBMS, they are used particularly to manage storage and buffers for those data objects consisting of a large volume of media data.

Media servers often control access to ensure that *resources* are allocated in a reasonable way. For this reason, they limit the number of requests that can be served concurrently. In addition, they use technologies for specific schedules in real-time and support QoS guaranties.

2.4.3   Multimedia Output Components

In an MMDBMS, the distribution of multimedia data is hidden from the user. The output is performed by special output components. From the view of the database, these components can be evaluated as additional component of the MMDBMS. This means that output mechanisms lack the capability of supporting the output of multimedia data. For this reason, MMDBMSs have to include a special output mechanism.

Generally speaking, output components have to enable the MMDBMS to exchange all types of multimedia data for a request in both transmission directions. In detail, the output of continuous data from the storage to the receiver is particularly critical, because such data have real-time requirements and data normally have to be represented to the user according to these requirements. This means that the admissible timeframe for playback has to be adhered to. The output of continuous data of the kind required to insert media objects is less critical, because no temporal limitation has to be observed.

2.5   Summary

Extensive work in the field of database technology has been dedicated to MMDBMSs as an important platform for many multimedia applications in recent years. In addition to the functionality for the management of conventional data, MMDBMSs offer storage expansions and system components especially for multimedia applications, particularly new language primitives, required for effective modeling of multimedia databases and their effective access. New system components, such as media servers and output mechanisms, consider the particular properties of media objects and allow the level of performance required for multimedia applications.

Issues requiring more effort include those related to the role of *transaction management* in MMDBMSs, a closer integration of retrieval techniques to the data management techniques, and the language and optimization of multimedia retrieval. In particular, more research work is necessary in the field of contents-based retrieval of continuous data. Queries like "Find a spoken text about the children song about the ten little Negerlein", or "Find a video section about Prince Andrew wearing an Andalusian dress" will be difficult to serve.

Programming

Many functionalities of modern multimedia applications, particularly the time-critical ones, which are available today as products, have usually been written in conventional procedural programming languages (e.g., C). Multimedia-specific functions, such as adjusting the volume while playing back an audio clip, are often still called or controlled via hardware-specific libraries. Also, parts of the application interfaces of operating system expansions for multimedia components still depend on hardware.

Unfortunately, most of the commercial multimedia application programs depend on the underlying hardware. The replacement of a device unit that processes continuous media often requires a new implementation of important parts of the application program. This is the case even when a device is replaced by a similar one, or by one that provides the same functionality but comes from a different vendor.

Some applications are implemented by use of *tools*. These tools generate the code either directly, or they handle routines supplied by the respective application, to integrate the device units into the corresponding application. In these applications, any change to the multimedia equipment requires fundamental changes to the tools, e.g., new interaction methods with the device units, and the renewed generation of the executable program each time.

This situation can be compared to the programming technique that uses floating-point numbers. The various computer systems supporting floating-point numbers differ in their architectures, their commands, and their interfaces. Sometimes, RISC architectures or parallel processors are used. Nevertheless, only few standard formats, e.g., the IEEE format to represent numbers, are used. Programmers normally use so-called *built-in functions* of higher programming languages, in addition to the usual operators, to encode floating-point numbers. Each hardware change will have hardly any effect on an application program, e.g., one written in Fortran.

Compared to the multimedia environment, we normally find relatively well-defined abstractions in higher programming languages, usually in the form of data types. This means that it is possible to hide the actual hardware configuration from the application, without an inherent loss of performance.

Object-oriented approaches are increasingly used in programming of multimedia systems and particularly for applications in this field. Early examples are [AC91], [Bla91], [GBD+91], [RBCD91] (a multimedia workshop in Heidelberg), or [FT88], [LG90], [SHRS90], and [SM92]. The object-oriented approaches are also increasingly being used for the interfaces to the communications system in use.

Although they have different properties, *multimedia objects* normally provide properties and functions which allow a faster integration into their environment. The development of an individual language or the expansion for a translator is not required. These two elements can be considered an integral part of the programming environment from a corresponding class hierarchy.

Unfortunately, the existing class hierarchies are very different. There is no consensus about a universally accepted or even *optimum* class hierarchy. Note that a multimedia product developed in an object-oriented programming language is still the exception to the rule.

This chapter describes the set of options available to access multimedia data, or their different representation possibilities towards the developer.

3.1 Abstraction Levels

When multimedia data are to be used in an application, then this normally includes the representation or processing on device units which are specialized for such data. However, as there is a large number of different devices even for one data type (such as audio or video), which offer the same or similar functionalities, but which have to be addressed in a different way, it is often useful to bind the communication of the program to the hardware. First, this allows the software to be independent of the hardware, and second, it simplifies program development by offering basic functions.

This solution can be achieved by introducing several *abstraction levels*, where each level offers a higher abstraction degree, compared to the previous one. This means that the functions provided on each level are more general and more independent of a special device, operating system, or programming language. Figure 3-1 shows a division into abstraction levels. The lowest level above the actual device unit is the *device driver*, handling communication with the hardware. The system software offers a uniform interface to the device drivers of a specific category, which, however, does not necessarily have to abstract from the specific properties of the device.

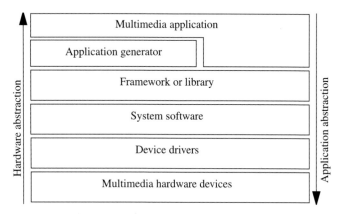

Figure 3-1 Abstraction levels.

A *framework* or *library* provides the interface used to address hardware devices from a programming language. This level can be further divided, depending on how much the framework or library abstracts from the special system software or the special device.

To implement a multimedia application, we can use another abstraction level: Various application generators for creating applications with multimedia contents offer proprietary or standardized *script languages* tailored to that application and offering the functions for these applications.

3.1.1 Device Drivers

A device driver is a software component responsible for communication with a special device unit within an operating system. The driver implements the conversion of the functions defined by the operating system for a device type to the special commands of a special device.

Addressing a hardware device requires very exact information about the hardware interface, so that device drivers for popular operating systems are normally developed and shipped with each device by the manufacturer.

3.1.2 System Software

The system software is responsible for forming a uniform interface between the actual hardware and the application software, so that application programs can be developed and used independently from the actual hardware configuration. This means that the system software defines a standard that all applications which need to access the hardware can use. In contrast to this solution, in older operating systems such as DOS, the programs were concerned with how to communicate with a wide range of different hardware configurations. In such an environment, a hardware interface often developed into a quasi standard that other hardware vendors had to accept, e.g., for audio output, to ensure that their devices could be used with the existing applications.

Depending on the types of devices and the functionality a system software defines for a device type, the software interface of the operating system can be allocated to various abstraction levels. For example, a very abstract, but (overly) simplified view is customary in UNIX systems. All hardware units are addressed and managed like files. Although this permits addressing a number of different devices, it has the major drawback that the system software hardly offers any device-specific functions. In UNIX, there is one single function call ("Fcntrl") available to address the special functions of a device drivers, e.g., the volume of audio devices.

For this reason, modern system software supports various types of multimedia devices. For example, Microsoft Windows offers a collection of hardware interfaces under the collective name of "DirectX". We will briefly describe DirectX as a representative example for this type of product below. Other system software defines proprietary interfaces, e.g., QuickDraw for graphics and QuickTime for continuous media for MacOS by Apple. OpenGL of Silicon Graphics is increasingly supported by other platforms (including Microsoft Windows).

Example: Microsoft DirectX   Microsoft *DirectX* is an advanced suite of multimedia application programming interfaces (APIs) built into Microsoft Windows operating systems. DirectX provides a standard development platform for Windows-based PCs by enabling software developers to access specialized hardware features without having to write hardware-specific code. This technology was first introduced in 1995 and is a recognized standard for multimedia application development on the Windows platform.

Simply put, DirectX is a Windows technology that enables higher performance in graphics and sound for PC games or videos.

The *DirectX Foundation* includes the interface specification for various types of hardware devices:

- DirectDraw offers functions for 2D graphics output, building on its GDI (Graphics Device Interface) predecessor.
- Direct3D supports three-dimensional representations.
- DirectSound offers playback for audio data.
- DirectInput supports access to user interaction devices (mouse, keyboard, joystick).

This collection of interfaces forms the so-called *hardware abstraction layer* (*HAL*). To achieve further hardware independence, DirectX Foundation additionally includes a *hardware emulation layer* (*HEL*). HEL provides software emulations of hardware functions (e.g., 3D functions in graphics accelerator cards), which are not directly supported by the actual hardware.

Building on the low-level functions of DirectX Foundation, the *DirectX Media Layer* includes additional high-level services to handle multimedia data, e.g., animations, media streaming, synchronization of multimedia elements, and user interactions. The DirectX Media Layer includes the following components: DirectShow, DirectAnimation, Direct3D Retained Mode, and DirectPlay.

DirectX is based on the *Component Object Model* (*COM*), developed by Microsoft and embedded in Microsoft Windows operating systems. COM offers essentially an encapsulation mechanism used to define interfaces. Objects that implement these interfaces can be reused in other applications, regardless of the implementation language used. These mechanisms are of fundamental significance for object-oriented application development. Consequently, the integration of object-oriented concepts into the system software forms the basis for the development of abstraction layers and reusable software.

Today, there are COM implementations available for other platforms and the embedding of COM objects in CORBA, so that COM in connection with DirectX could open up ways of developing multimedia applications independently of hardware and operating systems, similar to Java. Detailed information about DirectX is available at http://www.Microsoft.com/directx/default.asp.

3.1.3 Frameworks and Libraries

A *framework* is a collection of classes, providing a set of services for a specific application area. The classes and functions exported by the framework can be used by the application and adapted to individual purposes (e.g., [Cha03] [WGN02]).

The development of frameworks has been particularly facilitated by the increasing proliferation of object-oriented programming languages, because important concepts, such as encapsulation or specialization, are supported directly by the implementation language for the creation of frameworks. One example of frameworks is the Java Media Framework; visit http://java.sun.com/products/java-media/ for detailed information.

In addition, frameworks allow integration into *procedural high-level programming languages* (*HLLs*). In an HLL, the processing of continuous media data is influenced by a group of similarly-built functions. These calls are generally independent of hardware and drivers. This means that the integration into HLLs leads to a desirable abstraction, promotes a better programming style, and increases productivity. However, in addition to software engineering requirements, programs have to be able to effectively manipulate multimedia data. Consequently, in an HLL, the programs either access multimedia data structures directly, communicating directly with the executing processes in a real-time environment to control these processes, and/or the processing device units are controlled by a corresponding driver interface. Translators, binders, and/or loaders provide the required communication between the application program and the processing of continuous data. Currently, there is no programming language that includes the special constructs needed to manipulate multimedia data, except for a variety of programming languages in the field of digital signal processing which, at the assembler level, are usually able to encode the best time behavior of a program.

In addition, media can be regarded differently within a programming language (e.g., [BHK+02]). We will discuss a selection of variants developed by the authors below; initial results have been published in [SF92].

The following example shows the programming instructions embedded in a parallelism to describe a possible program code with media types:

```
a, b REAL;
ldu.left1, ldu.left2, ldu.left_mixed AUDIO_LDU;
...
WHILE ...
    COBEGIN
        PROCESS_1
                input(micro1, ldu.left1)
        PROCESS_2
                input(micro2, ldu.left2)
    ldu.left_mixed := a * ldu.left1 + b * ldu.left2;
    ...
END_WHILE
...
```

A first alternative to programming by using libraries is, for HLLs, the concept of *media as data types*. Here, data types are defined for video and audio. In a text, the smallest addressable element is a character (when not considering bits and bytes). A program can then manipulate such characters via functions and sometimes even directly via operators. They can be copied, compared to other characters, deleted, created, read from a file, saved to a file, displayed for the user, or become an integral part of another data structure. The question is now: Why should we not apply the same functionality to continuous media? In this case, the smallest unit would be the LDU. These data units can have a very different granularity (i.e., different size and duration). In the example above, LDUs are read in from two microphones and then mixed.

Our next example describes how text and a motion picture can be mixed. In this case, the text is interpreted as a subtitle of the motion picture. In this case, an application is the overlay of a video scene with subtitles which can be viewed by the user. This means that a distribution service could be transmitted, offering audio and subtitles in many different languages simultaneously. The user would be able to select the desired combination. This approach is extensively used for stereo sound for bilingual representations. However, the mixing of two visual media in this form is merely an *image within an image*. By using the teletext decoder integrated into TV sets, we could easily build such an application.

```
subtitle TEXT_STRING;
mixed.video, ldu.video VIDEO_LDU;
...
WHILE ...
     COBEGIN
             PROCESS_1
                 input(av_filehandle, ldu.video)
                 IF new_video_scene
                    input(subtitle_filehandle, subtitle)
                 mixed.video := ldu.video + subtitle
             PROCESS_2
                 output(video_window, mixed.video)
         ...
END_WHILE
...
```

Note that the example with the subtitle uses an implicit type conversion: Variables of different types are added and subsequently assigned to a variable of one of these types. When mixing or adding these two media, we could also define their relative position and duration. In addition to a previously specified standard value (e.g., centered across the bottom part of the screen), this relative position could be optionally defined by the programmer during the initialization phase. The duration is specified in the program itself by explicit masking, but it could also be defined in relation to the scene duration during the initialization.

3.1.4 Application Generators

When multimedia applications that focus on the presentation of multimedia data are to be created, then it is often not necessary to specifically write a program in a classical programming language. We could instead use application generators to specify and generate multimedia presentations, analogous to the processing of text in a word processor.

These application generators normally offer their own or a standardized *script language*, tailored to a specific application purpose.

Application Development Approaches requires little more than embedding multimedia data into the actual application. In fact, multimedia programming describes many more forms of application development.

Development tools, mainly for publishing documents in electronic form or the creation of presentations, have been used to allow authors with little or no knowledge of a (multimedia) programming language to create and edit such applications. These development tools are called *authoring systems*. Another approach is based on visual programming. This approach attempts to use audiovisual technologies to improve conventional software development.

Authoring Systems   Authoring systems are based on either of the following approaches:

- *Script-based systems*, such as the HyperCard system developed for the Macintosh in 1987, are the oldest authoring systems. They allowed programmers without knowledge of a high-level programming language for the first time to create applications which integrated text, graphics, and audio. Although the authors create their applications by use of scripts, similar to programming languages, the system hardware properties remain completely hidden from the authors. In addition, the language used is oriented to the creation of presentations, so that it can be substantially simplified. Script-based systems offer a very universal and flexible way of creating applications. The original goal, i.e., optimal support of non-programmers in their development effort, is not fully met.

- *Icon-based systems* represent an approach where the developer can create program flow diagrams by placing and linking icons. These icons serve as placeholders for text, commands, or complete animations.

- *Timeline-based systems* are characterized by their ease of use. Symbolic information objects are arranged on a time axis, defining the temporal flow of a presentation. The defined events can run consecutively or in parallel. In addition, the user can control the presentation flow.

Visual Development Environments   Visual programming, or the use of visual development environments for the development of applications, has become a concept representing intuitive software development, where graphical elements themselves are constructed and placed in relation to each other as representations of functionalities.

Current Developments   If we consider the authoring systems available in the market today, we can see that the boundaries between the individual categories are merging more and more. *Macromedia Director*, one of the best known systems, falls both into the time-based and script-based systems categories according to the classification described above. Applications created in Director observe a strict temporal or event-controlled flow sequence. At the same time, Director has its own powerful programming language, LINGO. This means that the transitions to visual programming environments are continuous.

The use of visual programming environments is still the subject of intense discussions. One of the most common arguments, that inexperienced developers can create applications quickly and easily by means of such tools, does not hold in practice.

The fact is that a professional application cannot be created unless the user has sound knowledge of the language used and the underlying concepts. In addition, changes or expansions in the architecture or the language often require some editing of the generated code, outside the development environment. Both the maintenance and the expansion of code created by another user is normally very difficult, particularly when the documentation is poor or non-existent.

With respect to the steady proliferation of object-oriented technologies, a major benefit of visual development environments is becoming increasingly important. If a (object-oriented) concept is used consistently, from the analysis and the design through to the concrete implementation, then development environments can support and facilitate the complete development process on all levels. Complex class hierarchies and relationships can be designed visually and converted into code, which merely has to be completed by the corresponding functionality.

As we progress through this chapter, we will discuss the concrete implementation of multimedia applications in more detail. First, we will describe the requirements for a programming language used to create multimedia applications, because this step forms the basis of program development.

Next, we will discuss object-oriented application development, because object-oriented technologies provide important concepts for reusability and expandability of software components. One of the increasingly significant aspects in connection with networked computer systems will be covered at the end of this chapter: the implementation of multimedia applications.

3.2   Requirements for Programming Languages

The use of multimedia data involves specific requirements, related to the environment (hardware and operating system), which can also be transferred to the implementation language, where they have to be specified.

Important properties characterizing multimedia applications, which have to be supported by programming languages, include the handling of very large data volumes, real-time requirements, concurrency control, and synchronization. In addition, a programming language should support reusability, expandability, easy maintainability, and robustness of programming components, to ensure efficient programming development.

3.2.1   Very Large Data Volumes

Multimedia applications are generally characterized by the fact that large data volumes have to be handled, because multimedia data also require large amounts of storage, even when available in compressed form. This requirement refers both to data held in the main memory and data handled by external devices (hard disk, network, sound card, or video card).

For a programming language, this means that the efficient processing of large data volumes is supported and the generated program code should not suffer from performance losses, e.g., when copying objects or passing parameters.

3.2.2   Real-time Requirements

Continuous media impose real-time requirements on programming languages, because exact timing has to be observed. On the other hand, both the processing and playback of multimedia data, e.g., audio or video data, may not have the desired quality.

This means that the language has to allow specification of time requirements, but it also has to provide mechanisms to handle exceptions, e.g., when a pre-set time limit cannot be maintained, due to insufficient processor performance.

3.2.3   Synchronization

When several media are to be represented concurrently, then it is often necessary to synchronize the presentation of various media. One example is video data, which contain audio information in addition to the image data, and where both have to be played out at the same time.

For this reason, a programming language should allow the formulation of conditions for synchronous representation, and ensure that they are enforced at runtime for the entire system.

3.2.4   Reusability

Multimedia applications often contain program components, such as routines to represent animated sequences, or to play back audio data, which are required in almost all applications. This means that these program components do not have to be created from scratch for each application. Instead, the corresponding components should be implemented once but in such a way that they can be reused in other applications. The programming language should encourage this reuse by offering a suitable *modularization concept*.

3.2.5   Expandability

The expandability of multimedia applications is another important factor. Developments in the area of multimedia are progressing at a fast pace, so it is important to be able to adapt applications to new features.

For this reason, the programming language should allow expansions, so that changes can be limited locally. Useful technologies include *encapsulation*, *abstraction*, and *hierarchies*, as well as modularization.

3.2.6   Maintainability

Multimedia applications are generally characterized by high complexity. For this reason, it is important to be able to build them in such a way that errors and the impact of changes can be easily limited. This is easier if the programming language provides suitable structurization mechanisms. In this respect, too, *modularization*, *encapsulation*, *abstraction*, and *hierarchies* can be important contributors to achieve easy maintainability.

3.2.7 Robustness

Robustness describes the way in which an application handles exceptions and unforeseen events. Such events can occur, for example, when computer performance is insufficient to represent the data, or when a network connection is too slow to transfer the data at the required speed. For this reason, the language level should also encourage both the design and development of robust programs.

3.3 Object-oriented Application Development

The previous section discussed requirements of programming languages. Considering that these requirements depend heavily on object-oriented languages, i.e., object-oriented languages are able to meet them, object-oriented techniques are used increasingly to design and implement multimedia applications. In particular, the flexible mechanisms for reuse of previously developed components (e.g., to manage and represent various multimedia data) and the easy expandability of existing applications and libraries (e.g., by new types of multimedia components), make object orientation well suited for use in this field.

Detailed information on object orientation is available in the literature, e.g., [Mey97].

3.3.1 Basic Terms of the Object Model

In this section we discuss briefly the fundamental terms of the object model, before we describe the properties and the application of this model in the area of multimedia .

Object and Class The basic term in object orientation is the *object*. An object has a unique identity, which distinguishes it from all other objects, and a specific behavior, which can depend on the state of the object. Objects with the same behavior are grouped into *classes*. A class describes, statically, the behavior and structure of objects. Objects are dynamically created (instantiated) as *instances* at runtime.

We normally distinguish between the *interface* of a class, which describes the behavior of objects visible to the exterior, and the *implementation*, which specifies how objects of a class are built internally. This distinction is important for encapsulation (see below).

Methods and Messages Objects communicate among themselves by exchanging *messages*. When an object receives a message, it executes a *method* that specifies how the object has to respond when it receives that message. Sending messages between objects can be compared to functional or procedural calls in functional or procedural languages.

Aggregation   When objects are built so that they use other objects, we speak of aggregation. Aggregation can be used to describe an *is-part-of relationship* between objects. One example would be a cart that has four wheels (among other parts). The internal static structure of the objects of a class described by the aggregation is normally not visible at the interface of a class, but it is specified in the implementation of that class.

Inheritance   *Inheritance* is used to describe two concepts frequently used together: the specialization of class interfaces and the import of implementations.

Specialization serves to build the structure of a system of classes by a subset relationship. Class *A* is then a specialization of another class, *B*, if all objects of *A* meet the interface defined by *B*, i.e., if *A* expands the interface of *B*. Note that a class with expanded interface describes a subset of objects, because the expanded description is more specialized. This is an important point that should not be forgotten.

In contrast, *import* describes the reuse of existing implementations (or parts thereof). When class *A* expands class *B*, then this could not only refer to its interface, but also to its implementation, to which more functions can be added, or existing functions can be adapted to a new context.

These two concepts are generally used together, because the implementation of a class should also be reused when it is specialized. Similarly, the implementation is also imported when there is also a specialization. However, because this is "only" the general case, modern object-oriented programming languages also support the separate use of the two concepts.

Polymorphism   We speak of *polymorphism* when a language allows a descriptor to reference objects of various classes at different times (or at runtime), or in a different context. This is the case, for example, when a variable in a multimedia application describes a selected object: At different times, this variable can point to images, audio data, or video data. Polymorphism offers an important concept for reuse and expandability of existing program codes, reducing both the implementation costs and the error probability.

Dynamic Binding   The reuse and expansion options introduced by polymorphism becomes really meaningful when the methods of a class are dynamically bound to the messages sent at runtime, in contrast to static binding, which is perfomed earlier, i.e., when the program is translated, and which is still used extensively in many programming languages.

Dynamic binding allows programming of a playback console for multimedia data, wwith which arbitrary continuous data can be played out. For example, this could be realized by sending a play message to a selected multimedia object. By use of dynamic binding, a play method to display video data could be called for video sequences. However, if the object is an audio file, we would use the corresponding play method for audio output. In the case of static binding, this difference would have to be addressed explicitly by the programmer, who would introduce a case differentiation for all possibilities. This would strongly limit the expandability of the program.

3.3.2 Object Model Properties

We can derive important properties of the object model: *abstraction*, *encapsulation*, *modularity*, *hierarchy*, *typification*, *concurrency control*, *distribution*, and *persistence*.

Abstraction   *Abstraction* is a fundamental human approach for handling complexity. This is achieved by considering only those essential properties of an object which distinguish it from other objects.

Therefore, an abstract description of continuous data would include only the properties that distinguish continuous data from non-continuous data, i.e., the total length of data. In particular, in connection with specialization hierarchies, abstractions can be used to make the complexity of problems more manageable.

Encapsulation   By distinguishing between the interface of a class and its implementation, as mentioned above, we can differentiate between the "external view" and the "internal view" of an object. More specifically, an object that sends messages to a specific object to obtain certain "services" is then called the "client" of that object. This means that the interface specifies for each object which messages it can understand and which services it will be able to offer (external view of the object). This concept is called the *contract model*, because each object guarantees a specific behavior to its clients at the interface. However, it is important that the realization of the behavior is not visible to the clients during the implementation of the object, i.e., only the object itself knows its implementation (internal view), because it ensures extensive independence between the objects of a system. Otherwise, reusability, maintainability, and expandability would not be ensured.

This becomes clear, for example, in the definition of interfaces for multimedia devices in an operating system: Applications that involve audio output can use only the functions specified for audio output devices at the interface, but they may not make any implicit assumptions about the device used. For this reason, an operating system interface like *DirectX* (see above) is based on the encapsulation properties of object models such as COM.

Modularity   The structure of a program is called *modular* when it can be divided into relatively independent components. This forms the basis for reusability and maintainability of program parts, in particular when the modularization is coupled to an encapsulation mechanism.

Within the object model, *classes* form an essential modularization structure, because each class represents an independent unit. Some programming languages additionally offer other modularization levels, e.g., by providing permission to group classes into packages or libraries. In Java, for example, there are packages for various application fields, which can also be structured in hierarchies. For example, the Java Media package offers a collection of classes to handle various media, including modules such as Java Media Framework (for continuous media), JavaSound, and Java 3D.

Hierarchy   Objects within the object model can be arranged in several hierarchies. The *aggregation* and *specialization* hierarchies are important in this respect.

Aggregation Hierarchy   *Aggregation* describes how the objects of a class can be combined with components of other classes, e.g., when a movie requires audio and video data. When we costruct new objects by using objects belonging to other classes, we build an "is-part-of" relation. We can use this relation to arrange the classes within a hierarchy, because the relation has to be directed and non-cyclic. (An object *a* that includes object *b* as a component cannot also be part of object *b*.)

Aggregation is an important concept for the reusability and handling of complex systems, because the classes created in this way can be reused, and the complexity can be gradually reduced.

Specialization Hierarchy   *Specialization* of classes introduces another way of forming hierarchies. Each class can be located somewhere between the more special and the more general classes. This hierarchy permits the reduction of the complexity of software systems, because each abstraction level only has to consider the classes belonging to that level. On the other hand, such a hierarchy is important for reusability and expandability, when program parts repeatedly access the appropriate level within the hierarchy, so that additional specializations can be added without having to change the existing code.

As an example, dynamic binding could be used to add another class for 3D animation, which also has a Play method and is also a specialization of the Continuous Media class. In this case, we would not have to change the existing implementation of the playback console.

Typification   *Types* describe a set of objects with the same interface. Many programming languages offer a type concept to verify automatically, by stating the types, whether or not an object will understand the messages sent to that object. This is important for the correctness of programs. In addition, the efficiency of a translated program increases when type information is available or can be automatically retrieved.

In a generational environment for multimedia applications, for instance, types would be available for reused multimedia data and multimedia devices.

Concurrency Control   *Concurrency* describes the ability of a system to execute several control flows (processes) concurrently (or quasi-concurrently). Concurrency has to be well modeled in an object model by assigning parallel control flows to various objects. These objects are then called active objects.

Concurrency is very important in multimedia applications, because this is the only way to represent continuous media concurrently without interrupting the actual program flow.

Distribution We speak of *distribution* when the objects of a system are distributed over different processing units (computers). As objects are independent units (modularity), they are well suited for distribution. The objects communicate by exchanging messages, so that it is easy to send these messages both within one computer and across a network.

Distribution is relevant for multimedia applications, e.g., because multimedia data can reside on various servers in the Internet.

Persistence *Persistence* is the ability of an object to maintain its temporal and/or spatial state. This includes a temporal persistence of the creator of an object, e.g., by storing and reusing it in another application. In addition, a persistent object can be moved onto another computer without changing its identity, behavior, or state.

3.3.3 Example: Java

Java is one example of object-oriented programming languages which are increasingly gaining significance in connection with multimedia applications. Java is a programming language developed by Sun in 1991; its main strength is the *portability* of the translated programs. Programs implemented in Java are translated by a translator into a neutral byte format, i.e., a format that does not depend on a specific architecture. The translated program is then executed by an interpreter. The main advantage of this approach is that, in contrast to applications written in languages like C++ and translated into system-dependent binary files by a translator, a Java program can run on any platform, once it is translated, as long as that platform supports a Java interpreter. However, machine-dependent and interpreted languages are not a new concept in programming language development. Only the combination of platform independence with an additional concept introduced by Java, the so-called applets, has led to an explosive proliferation of applications implemented in Java. An *applet* is a Java program embedded in HTML pages and executed in a browser by the user. The browser has to include a Java interpreter, which is the case for all currently available Internet browsers. In contrast to CGI (see also Chapter 5 on documents), this does not mean that there cannot be any user interaction with the rest of the page. Rather, the interpreter runs parallel to the actual browser. The applet is transferred from the server to the WWW browser on the client over the Internet and executed locally on that client.

The use of Java applets in connection with a browser offers a very easy way of letting clients use the services and functions of a server. All the user needs to access a program stored on the server is a Java-enabled browser and access to the Internet. The user does not have to install the executing program. This approach mainly facilitates the further development of an application, because the user does not have to bother about version updates. This means that new versions will be automatically available to the client when it starts the applet again.

Chapter 5 on documents includes more details of this approach.

3.4   Object-oriented Frameworks and Class Libraries

To represent multimedia applications it is important to have good class libraries and powerful frameworks readily available, because this domain has many reusable components that should not be implemented from scratch for each application. For example, this includes classes offering the functionality for various types of multimedia data.

All these classes represent *generic* abstractions, because they can be used for a broad range of applications. However, each application will expand this given set by additional *application-specific* classes, which are tailored to a specific application, i.e., which do not expand to other applications. When designing multimedia applications, the developer should be careful as to which program segments could be of interest beyond this special application.

This section discusses the different range of class categories offered by a class library or an object-oriented framework. In addition to classes for various types of multimedia data, this also includes classes for devices that handle multimedia data and for the modeling of data flows between different sets of multimedia devices.

3.4.1   Data Type Modeling

Different types of multimedia data have different properties and functions, so that it appears intuitive to describe them by different data types. This approach allows the specification of a class for each data type; normally, this includes classes like text, image, audio, and video.

When common properties from various data types are combined, then we can build a specialization hierarchy (see Section 3.3.2). One possible division could be drawn between *static* and *dynamic* data, depending on whether or not the data change over time. In turn, we could divide dynamic data into *discrete* and *continuous* data according to how they change over time. In this context, it should be noted that, due to the underlying principle, continuous data cannot really be processed on a computer, because we always have to perform a discretization. Figure 3-2 demonstrates this division.

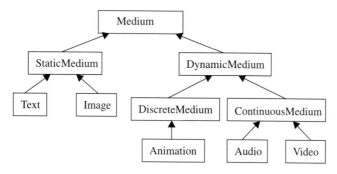

Figure 3-2 Typical specialization hierarchy for multimedia data.

For this reason, dynamic data are divided into *logical data units* (*LDUs*), which specify the value of dynamic multimedia data during a certain time. Within files, they are then stored in *time capsules* [Her90].

Another possible division could be according to optical and acoustic signals. However, such a division is normally less relevant for the application.

3.4.2 Modeling Devices

In addition to data, a framework should also make various multimedia devices available. This requirement includes not only real devices, such as monitor or audio card, but also *virtual devices*, which implement a function only in software and do not have a physical correspondence. One example would be an audio or video mixer, which combines a set of different signals into one signal by means of software.

A multimedia device can basically be divided into three parts, namely source, transformer, and renderer [deC98]. When the data flow between any set of devices is viewed, then the data is made available by a *source* device. A *transformer* handles multimedia data, and has both an input and an output. Finally, a *renderer* represents multimedia data, e.g., on a monitor or via an audio card.

This division provides a specialization hierarchy for devices.

3.4.3 Modeling Data Streams

The division or arrangement of multimedia devices by data flow suggests that the data streams between different devices should also be modeled. Each device has a certain number of inputs and outputs for *data streams*. When we connect these data streams, we can build a *data flow graph*, describing each data flow. The devices themselves are the nodes and the data streams are the arcs or edges in these graphs.

Figure 3-3 shows an example of a data flow graph.

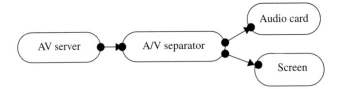

Figure 3-3   Example of a data flow graph.

3.4.4   Example: Java Media Framework

The *Java Media Framework* API of Sun, Silicon Graphics, and Intel is one example of a multimedia framework. This framework consists of a collection of various classes, allowing the display and handling of multimedia data streams. Thanks to the portability of Java, we can use this framework to develop Java applications or applets that can be used on these platforms. The currently available version of the framework (and a future version already announced) allows only the playback of multimedia data, which means that it is suitable for the implementation of prototype applications. Subsequent versions of the framework will include recording, processing, and implementing of video conferences.

3.5   Distribution of Objects

The increasing networking of systems and applications means that the need for and use of distributed applications increases. In the WWW, which is often praised as an interactive multimedia information medium, users are offered this multimedia information (audio and video) mostly only in *passive* form. The term *passive* here means that the user can only start and end the transmission of a desired information medium (e.g., a video transmission).

   For this reason, interactive applications should offer the user at least control options for the following four parameters [Flu95]:

   • The *time* when the presentation should start.
   • The *order* in which the information should be displayed.
   • The *speed* at which the information should be displayed.
   • The *type* how information should be represented.

The success of the Internet, or WWW, as a multimedia application can surely be largely attributed to the fact that a number of heterogeneous platforms are able to communicate with each other.

   Object-oriented programming languages and middleware platforms like [CBM02] are very useful for implementing multimedia applications. Standards like CORBA allow remote communication of objects, which will be briefly discussed below. Later, we will introduce DAVIC and DSM-CC.

3.5.1   Example: OMG and CORBA

Like the *Open Software Foundation* (*OSF*), the *Object Management Group* (*OMG*) is a non-profit consortium, established in 1989, to formulate a suitable architecture for the distribution and cooperation of object-oriented software components in distributed systems. This work has been based on the approach of the *Remote Procedure Call* (*RPC*), realized by Sun in 1987, which is used to call methods from a remote computer. This architecture allowed, for the first time, the transition from the development of communication-oriented implementations to application-oriented distributed applications. The goal of the OMG was to allow an architecture for the distribution and cooperation of different software components in networked heterogeneous systems. The OMG itself does not produced readily-implemented solutions; it exclusively elaborates specifications. The *Object Management Architecture* (*OMA*) was published as a reference architecture in 1990. This architecture consists of four components (see Figure 3-4).

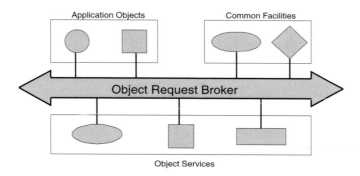

Figure 3-4   The Object Management Architecture (OMA).

- Like the *External Data Representation* (*XDR*) in RPC, the *Interface Definition Language* (*IDL*) serves for platform- and language-independent declarations of communication objects. The syntax is very similar to C++. In OMA, the mapping of IDL specifications to concrete implementations, e.g., in C++, Smalltalk, or more recently to Java, is defined in addition to the syntax. This means that it is irrelevant for objects what programming language was used to implement other objects which they use to obtain services. These objects could also offer other methods that are not declared in IDL. Although these methods cannot be accessed from another computer, the can be used locally.

- The *Object Request Broker* (*ORB*) is the central brokering component of the CORBA architecture. A client object does not contact one or several server objects directly, but handles all communication with the intermediate object bus. All requests are sent to ORB, which passes the method call automatically to the required object and ensures that the function value is returned correctly. This means that the client object does not need to have any knowledge of the transport protocols used, or how objects are created and stored on the server side. In contrast to RPC, the role of the client and the server is not rigid, but all objects participating in the communication can use other objects to obtain services.

- The *Object Services* are defined in the *Common Object Services Specification (COSS)*. These services include basic operations for logical modeling and physical storage of objects or services required in almost all distributed applications (e.g., security, transaction monitoring, lifecycle). OMA has published several requests for the definition of new services since 1990. Members can submit implementation proposals, but they have to submit one reference implementation. To date, there are no services implementing special services required for multimedia applications and data transmissions. All services defined by OMG have to be contained in CORBA-compliant products. Virtually no manufacturer meets all of these requirements.

- The *Common Facilities* are a collection of classes and objects including general, useful higher-level services for a range of different application types. In contrast to the Object Services, they do not have to be included in each CORBA-compliant product, but are merely a recommendation of OMG. These facilities are a further development of the software components or libraries described above. However, these facilities do not reuse only individual objects, but complete process flows, mapped to objects and object relationships. This allows the integration of complete application frameworks, e.g., the TIVOLI network management tool or IBM's OpenDoc specification in CORBA.

In summary, we can see that the CORBA specification offers an architecture which, together with its Interface Definition Language, allows a clear separation between the design and the implementation of distributed applications. In addition, all the benefits of object-oriented programming, such as inheritance, isolation, and encapsulation, can be used. Moreover, the architecture is independent of any special programming language and platform, so that it is very flexible and interoperable. Most importantly, the CORBA architecture is widely accepted in practice and supported by many vendors.

Maximum flexibility in the development of distributed applications can be achieved by combining CORBA and Java. Since the publication of the *Internet Inter ORB Protocol (IIOP)*, which is part of CORBA 2.0 and has to be supported by all ORB vendors, it is ensured that objects bound to an arbitrary ORB can be addressed by each CORBA-compatible ORB. An ORB implemented in Java offers programming-language independent use of distributed objects and, additionally, the platform independence inherent in Java. Most browser vendors also announced that they would support IIOP, so that the implementation of ORBs running as applets within a browser can be expected. We are thus talking about a portable ORB that can be loaded upon request and used to access remote objects. Figure 3-5 shows an sample scenario for the use of this Java ORB in connection with a Java program on the client side, and server applications written in different programming languages to realize a distributed application.

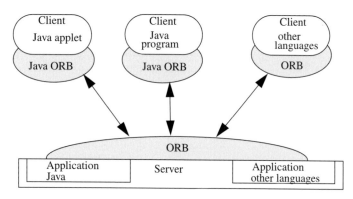

Figure 3-5   Example of a combination of CORBA and Java.

This approach allows the use of multimedia capabilities of Java to implement distributed applications. However, it would be desirable to support multimedia applications in CORBA itself, which is not possible at present. To facilitate the creation of such applications and data exchange between them, special standardization boards have been formed, which will be briefly introduced below.

3.5.2   Example: Digital Audio Video Council (DAVIC)

DAVIC (Digital Audio Video Council) was a non-profit Association based in Switzerland and formed in 1994, with a membership which culminated at 222 companies from more than 25 countries. It represented all sectors of the audio-visual industry: manufacturing (computer, consumer electronics and telecommunications equipment) and service (broadcasting, telecommunications and CATV), as well as a number of government agencies and research organizations. The association was disbanded, according to its statutes, after five years of activity and presently it is only active through its website http://www.davic.org. The DAVIC approach consists of five independent units: the Content Provider System (CPS), the Service Provider System (SPS), the Service Consumer System (SCS), the CPS-SPS Delivery System, which connects CPS to SPS, and the SPS-SCS Delivery System, which connects SPS to SCS (see Figure 3-6).

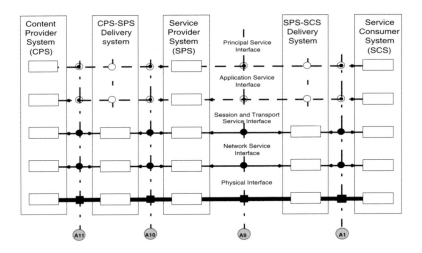

Figure 3-6   The DAVIC architecture.

Each of these subsystems, shown in Figure 3-6, and other parts of the system, e.g., information representation, are described in the DAVIC 1.0 specification. DAVIC 1.0 is organized into 11 elements, classified in three groups. Elements in Group 1 identify all the tools that are necessary to build DAVIC-conforming systems. Elements in Group 2 describe how the three main DAVIC subsystems can be assembled using the tools of group 1. Finally, elements in Group 3 address system-wide issues. More specifically, the DAVIC 1.0 specification describes the following DAVIC system tools:

- ·*Group 1*: High-layer and mid-layer protocols, lower-layer protocols and physical interfaces, information representation, security, and usage information protocols.
- ·*Group 2*: Service Provider System architecture and interfaces, Delivery System architecture and interfaces, and Service Consumer System architecture and interfaces.
- ·*Group 3*: DAVIC System functions, system reference models and scenarios, and dynamics, reference points, and interfaces.

The full specification would go beyond the extent and scope of this book, so that we will limit ourselves to just a brief description of the subsystems shown in Figure 3-6, which represent important general concepts of DAVIC:

- *Content Provider System (CPS)*: This system generates multimedia data (e.g., audio or video data) and applications and makes them available in a format supported by the end-user systems. In addition, the CPS can support mechanisms such as database queries, message transmission, or transaction management.
- *Service Provider System (SPS)*: This system is responsible for storing, updating, or deleting contents and their delivery to the end-user upon request. In addition,

the system supports services for selection of applications and access to external data and services (e.g., WWW).

- *Service Consumer System (SCS)*: This system is used to transmit and represent the (multimedia) data requested by the end-user. It can be either a regular PC or any other device suitable for data playback (e.g., TV and set-top box). The SCS is responsible for requesting, receiving, interpreting, and presenting the desired contents.
- *CPS-SPS Delivery System*: This system is a broadband system used to transmit the data from the contents provider to the service provider.
- *SPS-SCS Delivery System*: This system is responsible for the transmission of data from the service provider to the end-user, where a local area network (LAN) or metropolitan area network (MAN) is normally used as the underlying network.

Traditional standardization tends to define vertically integrated systems with little or no attention to similar systems in other domains. DAVIC's goal of interoperability across applications systems cannot be specified, but "components" (tools) that are non-"system-specific" can be, because they have to be able to be used by different industries in different systems and still guarantee interoperability.

The need to support business and service models of multiple industries requires not only that tools should be usable in a variety of different systems but also in different parts of the same systems. Therefore DAVIC defines its tools in such a way that they can be relocated, whenever this relocation is technically feasible and practically meaningful.

Tools should be unique, a principle sometimes hard to enforce, but compliance to this principle provides substantial benefits in terms of interoperability and availability of technology, thanks to the easier achievement of a critical mass because of a wider field of applicability of the technology. Sometimes, tools can contain normative improvements to specifications that do not affect backwards compatibility. What constitutes a tool is not always obvious, as tools may depend on the particular technological situation: A video decoder today must be implemented in dedicated silicon, but in a few years time, it will be possible to have programmable processors in which decoding algorithms are "downloaded".

That a standard should specify the minimum that is necessary for interoperability seems obvious. But this was not always so. When standards were produced by associations of particular industries, it was natural to add to the "minimum" those nice little things that bring a standard nearer to a product specification. The border of "minimum" then became blurred. This approach was fostered by the concept of "guaranteed quality" so dear to broadcasters and telecommunication operators alike because of their "public service" nature. A multi-industry environment like DAVIC does not have a single constituency to satisfy but rather tens of them, so it has to specify the very minimum that is needed for interoperability.

3.5.3 Example: DSM-CC

DSM-CC (Digital Storage Media—Command and Control) is a recent ISO/IEC standard developed for the delivery of multimedia broadband services. Open protocols in this area are essential for the widespread deployment of such services. Total interoperability between service providers and consumers will require many different aspects of broadband service delivery to be addressed. What follows is an introductory overview of the different functions covered by the DSM-CC standard. Its purpose is to convey the scope of the DSM-CC standard and the basic reference model that underpinned the development of the standard.

Of particular interest for the development of interactive multimedia applications is the user-to-user interface of DMS-CC. This specification describes interfaces between clients and services and interfaces for the portability of client applications.

The current DSM-CC standard described in ISO/IEC 13818-6 offers protocols required for the development of movies-on-demand, near-movies-on-demand, distance learning, movie listing, or news-on-demand. Note that the DAVIC 1.0 specification also specifies the user-to-network and user-to-user communication modules of DSM-CC, in relation to DAVIC's Service Consumer System.

DSM-CC includes the following protocol areas, which will be briefly explained in the sections below:

- Network Session and Resource Control
- Configuration of a client
- Downloading to a client
- VCR-like control of the video stream
- Generic Interactive Application Services

The key to DSM-CC is its flexibility: Each protocol area can be used standalone, or in concert with other protocol areas, depending on the application(s) being addressed.

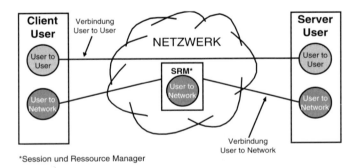

Figure 3-7 The DSM-CC reference model.

Figure 3-7 shows connections for carriage of User-to-Network (U-N) information and User-to-User (U-U) information. A U-U information flow is used between client and server. The U-N information flows between the network and the client or the server. U-N messages are exchanged over U-N connections, and their purpose is to control sessions and network resources. Figure 3-7 also shows that the network contains a *Session and Resource Manager (SRM)* entity. The SRM is the entity that terminates the U-N connection from a user. An SRM could be distributed over a geographical area, in order to cover the spread of a global network spanning many network providers. The U-N part of DSM-CC defines a User-Network Interface protocol: it does not, at present, define any intra-network communication required.

The SRM can police client/server connections based on policies set at service subscription, it can be the point in the network that provides configuration information to users, and it can authenticate the clients.

- *U-N Messages*: DSM-CC defines a standard message header for all U-N messages. The assumption is that these messages will be carried over some transport layer protocol. Minimum requirements are placed on any such protocol. It need not reliably deliver messages, but it must detect and discard corrupted messages. The transport service must be able to deliver entire U-N messages (i.e., lower layers perform any segmentation and re-assembly) but it need not be responsible for delivering messages in order. These requirements are met by common protocols such as UDP over IP and, indeed, by AAL5 over ATM.

- *U-U Connections*: It is expected that there will be multiple U-U connections between a client and a server. In general, the protocol carried over these connections is not specified by DSM-CC, it is instead a matter of agreement between the client and the server. However, DSM-CC defines a set of generic services that a server may provide in an interoperable fashion to clients. Invocation of these services is performed by a Remote Procedure Call (RPC) protocol carried over a U-U connection.

The following sections describe each of the different protocol areas that DSM-CC defines.

Network Session and Resource Control   A key concept in DSM-CC is that of a *session*. A session is defined as an association between two users, providing the capability to group together the resources needed for the instance of a service. In other words, a client accesses a service, say home shopping, by setting up a session with a server. At the end of the service, when the client no longer needs an association with the server, the session is torn down. Figure 3-8 shows the DSM-CC U-N messages used for session setup.

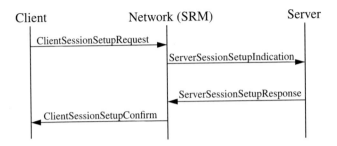

Figure 3-8   U-N session setup.

DSM-CC is intended to operate in an environment where network resources are not necessarily either free or bountiful. Rather, it is assumed that resources will be acquired when needed to deliver a service, and released after a service has finished. Different services will require different resources. Resource allocation is tied to sessions. A Network-wide unique *sessionId* identifies a session in the network. All resources belonging to an instance of a service are tagged with the sessionId, and can thus be easily identified. This is useful for billing and administration by the network, and for disposing of all resources associated with a session when the session is torn down. The DSM-CC session setup protocol is designed to allow client authentication by the network, and to ensure that the client is aware that a session has been set up, and thus accepts responsibility for it.

During a session, the server can request that the network add to the session more resources (or remove existing resources), depending on the phase of the service. This is done with the *AddResource* message set (respectively, the *DeleteResource* message set). In these messages, the server describes the resources it needs from the network by using *Resource Descriptors*.

Connections for User-to-User information flows are the main network resources that make up a session. A DSM-CC session will usually contain more than one U-U connection. Often, sessions are shown as having a control stream, for RPC messages, and an MPEG-2 stream. Sophisticated applications may use more connections, for example, a connection to carry video that is shown in a window whose surrounding background is sent over another high-speed connection. Note that the server-end connections within a session do not all need to terminate at the same Network Service Access Point (NSAP): a client may be receiving information from more than one source within a given session.

VCR-like control of the video stream   The MPEG-2 standard for video encoding/ decoding does not address the issue of play times for any particular video. MPEG-2 streams include their own internal clock times in the encoded streams that relate the encoded video to the encoded audio, to allow the synchronization of the two. However, video playback requires more than this: To support random positioning within a stream and a variety of play rates, the DSM-CC media stream interfaces make use of a temporal addressing scheme created for DSM-CC, called *Normal Play Time* (*NPT*). NPT is the "clock" a viewer associates with a "program". NPT advances normally when in normal play mode, advances quickly when a user selects fast forward for a stream, or decrements quickly when rewind is selected.

Generic Interactive Application Services The DSM-CC User-to-User part provides a generic set called *Multimedia User-to-User Interfaces*. These interfaces provide modular building blocks that can be used to enable a wide range of multimedia applications, from movies on demand, over teleshopping, to games and distance learning.

Interface definitions are written in the *Interface Definition Language* (*IDL*) and provide two distinct interfaces: an *Application Portability Interface* (*API*), defined for programmers writing applications that run on Clients, and a *Service Interoperability Interface* (*SII*), defined to allow clients and servers from different manufacturers to operate together. The IDL of the SII leads to a fixed bit pattern on the wire, once the Remote Procedure Call (RPC) encoding scheme and message set have been chosen. Figure 3-9 shows the two DSM-CC interfaces.

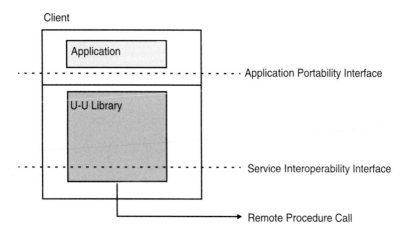

Figure 3-9 The Application Portability and Service Interoperability Interfaces.

DSM-CC does not specify which RPC scheme is used. However, its aim is to permit interoperability with CORBA 2.0, the Common Object Request Broker: Architecture and Specification, Revision 2.0. DAVIC has chosen CORBA 2.0 RPC (UNO—Universal Networked Objects) and encoding (CDR—Common Data Representation) for its specification of DSM-CC.

Core Client-Service Interfaces The DSM-CC Core U-U interfaces are a collection of minimum requirements that have to be supported by a DSM-CC server complex. The basic functions of these core interfaces are briefly outlined below:

- The *Stream* interface provides VCR-like control to the client.
- The *File* interface allows a client to read and write files stored on a server.
- The *Directory* interface provides navigational facilities.
- The *BindingIterator* interface allows the client to process lists of information .
- *Session* interfaces provide attachment to (and conversely detachment from) ServiceGateway services.
- *ServiceGateway* interfaces form the access point to the services for the end-user. This is the location where services of a contents provider are registered, or registrations are removed.

The abstract interfaces, *Base* and *Access,* provide interfaces common to more than one instantiable interface. The abstract interface *First* enables clients to obtain their first objects.

Summary   DSM-CC is a collection of protocol areas for the delivery of multimedia services over broadband networks. DSM-CC defines a protocol for User-to-Network messages to realize session and resource management. It provides protocols for both client configuration and download. DSM-CC includes an interface for VCR-like control of video streams, and interfaces for a multitude of other generic interactive application services. Through the definition of a Data Carousel and a U-U Object Carousel, DSM-CC provides protocols for generic broadband application services. For channel changing in broadcast networks, DSM-CC includes a protocol for switched digital channel change.

DSM-CC is widely applicable. It is based upon a very general model of client, server and network entities. It does not dictate how each entity must be realized (although it provides some examples of possible organizations). Rather, the DSM-CC specification focuses on the User-to-Network interfaces and the User-to-User interfaces. DSM-CC is very flexible. A network supporting DSM-CC can offer a wide range of broadband applications. Each protocol area can be implemented separately, thus aiding in the integration of the DSM-CC standard with other standards. Similarly, the DSM-CC Switched Digital Broadcast (SDB) Channel Change Protocol can be implemented without implementing the DSM-CC U-N or U-U messages.

Other approaches for the development of distributed multimedia applications based on CORBA, which are clearly more oriented to the respective problems, are found in print or online , e.g., TANGRAM project [EFSS] or MASH [MS97].

Security

This chapter deals with the security aspect in multimedia systems. We will begin with a discussion of the term *security*, as opposed to the term *failure safety*. As mentioned in other chapters, no arbitrary combination of media deserves the term *multimedia*. To particularly emphasize requirements in multimedia systems, our descriptions and discussions of security problems and solutions concentrate mainly on multimedia components. We will not discuss pure text components in detail, because they do not have any particular requirements, and are normally subject to well-known cryptographic methods frequently discussed in the literature. After a definition of the terms, we will present general security requirements in multimedia systems, followed by an introduction and discussion of various solutions for image, video, audio, and 3D data. To better explain the security approaches introduced here, we will close this chapter with several application examples to illustrate such security problems and practical security system solutions.

4.1 Definition of "Security"

More and more current applications are executed on several computers within cooperative tasks in networked environments, some forming internetworks with functional units distributed over several local and remote locations. The trend towards networking, particularly for communication over public networks, increases the risk of damage caused by intruders or malicious users [Sch03]. The acceptance of new information technology systems depends largely on the security offered by the distributed application. This means that the requirements with regard to technical data protection and data security become increasingly important, so that the continuous design of technical systems based on the criteria of safe telecooperation gains ever-increasing importance.

Security   The term *security* means actions or measures to prevent potential attacks on computers, stored and transmitted data, and communication relationships. These actions can be of an organizational or a technical nature. Technical protection measures are involved either in the network or the application level and can be implemented by configuring and/or using cryptographic methods.

Failure Safety   In contrast to the above definition, *failure safety* attempts to limit or reduce the impact of inadvertent events that can lead to a failure of or damage to computers, stored or transmitted data, and communication relationships. This area includes data protection, data recovery, or improvement of a computer's failure safety. Inadvertent events include storm, fire or water damage, as well as power failure and hardware or software defects. Failure safety in multimedia systems does not translate into media-specific requirements or properties, so that we will not discuss failure safety strategies any further.

4.2   General Security Requirements and Properties

The conception and design of new information technology systems introduces *chances*, but also *risks* which arise with any new information technology. This section discusses potential risks and the resulting security requirements for multimedia systems.

The worldwide deployment and proliferation of digital networks opens many vulnerability points for all kinds of attacks, i.e., eavesdropping, flooding, spoofing, manipulating, or deleting of data by unauthorized or malicious users. This means that the use of new technologies offers many chances, but also entails considerable threats, ranging from immediate financial and/or legal damage to corporate image loss. The equipment an attacker needs to devise and cause such damage is not complicated and is commercially available; in fact, a PC with modem and telephone line is often sufficient. The lack of higher-level control instances, the extensive free access, and the frequently poor or non-existing security standards among system operators and users open up additional vulnerabilities, encouraging misuse. In addition, attacks are often detected too late or not at all, leading to considerable damage. Finally, it should be noted that the legal investigation and law enforcement procedures in such high-tech criminal cases are very difficult, in particular in case of international offenders, in view of the global cyberspace. It is often the case that, when distributing new technologies, the security risks and potential criminal misuse are either not dealt with in a timely fashion, or not at all. Of course, this means that, once a system has been introduced and the first cases of misuse become known, either service providers and distributors search for solutions because of possible liability claims, or users search for solutions to protect intellectual property. Then it is very difficult to remove the deficits incurred. Therefore, it is meaningful to use preventive concepts which offer high protection from the very beginning. This concerns both the handling or storage of data, which are subject to a higher risk due to unauthorized knowledge, and the transmitted data, which have to be protected by effective protection measures.

Data protection is divided into legal, organizational, and technical protection measures.

Legal data protection formulates laws with special criteria, such as the German Data Privacy Act [BRD91], which regulate technical and organizational measures in the automatic processing of personal data, depending on the type of data to be protected. Within the scope of legal data protection, there could be a connection to copyright, an option which is gaining increasing importance in multimedia systems. Such a law does not deal with personal information, but with the significance of data as intellectual property. In Germany, for example, the legal basis for this Act is the Law of Proprietary Rights [Hoh93].

When a piece of work is to be additionally protected by the US copyright act, then a copyright notice should be added to the imprint of that work, and registration with the Register of Copyrights is necessary (address: Register of Copyrights, Copyright Office, Library of Congress, Washington, D.C., 20559). In addition, efforts have been made to introduce a copyright system in the European Union (EU) [Hoh93].

Organizational data protection attempts to protect data against unauthorized access by organizational measures. Here, the four-eye principle is applied, i.e., certain activities may only be executed in the presence of (at least) two persons, but never by one person alone. In connection with computer systems, this approach could be implemented by two passwords; the user would have to enter both passwords, before he or she can perform such an activity. We will not discuss organizational data protection any further in this book, because multimedia systems behave like traditional systems in this respect.

Finally, we will discuss *technical data protection*. If we want to introduce technical data protection measures, we first have to think about the level at which the security concept should be implemented. We distinguish between two levels:

- The network level, where data is transmitted; and
- The application level, where data is processed and stored.

One of the issues relevant at the network level is how specific services can be accessed by certain user computers, while excluding other machines. Most of the mechanisms used today do not allow the direct integration of security functions. Some of the newer services and protocols support the integration of data encryption methods, including:

- *RTP* (Real-Time Protocol) [SCF96]: This protocol supports a simple implementation of data packets, from multicast to unicast routing, and vice versa. One bit in the header specifies that the payload contained in the packet is DES (Data

Encryption Standard) encrypted [Sch96]. The key can then be exchanged by use of *RTCP* (Real-Time Control Protocol), defined for RTP.

- *IPv6* (Internet Protocol Version 6) [DH95] handles encrypted data packets in a so-called *extended header.* The *ESP* (Encapsulated Security Payload) header defines that the packet arriving next is encrypted. The *authentication header* (AH) can be used for authentication and integrity.

- *ATM* (Asynchronous Transfer Mode) defines its own security model for end-to-end encryption and line encryption [ATM97].

Other work in this field concerns *firewalls*, *packet filters*, and *router configurations*, which do not have media-specific properties. We will discuss security concepts at he application level, involving security issues at the level of objects and users, in the following section.

Interests of the users   The security interests of the users of a multimedia application result mainly from potential abuse in open communication environments. Communication normally proceeds over different types of communication networks, which means that the transmission channels cannot be safely controlled and unauthorized persons may gain access to data. Most cases of abuse are based on economic interest, while cases based on intellectual interest in gaining information or manipulating information are rare. Basically, protection measures have to be directed against *external and internal abuse*, i.e., against both unauthorized and authorized network and system users and operators. The interest of authorized users is to protect their data and communication against unauthorized access by other user groups and network users and to communicate safely.

We will now describe data security aspects in the form of *access protection, authenticity, confidentiality, integrity, nonrepudiation, copyrights,* and *privacy and anonymity.*

Access Protection   Access protection means the control of access to the system and protection of data against unauthorized inspection. For this purpose, access rights and access limitations are defined for certain system functions and data inventories. More specifically, special access profiles have to be developed for each system user, whereas password control and protocol functions fall into the area of identification. One example is the well-known Kerberos utility for UNIX systems [Sta95].

Although the security of applications depends on other specific criteria within access protection, e.g., password control, trustworthy booting, protocol functions, and advanced access rights, they are not further discussed such as user authentication (authenticity check) and confidentiality, as well as cryptographic protocols.

Authenticity   Authenticity means the proof of the identity of an originator and the proof of the originality of the data material or a communication relationship. More specifically, authenticity involves the declaration of the originator or the authenticity of data, as well as the authenticity of the user. In a conventional paper document, the manual signature of the originator authenticates the originator and the originality of data. In the electronic context, this is replaced by a so-called *digital signature*. This means that it should be possibile to verify the authenticity of the sender, the data, and the system messages (e.g., receipt and forwarding acknowledgements, send requests, user identification, user classifications) based on certain criteria.

Confidentiality Confidentiality is a security measure which prevents unauthorized third parties from reading data. Confidentiality can be expanded to secrecy of data, so that even the knowledge of the existence of data is confidential.

Integrity Data integrity means the correctness and completeness of stored and trans- mitted data. When storing and forwarding data, integrity measures should ensure that no undetected changes have been made to these data. Integrity measures merely enable users to detect any manipulation. This means that integrity measures alone cannot restore the original information. Instead of marking the entire data material as falsified, integrity measures should include an exact reference to manipulated sections of data, so that the transmission can be repeated, or compromised information can be corrected.

Nonrepudiation Nonrepudiation involves allowing authorized third parties to verify the authenticity and integrity of data, in addition to the data receiver, which means that an authentication is performed. Nonrepudiation also ensures the binding character of a communication. This means, for example, that two communication partners who put their digital signatures under their documents cannot repudiate their signatures. This aspect deals with the acceptance of the origin and the receipt. The legal background of this requirement is obvious and is especially targeted at digital signatures.

Transparent Representation Possibilities It may be of some interest to users not to keep all data secret, to make data illegible to unauthorized persons, or to protect their data. This issue arises in so-called *Try&Buy transactions*. For example, data should be made available to a client so that he or she can evaluate that data's quality and usability. On the other hand, the client should not obtain the full package in its original quality before the parties have agreed on certain terms and prices, or come to another form of agreement. One practical solution to this problem is called *transparent encryption*.

Copyrights In addition to eavesdropping and tampering with data, the illegal produc- tion of copies from digital data represents a further problem, which, of course, has become very pressing in the electronic world. The methods known for access control can be used to prevent unauthorized access to data, but once a user has acquired the necessary access rights, there is no way to control his or her actions. The digital nature of data allows easy production of copies which are absolutely identical with the original. To prevent this counterfeit, specific measures are required to both identify the original data owner and the distributor of illegal copies in a unique way, so that damage compensation claims may be made (e.g., [EK03]). Copyright law has already been mentioned in a previous section; it forms the legal basis for a solution to this problem [Hoh93].

Privacy and Anonymity   The protection of privacy and anonymity is closely related to the area of legal data protection. We will discuss it briefly, because a user may have a justified interest in working in a system anonymously. For this purpose, mechanisms for sender and receiver anonymity and anonymity of the communication relationship should be provided to prevent the creation of communication profiles [PWP90]. To prevent such analyses, so-called *mix models* have been suggested [FJP97]. Measures for the protection of personal data will be discussed in connection with legal data protection.

One final note about the Common Criteria (CC) in the information processing industry [Bra96]: CC deal with international security criteria and are expected to offer generally accepted security criteria upon their completion. One important characteristic of CC is the separation between functionality and confidentiality.

Summary   Table 4-1 presents a summary of the security aspects discussed above.

Security Aspect	Short Description	Example
Access protection	System access control and access limitations for system functions and data inventory.	Firewall
Authenticity	Evidence of the identity of an originator/author and authenticity of the data material.	Digital signature, digital watermark
Confidentiality	Prevents access to data by unauthorized third parties.	Encryption
Integrity	Provides evidence that data have not been manipulated or compromised.	Digital signature, trust center, time stamp
Nonrepudiation	Verification of the authenticity and integrity of data, also against authorized third parties, to ensure reliable communication.	Digital signature
Transparent representation possibilities	Data material should be available in reduced quality.	Transparent encryption
Copyrights	Protection of intellectual property, copyright marks with ownership details, identification of distributors of illegal copies.	Digital watermark, fingerprint

Table 4-1   Summary of security aspects.

The next section discusses solutions to protect multimedia data, i.e., how the required security aspects can be implemented. We will begin with approaches based on cryptographic protocols to implement security services, such as confidentiality, authenticity, and integrity. Subsequently, we will deal with specific problems in connection with digital signatures and certificates for multimedia data. We will then introduce steganographic methods as a solution to protect intellectual property. This solution is the so-called *watermark* embedded in image material. Finally, we will show how firewalls can be used to implement effective access protection measures against external computer networks in local computer networks.

4.3 Solution: Cryptography

Cryptology has a long history and deals with algorithmic methods to protect or disguise information. There are two main disciplines in cryptology, namely *cryptography* and *cryptanalysis*. Whereas cryptography deals with the development of new systems to secure information, cryptanalysis is aimed at attacking and breaking these systems to evaluate their security. This section describes the use of cryptographic protocols and methods for multimedia data. Detailed discussions of cryptography can be found in the literature, e.g., [Sch96] and [BSW95].

4.3.1 Definition of Terms

A *cryptographic algorithm* or *cipher* or encryption method is a mathematical function used to encrypt and decrypt data. Data to be sent are called *plaintext* and encrypted data are called *ciphertext*. Let the encryption function be E, the decryption function D, and the key K; then $E_K(P)$ means that the plaintext P was encrypted by function E using key K.

When the communicating parties use the same secret key, then they use a *symmetric* or *private key system*. In contrast, in *asymmetric* or *public key systems*, the communicating parties use a pair of keys, where one key is known to both parties and the other key is known only to one of the parties. Public key systems also offer a way of using digital signatures to ensure the authenticity of a message. For this purpose, the message is encrypted with the sender's private key. As the key is secret, the sender can be sure that nobody else can read this message. The receiver, (or any other person) can use the sender's public key to decipher the message. If the deciphering attempt is successful, then the receiver can be sure that the message was indeed sent by the presumed sender. In practice, users do not sign the entire document, but instead apply their digital fingerprint, which is normally a cryptographic hash value. Digital signatures are based on the *DSS* (Digital Signature Standard) standard. In Germany, for example, there have been legal provisions in force since 1997 for the use of digital signatures [Str97].

We can identify the following *advantages* of public key systems:

- The communicating parties do not have to exchange secret keys.
- Each party has its own secret key.

- The pair of keys can be used for all communication relationships.
- The origin can be proven to third parties.

When verifying the authenticity of a document, determining the time at which a signature was made may present a further problem (digital timestamp).

Errors can occur during the transmission of messages (or an intruder can introduce errors). Hash functions are used for integrity control. They determine checksums of messages, which can then be protected with a digital fingerprint for additional authentication. If it is hard or impossible to determine a colliding message, then it is a secure hash function. In this case, an attacker cannot generate a message that has the same hash value, and bit errors can be detected.

The following sections introduce some methods used to protect confidentiality and transparent representation possibilities for Try&Buy transactions. This discussion is limited to a choice of methods for video data. The fundamental approaches can be applied to all media.

4.3.2   Partial Encryption

The encryption of messages by means of a secure cryptographic method is very time-consuming, due to the complexity of these methods. In contrast to pure text components, the cost of encrypting multimedia data, e.g., video data, is very high. For example, if video applications are to reach private users with PC terminal equipment, then this equipment's processing capabilities should be taken into account. When decoding and displaying video data, these machines often reach their performance limits. An additional time effort for encryption algorithms, which is relatively large due to the extensive data volumes involved in a video data steam, is normally not possible in such cases, without risking a loss in the presentation quality of video data.

One solution to this problem is based on the use of *partial encryption*. This means that only sections of the entire data volume of a message are encrypted. This solution results in the following *benefits*:

- Machines with a performance capability insufficient to encrypt and decrypt the entire data stream in real-time can participate in the communication relationship.
- In machines with capacities for an encryption of all the communication data which arise, reduction of encryption costs can free additional computing capacity; this capacity could then be used for other applications in a multi-user system.
- With targeted encryption, e.g., only of the image information contained in a video data stream, an application can still process the entire stream. It can skip the parts it cannot represent, due to insufficient computing time or lack of hardware possibilities. The synchronization with data important for the application will not be lost, because the control information contained in the video data stream is available in non-encrypted form.

- Targeted partial information within a data stream can be protected, e.g., by *transparent encryption* of video data streams. (Transparent encryption is described in more detail below.)

Partial encryption also has some *drawbacks*:

- In most cases, additional information about the position and extent of encrypted data within the total data stream has to be added to and transmitted in the payload, increasing the data volume.
- In most cases, changes have to be made to the code of the sending and receiving applications to integrate partial encryption and ensure efficient implementation.
- Many data types, mainly text or control information, do not allow a division into confidential and non-confidential parts.

The last point in the list of drawbacks addresses a problem that can be solved by partial encryption, e.g., for video data. We will use JPEG, H.261, MPEG-1, and MPEG-2 encoded data streams as examples to introduce these partial encryption concepts. Readers with a particular interest in these concepts are referred to [KVMW98].

Special Methods for Video Data Encryption   The selective encryption of video data has been studied more intensely in recent years. One reason for increasing efforts in this field is that progress in the development of hardware has enabled the integration of digital video technology into consumer products and home PCs in recent years. In these systems, security requirements are less critical than in other areas, e.g., in military or intelligence services systems. For this reason, they are normally not equipped with special hardware to support encryption mechanisms. In these systems, encryption is normally done by software, which imposes additional loads on many current low-end systems.

Systematic Encryption of Message Blocks   The easiest method to reduce e encryption costs is the selective encryption of fixed-length data blocks, followed by a series of non-encrypted blocks in the data stream. To keep the implementation cost to a minimum, we would normally select the data block length corresponding to the block length of the encryption method, if block ciphers are used. The cost involved in the encryption is optionally scalable. This method has the advantage that is is easy to implement and it does not exchange signaling information between sender/encryption unit and receiver/ encryption unit.

Partially protected data can no longer be played back in a regular hardware or software video decoder. However, if such a decoder program is protected against potential crashes by use of page errors and field index threshold values, then we can detect a few details in the video data stream during playback, depending on the selected encryption costs (see Figure 4-1). Note that such a method never offers real protection against extensive code-breaking attacks.

Figure 4-1   Partial encryption at the data stream level with 1% (left), 5% (center), and 10% (right) encrypted data, respectively. Video clip Miss America, QCIF resolution; from [KVMW98].

Encryption of Reference Blocks (I Frames)   One of the first special methods to reduce encryption costs for MPEG video data streams was proposed in 1995 in the form of I frames of a video to limit the amount of encryption [MS95]. MPEG-encoded video data can be easily separated on frame level, because a unique frame start header can be easily located in the video data stream.

At first sight, this method seems to offer a relatively large amount of confidentiality in video communication. The data contained in the unprotected P and B frames normally refer only to changes versus the previous I frames, and the data contents of the I frames are well protected by encryption. This means that this additional information cannot be used to disclose anything. The limitations of this method are discussed in the next section.

Encryption of Intra-Coded Blocks (P and B Frames)   [AG96] illustrates the vulnerabilities introduced by selective encryption of I frames only. In most cases, the P and B frames of an MPEG video contain a large number of intra-coded blocks, mainly in abrupt scene transitions in the video data. Because the information from the previous I frames deviates so strongly from the actual image content, encoding just the changes in an image is no longer reasonable.

One improvement of the method of [MS95] is that the intra-coded macro blocks contained in the P and B frames are also included in the encryption. One example of this method is SEC-MPEG [MG94].

[AG96] also includes examples of this type of encryption. At the same time, it is emphasizes that this form of partial encryption still does not offer very good protection. On the basis of the movements vectors in the unprotected inter-coded macro blocks alone, we would still be able to make contours of moving objects in the video scene visible. Also, the difference information in the inter-coded macro blocks discloses a relatively large number of details about the objects contained in the original video data. Figure 4-2 shows reconstructed example frames from this type of "protected" video sequences.

Figure 4-2 Cryptoanalysis to code all intra-coded information. Left: all I frames are encrypted; right: all inter-encoded blocks are encrypted. Video Flowergarden, reconstructions of frame 29 (last P frame in GOP).

To make the confidentiality of the method described here scalable, the authors propose an increase of the I-frame density in the encoder, as this would increase the security level. In addition to the inherent problems (the frame sequence is hard-coded in most MPEG encoders, e.g., *IBBPBBPBBPBBI...*), this proposal results in a significant change of the bandwidth, which is not desirable in many applications, and also violates the bandwidth limits specified in the MPEG standard.

The selective encryption of I frames as well as I and P frames was implemented in 1993 on the basis of the Berkeley MPEG decoder [PSR93] and tested for use in WWW applications in 1995 [YLTC96].

Permutation of DCT Coefficients Another approach, especially for video compression methods has been proposed [Tan96]. It is based on the JPEG image compression algorithm (i.e., MPEG and H.261/H.263). This method does not introduce any significant delay for encoding and decoding of a video data stream. The method is based on a permutation of the DCT coefficients occurring in the JPEG compression. The key for the cryptographic method used is then exactly this permutation. The method does not impose delays, because when encoding or decoding video data, the DCT coefficients are normally arranged in a zigzag pattern, via an index table, which then simply has to be permutated once before encoding the video data.

However, the permutation of DCT coefficients has the following *drawbacks*:

• The permutation of DCT coefficients causes a clear deterioration of the entropy encoding of a video data stream. Test results have shown that all of the tested video sequences are larger by a factor of approx. 20 to 40%, compared to the original encoded video data.

• The method is vulnerable when statistical analyses of the DCT coefficient structure are performed.

• Due to the strong coupling of the encryption (permutation) with the compression algorithm (JPEG encoding), the method can only be processed in a video encoder or decoder written especially for this purpose.

Using a Partial Video Data Stream as a Cryptographic Key   [QN97] introduces a video encryption method that is said to offer secure encryption for the entire video data stream. The method can encrypt a complete data stream in approx. 55% of the usual time.

First, the video data stream (MPEG) is divided into data packages with a block length corresponding to the encryption method used (64-bit DES). Then, each respective 64-bit block of the video data stream is XORed with the next block to form a one-time disposable key, and written to that block's position within the video data stream. The DES-encrypted content of the first block is written back to its position. This explains why the method requires only half of the time otherwise required by DES operations on the video data stream.

4.3.3   Commercial Tools for Selective Video Encryption

The significance of confidentiality in video transmission has been recognized by companies and organizations, and a number of projects have been developed in this area. One of these efforts is a software packet by the name of *SEC-MPEG* for video data encryption.

SEC-MPEG   The SEC-MPEG project was first initiated at the TU Berlin as a study of security mechanisms for MPEG video data [MG94]. The implementations of protection methods and integrity checks developed within this project form the basis of the SEC-MPEG tool now commercially available.

The program package offers functions to protect confidentiality (encryption) and verify the data integrity of MPEG video data streams. The product offers four levels with increasing confidentiality (*Confidentiality* or *C Level*) and three levels for integrity control (*Integrity* or *I Level*). The individual levels differ in the extent to which they implement security functions:

• C level (confidentiality level):

  • 0: no encryption
  • 1: encryption of all MPEG headers
  • 2: additional encryption of a partial set of the intra-coded macro blocks
  • 3: additional encryption of all intra-coded macro blocks
  • 4: complete encryption

• I level (integrity level):

  • 0: no integrity check
  • 1: integrity check of header data (playback protection)

- 2: integrity check of all intra-coded data blocks (originality protection)

- 3: complete integrity check (data stream protection)

An SEC-MPEG-protected data stream uses its own data format, and SEC-MPEG headers as well as information fields specifying the size of the encrypted data packets and the check sums for the integrity check, in addition to the MPEG headers. However, this has the drawback that the data stream cannot be displayed with a standardized MPEG player.

4.3.4 Scalable Adaptation of the Encryption Cost

Kunkelmann et al. (1998) propose a method for partial video encryption which is scalable to the security requirements of an application [KVMW98]. At the forefront is the use of a secure cryptographic method. DES based on 64-bit blocks could be an alternative. In addition, the RC4 stream cipher could be used [Sch96].

The relevant data occurring in a video stream can be summarized as follows: header data, coded-block pattern (CBP), macro block type, movement vectors, and DC coefficients. The index n of the coefficient encoded last is passed on to the method as a scaling parameter to specify the encryption cost. The algorithm starts the encryption at the beginning of a DCT block and encrypts interrelated blocks from the video data stream in a block length corresponding to the encryption method used. Figure 4-3 shows the data segments of an MPEG video data stream encrypted by this method. We can see that the third DCT block overlaps the data from the second block.

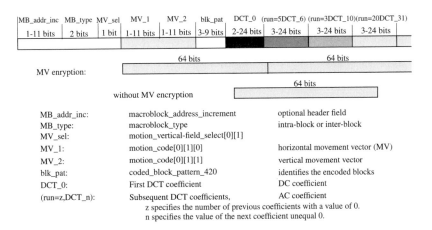

Figure 4-3 Parts of an MPEG data stream protected by the partial encryption algorithm.

4.3.5 Transparent Encryption for Try&Buy Transactions

Another practical requirement is to make data material available so that an interested party can obtain an initial impression, but should not obtain the full quality before that party pays the price and meets certain conditions. This situation means that the data cannot be encrypted fully or in an illegible way, but have to be represented in part and in poor quality. With a key obtained upon payment, the client should then be able to view the image material in its full quality.

One solution to meet this requirement is to encrypt the data transparently. This means that the encryption does not make the data fully illegible. Instead, a noise factor or interference is introduced into the data, which can be removed with a secret key.

Tool for Image Encryption (TIE)   Storck proposed a Tool for Image Encryption (TIE) in 1995; this tool was one of the first approaches to encrypt vector images [fGD95]. TIE can encrypt parts of an image, which then appear in a lower resolution or as a black box. TIE handles the image areas to be replaced in so-called *application extension blocks*. To provide security, this data is DES-encrypted, where the user can optionally select a key space in a size to the order of 2^{56}.

Transparent Encryption for MPEG Video Data   The TIE method was developed for JPEG images and expanded only for MPEG-1 video data. MPEG-2 offers another interesting approach: It allows the use of the scalability of the data format for transparent encryption and the development of mechanisms to enhance scalability to obtain transparent representation options [DS97b].

The scalability is intended to influence the error behavior of a transmission or its quality. We will describe the SNR (signal-to-noise ratio) scalability derived from the scalability modes defined in the standard.

To see the modus concerned, there is a so-called *sequence_scalable_extension*, including a *scalable_mode* field. Table 4-2 shows the possible initializations and their meanings.

scalable_mode	Meaning
00	data partitioning
01	spatial scalability
10	SNR scalability
11	temporal scalability

Table 4-2   Definitions of the scalable_mode field [Org96].

We will now briefly describe the options of *SNR* (signal-to-noise ratio) *scalability.* These modes also allow several transparent encryption approaches. Moreover, the MPEG-2 standard allows one to combine scaling modes, so that a multi-level error behavior or quality scaling is possible.

SNR scalability is a tool used to support video applications in connection with telecommunication or video services at various quality levels. SNR scalability generates two video layers with the same spatial resolution, but in a different video quality, from one single video data source. There is a *base layer* for basic video quality and an *enhancement layer* to improve the video quality of the base or lower layer. We can increase the quality reproduction of the input stream by adding the enhancement layer to the base layer,

The quantization level should be selected so that it is coarser for the lower layer, i.e., higher quantization steps should be used. In contrast, smaller or finer quantization steps should be used for the enhancement layer, where 1 is the minimum value; this allows us to fully compensate for the lower-layer quality loss.

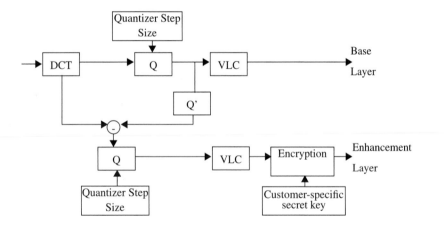

Figure 4-4 Transparently encrypted MPEG encoder.

The composite data stream should generally be calculated for luminance and chrominance blocks; it offers an interesting approach for transparent encryption. More specifically, we can either code the video data stream in the SNR scalability mode and send only the lower layer, or we send both, where the enhancement layer would then be symmetrically encrypted. To use the first method, we have to extract the enhancement layer after the encoding process. When a client wishes to receive the full quality, the complete enhancement layer has to be subsequently transmitted. The second method codes to the SNR scaling mode, then encrypts the enhancement layer, and hides the enhancement layer from the decoder, so that only the base layer can be accessed from the decoder (see Figure 4-4). To achieve this, we set the decoding mode from SNR-scalable to the non-scalable mode.

If a client wishes to obtain the full quality, then the key will be sent to him or her, in order to decrypt the enhancement layer. The scaling mode is reset to SNR-scalable, and the desired quality can be obtained (see Figure 4-5).

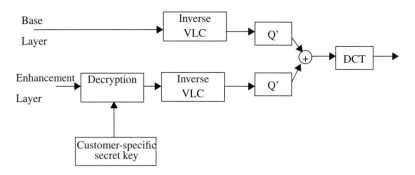

Figure 4-5   Transparently encrypted MPEG decoder.

Of course, this method requires a separate tool for encryption and decryption, similarly to TIE, which has to be given to the client, together with the key. Once the client knows the secret key, he or she can switch between the different quality levels.

4.4   Solution: Digital Signatures

4.4.1   Methodology and Applications

Digital signatures offer a way of verifying both the authenticity and integrity of a message. In combination with timestamps, they can be effectively used in electronic business. Today's digital representation of media allows simple changes to the data material. For example, image manipulations range from scaling, rotation, and production of sections to direct changes to the image contents. Especially in the movie and video industry, persons who have never before stood together in front of a camera are shown together. One famous example is the award-winning movie "Forrest Gump" (J. F. Kennedy together with Tom Hanks). What still falls within the area of art, as in this example, can easily cause problems in movies or photos, when the data material is to serve as a piece of evidence.

Digital signatures are well known from cryptography [Sch96] [Pet96] and are adequate to ensure the origin and authenticity of data materials.

There is a large number of algorithms for digital signatures. Most of them are based on public-key systems, where secret information is used to sign documents and public information is used to verify a signature. One exception is the RSA algorithm

[Sch96]. To sign it, the document (i.e., normally a one-way hash value of the document) is encrypted with the private key of the signer. The digital signature produced in this way is appended to the document, and can then be decrypted and verified with the public key. The entire protocol used to verify the receiver of a message, the identity of the sender, and the integrity of the message is called *authentication*; see [Sch96].

However, if we use the conventional signature technology, where the data material is signed as a binary data stream, we will meet problems, e.g., with video data: Data transmission is often subject to errors which do not cause any major quality loss in the representation of the image itself. The viewer will merely perceive a slightly poorer quality, or noise, but the contents of the video data remain unchanged. What appears as noise to the viewer leads to an error when the digital signature is verified and lets the image material appear invalid. Moreover, MPEG streams are often subject to multiple encoding steps to adapt the data rate to the transmission channel, e.g.; keywords include noise or spatial scalability and bit rate reduction. Also, the binary data stream is changed without influencing the image contents.

For these reasons, it is desirable to either construct fault-tolerant signature methods or to design content-based signatures. We will discuss the latter method in more detail below, because no extensive mathematical considerations with regard to fault-tolerant signatures seem to be available.

4.4.2 Content-based Digital Signatures for Single and Motion Pictures

The content-based digital signature is a combination of protecting the image contents with the proof of authorship. To create the signature, information about the core statement of the image is summarized by means of a cryptographic hash function. The resulting hash value is signed (encrypted) with the author's secret key and can be decrypted by means of the public key, which is generally accessible. If the hash value matches the hash value newly determined by the checker, we can assume that the image is unchanged and originates from the identified author. If the check is not successful, we can prove neither that the image has not been tampered with, nor its authenticity.

The principle of a digital signature has been known for some time and was formulated by [Fri93] as a theory. Problems arising in connection with digital signatures include the selection of the information about the core statement of the picture or the question of what actually should be protected and authenticated in a picture. In addition, it would be desirable to be able to find the image material authentic during further processing steps that do not concern the image contents, such as noise reduction, signal conversion into various formats, λ correction, scaling, and similar steps.

The problem is that we allow certain changes but would also like to detect other manipulations.

Today, various approaches are used to filter representative information from the image to yield an image core statement. In [SC96], Schneider and Chang (1997) describe possibilities based on histogram technologies (intensity and color histogram technologies). These methods are applied to the picture block by block, which means that they are very complex. Depending on whether or not the hash value is based on a per-block basis or on the entire picture, we obtain hash values of different order. Moreover, the formation of a hash value is not possible for compressed material, so that compressed data formats would have to be fully decoded. Problems arise mainly in color conversions, which do not change the actual picture content.

Storck (1997) describes a method for DC and AC coefficients of DCT for image data. Changes of the DC coefficients and the first AC coefficients following them have a major impact on the visual appearance and the content of an image [Sto96]. The luminance components are used for visualization to provide for insensitivity to color changes. Note that even the smallest changes in the DC values have a strong impact, so that absolute DC values are not taken into account, instead only the differences between two consecutive DC values are considered.

The method is insensitive to minor changes in the image which can result from transmission errors or luminance adaptations, because only the difference is taken into account.

One major drawback is that the method fails when the image statement depends essentially on the color. In addition, the method is not resistant to compression and scaling. The method can be applied successfully only once the original size is then restored. Considering that one single hash value is assigned to each image, we cannot identify the regions where changes have occurred. For this reason, hash values are used for different image regions.

If we want to make sure that the contents of individual images can be verified, then we have an additional requirement for motion pictures: the capability of verifying the authentic picture sequence.

Zhong and Chang (1996) enumerate possibilities for video data to yield representative information for the core statement of the picture and the picture sequence from color, texture, and movement [ZC97]. Due to the sheer inspection for regions of equal color, we obtain a large number of smaller regions per picture. To facilitate their handling, we try to put them together to a group (including entire objects). The same movement vectors from picture to picture serve as grouping criteria. To implement this with a high probability of matches, we need long observation times, which excludes the use of real-time applications. Other criteria for object interrelations are geometric relationships. One drawback of this method is that the inspections are complex and costly. Moreover, the method functions only in the picture space and is sensitive to picture changes caused by lossy compression and color conversions.

Another possibility is to use the method described by Storck (1997) with an expansion to motion pictures, forming an additional signature to neighboring picture signatures (predecessor and successor signatures). This yields hierarchically verifiable signatures that authenticate both the picture material itself and the picture sequence [DH98].

4.4.3 Problems with Hypermedia/Multimedia Formats

The capability of verifying is more difficult for media compositions than for single images or motion pictures. Each medium has to be verifiable, both individually and in an arbitrary composition. For example, in addition to the motion picture verification, the synchronized audio data have to be authenticated individually and as a whole (video and audio data together). One problem is the verification of so-called link structures, because information both about the link and the relevant document has to be verified.

4.4.4 Certification—the Trusted Third Party

To ensure the authenticity of the public parameters used, the existence of a trusted third party, the so-called *certification authority*, is of central significance. One problem in the use of asymmetric encryption technologies is the unique allocation of the public key to persons or organizations. A digital signature is meaningful only if it can be allocated to a certain person in a unique and incontestable way. The common solution to this problem is the cooperation or involvement of a neutral trusted authority. This authority issues a certificate: It adds the name of a user, his or her public key, and other information to form a data structure and then signs this data structure.

In particular, a certification authority enters the public key of the system users as a certificate into a list. The certificates added to the list are tamper-proof; they can be verified by the users, and they form the security basis of the entire system. Recommendation X.509 for authentication in the area of directory systems proposes a suitable structure for authentication certificates [HSF97].

Certificates can be realized by means of RSA or ElGamal signature methods, where entire trust centers can be formed. In addition to providing the directories, the trusted third party is also responsible for locking and revoking keys and providing information (see Figure 4-6).

Instead of "certification authority", a trust center is sometimes called *confidence authority*, because trust centers handle these important functions. Problems and infrastructure solutions in connection with trust centers are discussed in [Ham95].

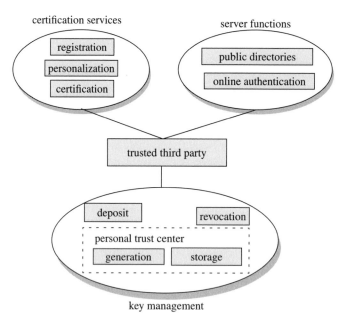

Figure 4-6   Allocation of tasks in a trust center: trusted third parties and personal trust centers.

4.5   Solution: Steganographic Methods

4.5.1   Methodology and Applications

In addition to the problems of data eavesdropping and tampering, the illegal production of copies from digital data plays an increasingly important role in the online world. To prevent this abuse, special measures are required to identify the owner of a file and identify the distributor of illegal copies [FSBS98].

The sole addition of a digital signature or insertion of visible information into the video material is not sufficient. This information can be easily removed. Although the MPEG-2 system stream offers the possibility of embedding copyright information in a data stream, this approach does not provide effective protection, because this information can also be easily removed. The option provided by the MPEG-2-standard to embed copyright information into the data material is based on the principle that the information is available to the user, so that the user is informed about such rights in connection with the product [DS97a], i.e., the author declares his or her legal right. However, this information can be easily removed by an attacker, because it is not connected to the image material, i.e., it does not incorporate additional information from the image. The marking is attached and a CRC is applied to the corresponding descriptor and the PES package, so that changes to the marking can be checked.

However, an attacker could also remove the marking or modify it to subsequently adapt the checksum. Even an encryption of the data would be unsuccessful, because an attacker could also remove this data. This means that criteria would have to be created to bind a copyright marking, so that the data material would become incomplete as soon as the attacker attempts to remove it. Such dependencies have not been defined in the system section of the MPEG-2 standard.

One appropriate approach integrates the copyright information into the data in such a way that they are not visible to the user. This technique is called *steganography*; it is a type of communication that hides the existence of secret communication. We distinguish between two basic approaches. The first approach integrates copyright information by means of a secret key, where the algorithm is known. This means that only the owner of the secret key can retrieve this information and produce evidence of ownership. The second approach does not use secret keys, which means that anybody can retrieve the information. The latter method requires secret algorithms and will not be discussed any further in this section.

In practice, steganographic methods are based on the fact that they replace a noisy component in the digital message by an encrypted secret message. This method is called *substitutional steganography*. In contrast, *constructive steganography* is a method that does not insert the secret message by replacing noise components, but reproduces noise signals based on the original noise pattern.

4.5.2 Digital Watermarks—Methodology

Some solutions for such methods are already available for image data. The key required to reproduce the copyright information is deposited with a trusted authority, so that irregularities or disputes about copyrights in an image can be settled by simply reading out the copyright information from the material.

Similarly, a piece of information about the user can be coded within the image, so that the producer of illegal copies can be identified. Of course, this violates the user's privacy, so that the user rights have to be encrypted.

Existing methods are based on substitutional steganography and are called *digital watermarks*. A good description of this technology is found in [Pfi96].

Requirements for digital watermark algorithms and the properties of the inserted marking are described in detail in [CL97]. Digital watermarks make it possible to integrate copyright and client information into the data material. Note that there are many different possible points of attack against such integrated information. [PAK98] describes a number of variants that prevent the reading or extraction of integrated data in most of the methods used today. The actual embedded information is maintained in the majority of the methods; only the extraction is rendered more difficult, for example, by destroying important features of the picture. Nevertheless, digital watermarks should be used, because the marked data do not disclose whether or not such information is actually included. This means that an attacker would have to read and modify each piece of data material to disguise the information. In addition, it can be assumed that future methods will be more powerful and resist such attacks.

4.5.3 Methods for Single Images

To avoid falsification, abuse, and violation of copyrights, the embedded information has to be invisible, non-removable, undetectable, and unchangeable. In particular, it should also resist methods that deteriorate the quality of the data material.

In 1995, Zhao [ZK95] and Koch [KZ95] described a first possibility to embed copyright information in an image. The approach is called *Randomly Sequenced Pulse Position Modulated Code (RSPPMC)* and is based on the well-known fact that the digital representation of people, buildings, and natural backgrounds can be considered a non-stationary, static process, which is highly redundant and tolerant to noise. This means that changes to the data material within a certain level are difficult to detect, even when comparing the modified image with the original.

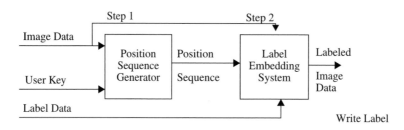

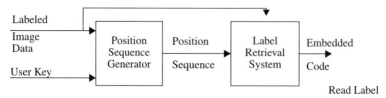

Figure 4-7   Write and read steps.

The embedded markings appear as a natural part of the original image. The system consists of two basic functions for writing and reading of markings (see Figure 4-7). The *first step* creates the actual copyright code and a pseudo-random sequence for the positions of the secret messages to be embedded or retrieved. This component uses existing techniques for encryption and pseudo-random number generation. The image material and a secret, user-specific key are read into a position sequence generator. The *second step* reads or binds the generated secret message to the positions determined in the first step. The insertion methods depend on the data format used.

A JPEG-based method which works in the frequency space was developed for gray-scale and color images. More specifically, a sequence of 8×8 blocks is pseudo-randomly selected, depending on a user-specific key and the data material. In its current form, the mechanism uses only the height and width of the image to generate positions, which means that embedded copyright information can no longer be detected once the image is scaled. This is a major drawback of the method. Next, the method applies a discrete cosine transform (DCT) and a quantization step to each of the selected blocks. For this purpose, three randomly selected elements of each 8×8 block are quantized within a three-part frequency space: low, medium, and high. Subsequently, they are inspected for existing relations and evaluated with a 1- or 0-bit label code or an invalid pattern. The invalid pattern shows that the corresponding block should be ignored when the copyright information is retrieved. The elements are completed on the basis of these criteria. The quantized frequency coefficients in the center of the frequency range of a block are slightly modified, so that a skew of exactly 1 or 0 is included. The minor change caused by this method is hard to perceive visually.

This method was implemented for JPEG images and expanded to the MPEG-1 video data format, because this format also uses intra-frames. (For wavelet-based approaches the reader is referred to, e.g., [GG02] and [PU03]). However, the method introduces *two additional insecurities* that an attacker could use to remove the embedded copyright markings from the data material. First, there is a potential risk that individual frames can be deleted, and second, there is a potential risk of recompression using different patterns. To prevent these potential threats, the marking is repeatedly embedded in each frame. This allows the retrieval of the markings from all intra-coded frames, without having to consider recompression with different patterns.

The level of security offered by the method described here depends mainly on whether or not the embedded information can be deleted or modified to ensure that no copyright information can be retrieved from the data material. There are many different variants to these types of attacks, e.g., format conversions, data compression, or low-pass filtering.

Altogether, the current method is *resistant* to lossy compression, low-pass filtering, color reduction, and the production of image sections. However, the method is *vulnerable* to physical damage, e.g., cutting a pixel line. This problem is currently solved by letting the user specify valuable or sensitive areas of an image in which multiple markings can be embedded.

This means that cutting a part of these areas would not damage the embedded marking. However, the algorithm used introduces the potential risk that the copyright information can no longer be found when the data is scaled, because a *position sequence generator* calculates the corresponding pixels that hold the copyright information, based on the image size. This is a critical drawback. An attacker aware of this vulnerability could easily remove the marking.

Several improvements of the Zhao-Koch approach have been developed [BMBLY97]. A totally different approach is described by Fridrichs (1997). This method requires that the original image retrieves copyright information [Fri97]. Fridrichs uses pseudo-randomly generated black-and-white patterns, which are integrated into the image. This approach was expanded to MPEG video data by Dittmann et al. (1998). Here, the original image does not have to retrieve copyright information [DSS98]. Other methods for single images are discussed in [CKLS97], [KJ97], [RP97], and [Pit96].

Dittmann et al. (1998) developed a 3D watermark, which generates a 3D model of the marked image [DNSS98]. Figure 4-8 shows an example.

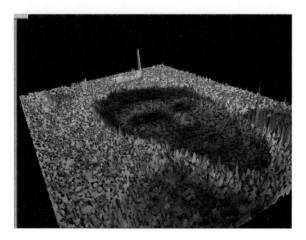

Figure 4-8   Example of a 3D watermark.

The model shows the changes left by copyright information in the image. The 3D watermark is a tool from a series of applications used to support and represent the inclusion of digital watermarks. For example, the intensity and robustness of the embedded marking can be evaluated, i.e., we can see which areas of an image are marked, so that the visual changes can be measured.

Yet another method is mainly used to code *information about the user*, so that the producer of illegal copies can be identified. This method was introduced by Caronni in 1995 [Car95]. For each client, a very special copy of the image is created with invisible client-specific information. This information can be used to allocate copies emerging in the market to a client. For this purpose, the brightness of the image is modulated in certain rectangular areas to add a user-specific marking. An independent modulation of the RGB color values is less suitable for this purpose, because images with many high-quality gray levels suffer from considerable information and quality loss when RGB color values are transformed to these gray levels.

The marking process adds a user-specific noise to the image material, so that the quality decreases. This quality loss has to be measured. To measure the quality loss, we can use the correlation coefficient between the original and the modified image. This coefficient is calculated over the brightness values of each corresponding pixel in both images: $b_o(x,y)$ for the original and $b_m(x,y)$ for the modified image. The correlation coefficient R is calculated as follows:

$$R = \frac{v_{om}}{v_o v_m}$$

$$v_{om} = \frac{1}{XY-1}\left(\sum_{x=1}^{X}\sum_{y=1}^{Y}(b_o(x,y)-m_o)(b_m(x,y)-m_m)\right).$$

In this equation, R is the correlation coefficient, v_{om} is the covariance of the two images, v_o and v_m are the variances of both images, X and Y are the maximum values for width and height of the image, $b(x,y)$ is the brightness value at pixel position (x,y), and m_o, m_m are the mean brightness values of both images.

The above equation represents the covariance between the original and the modified images. The variances of both images, v_o and v_m, are defined as follows:

$$v_o^2 = \frac{1}{XY-1}\left(\sum_{x=1}^{X}\sum_{y=1}^{Y}(b_o(x,y)-m_o)^2\right),$$

$$v_m^2 = \frac{1}{XY-1}\left(\sum_{x=1}^{X}\sum_{y=1}^{Y}(b_m(x,y)-m_m)^2\right).$$

When comparing two identical images, we can see that $|R|$ is exactly 1: The more differences that are found between the images, the closer the value $|R|$ approximates 0. The problem is, however, that this comparative method is meaningful only if both images have the same size, which means that some preparation or preprocessing may be needed.

When an author adds some *user-specific identification* to his or her work, an attacker could attempt to make this marking ineffective to prevent identification of the origin of the image data. This could mean a large number of different modifications, which make it hard for the author to recognize the client-specific noise. In general, it is very difficult to evaluate the strength of an algorithm, considering the wide range of potential attacks.

For example, a *group of cooperating attackers* could initialize a very strong attack [Car95]: They could simply mix all their image materials by swapping pixel values. This would make the recognition of the client-specific marking generally impossible, because the profile of the corresponding rectangle in the image is flattened out. In addition, the attackers could compare their image material to detect differences. Once they discover the differences, the attackers can falsify their identifications. As long as the number of attackers is small, the author of the image material could still obtain some identification by checking the bits that are not as easily detected. However, with a larger number of attackers, it becomes increasingly difficult or even impossible to identify the sequence.

In contrast, a *lone attacker* would be unable to obtain information about the identification sequence in the image material. For this reason, the potential attacks of a lone attacker can be divided into two classes: modification of the image material size and modification of the image content. Caronni's results have shown that this marking technique still requires some improvements.

4.5.4 Methods for Motion Pictures

Commonly used methods for motion pictures are essentially based on the algorithms for single images and adapted according to the video data format used. Of course, a complete video can accommodate much more information than a single image. However, if we want to protect image sequences or even single video pictures, the requirements for these methods are much more complex than those for single images. We need special mechanisms to accommodate the required information quantity per picture and to simultaneously ensure resistance to video compression methods. An additional requirement for these mechanisms is that they subsequently embed markings in compressed data formats.

Dittmann et al. (1998) developed two marking techniques for MPEG video data: one in the picture space and a second one in the frequency space [DSS98].

The *picture space* method is based on a modification of the Fridrichs algorithm, so that much more information can be embedded in each video single picture and the marking information can be retrieved without using the original picture. To achieve this goal, a black-and-white pattern generated from a secret key is not embedded over the entire picture just once, but repeatedly and differently, according to the binary sequence to be embedded. Statistical correlations can then be used to retrieve the marking information without using the original. The method has proven resistant to MPEG compression, format conversion, and low-pass filtering. The integration of a concrete black-and-white pattern also offers resistance to direct picture manipulations, e.g., scaling and production of sections, and watermark information can be read successfully.

The *frequency space* method is fundamentally based on the Zhao-Koch approach introduced in 1995, but it uses error-correction codes, which makes the method additionally resistant to multiple MPEG compression. In addition, it takes smooth edges and homogeneous surfaces into account, so that much fewer visual artifacts occur. The two methods introduced by Dittmann et al. (1998) can embed approx. 50 to 100 bits per frame, without sacrificing resistance. If the data rate increases, either visual artifacts become visible, while the resistance remains the same, or one attempts to reduce the artifacts, but at the cost of less resistance to modifications.

Hartung and Girod (1997) describe a method for embedding watermarks in compressed video data [HG97b] [HG97a]. The fundamental idea behind this method is also the additive overlaying of a signal with smaller amplitudes, which cannot be visually detected. However, if we attempt to use higher frequencies than those recommended by Dittmann et al. (1998), we may expect less artifacts, but we would have to compromise with regard to the guarantee of resistance of the embedded data set. In this method, the bits are not measured per frame, but per second of the entire video data stream, so that approx. 4 bits per frame are lost. Due to the small volume of the watermark information per picture, this method is not suitable to protect single pictures, but it is suitable for embedding information for the entire video stream. Subsequently, the watermark information is applied by modifying the DCT coefficient during the decoding process. The accumulation of visible interferences is prevented by adding a drift compensation signal.

DCT-based methods can be easily applied to MPEG, H.261, H.263, and H.263+. Image space methods can basically be applied in all cases. For compressed video data formats, the pattern to be embedded is converted accordingly and transformed, so that it can be easily added to the compressed video data.

Considering that MPEG-4 unifies various video planes and virtual objects, we have to embed a digital watermark in each one of these objects, because they can be combined in many different ways. It should be possible to retrieve the marking both from a single object and from entire scenes. An initial approach in this respect was described by Hartung et al. (1998) for face animation parameters [HEG98]. A general method for object marking is introduced in [DNSS98].

4.5.5 Methods for Audio Data

This section introduces, as a representative example, a method for the accommodation of digital watermarks in audio data. This method is based essentially on the MPEG compression method [BTH96]. While MPEG calculates how many bits can be saved in the resolution, to reduce the data word length, the method described here uses these "free" bits to accommodate additional information. However, if we were to accommodate a watermark "directly" in these bits, we would compromise its robustness. A more or less strong MPEG compression would eliminate exactly these bits. However, we can generate a robust watermark by taking certain criteria into account:

- The watermark has to be unique (copyright).

• The watermark has to possess a noise characteristic, because noise is easier to hide than a tone signal.
• The watermark should ideally have the maximum level that can be hidden to achieve maximum resistance to compression.

This means that we have to generate a unique noise that exactly occupies the surface under the respective hiding curve (see Figure 4-9).

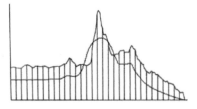

Figure 4-9   Division of the signal spectrum in sub-bands in a sample hiding curve.

The watermark (W) generated in our example is mixed with the original signal (S), and the resulting sum is MPEG-encoded and decoded at a high compression rate ($S+W$ CoDec $S'+W'$). Next, the original signal is run through a CoDec separately at the same compression rate (S CoDec S'). The difference of the two resulting signals is the part of the watermark that has survived the compression ($S' + W' – S' = W'$). This result is the actual watermark added to the original signal ($S+W$). This type of marking has proven resistant to compression and noise in tests and can be retrieved with a probability of approx. 95%.

Robust and efficient content-based digital audio watermarking for other coding schemes has also been introduced and discussed in [XF02].

4.5.6   Methods for 3D Scenes

3D models or entire 3D scenes can consist of a large number of objects, including polygons, lines, or predefined shapes. All of these objects have attributes describing color, transparency, surface, or textures. Digital watermarks can be integrated in a number of different ways. Geometries are particularly useful for integrating robust additional information into the data material. Initial studies have been introduced by Ohbuchi et al. (1997) for polygon models [OMA97]. Such methods distinguish between inserting or modifying the geometric or topological properties of single objects or the entire model. Ohbuchi et al. (1997) describe a total of five different marking strategies.

4.5.7   Digital Fingerprints

The term *digital fingerprint* [Pfi96] appears often in the context of digital watermark technologies. Digital fingerprints usually designate *what* type of information is embedded. The way *how* this information is embedded is similar to the common digital watermark algorithms. In general, this involves client-specific information to prove or trace the legal use of data material.

Embedding client-specific, i.e., different information, in data material, e.g., a picture, means that various copies of that picture are formed. This makes it easy for cooperating attackers to destroy the marked information or make it illegible by comparing their picture copies and manipulating them in various ways. This produces a situation which makes it harder for producers or authors to verify a client who acquired the picture legally, or one who reused it in illegally, when they find a copy of their work. Schwenk and Ueberberg (1997) describe algorithms that use finite geometries to make such attacks harder by generating very similar patterns for each client [SU97]. However, this method has the drawback that it is very complex, and a large number of bits have to be introduced into the data material, which impairs the robustness of the marking method, compared to normal data transforms.

4.5.8 Copyright Protection Architectures

If litigations arise due to digital watermarks when verifying copyrights, then trusted third parties are needed, as in the case of public key systems, to guarantee a unique allocation of persons to keys and multimedia data. Based on this requirement, so-called *copyright offices* have emerged in connection with public key infrastructures. An interesting approach is introduced in [PHR97].

4.6 Sample Applications

Multimedia data are increasingly found in a network environment today. This means that the data material is available almost everywhere. In addition to the opportunities offered by a distributed work environment, considerable security threats also exist. All security aspects mentioned at the beginning of this chapter play an important role in a distributed production environment, i.e., access protection, authenticity, confidentiality, integrity, nonrepudiation, transparent representation possibilities, copyrights, and privacy.

A user wishing to protect his or data material under the intellectual property right law has to do this before considering any other protection measure. Subsequently, the user can apply integrity-protecting methods. Next, there could be a general or transparent encryption to ensure confidentiality, authenticity, and, in the asymmetric case, also nonrepudiation [DS97a].

The modules discussed here can be configured so that the user can select from various security levels with respect to efficiency and performance. A practical implementation of the modules can be constructed on top of existing cryptographic and steganographic methods. This approach offers a layered security concept, which can be applied individually by the user, so that the acceptance of the technology can be further increased by an optional design element. Each end component, either in the client editing system, or in a video database, or in a metadata base, has to have the information required to implement a security policy at its disposal locally. Each component is responsible for the local security.

4.6.1 Unidirectional Distribution Services

Communication Model In unidirectional distribution services (broadcasting), information providers send their data over public channels (satellites, cable network, radio) to to the general public. The data are encrypted to protect the transmission, e.g., in pay-TV systems. An attacker is a person who attempts to gain access to a provider product without being authorized to do so by the provider.

Basically, anybody can start an attack, e.g., in radio transmissions, because anybody can receive the signal. We will describe a few examples in which unidirectional distribution services are used.

Broadcast distribution channels, satellite and antenna (terrestrial) and cable TV paths or radio systems are used to distribute information over *DVB* (Digital Video Broadcast) and *DAB* (Digital Audio Broadcast). *NVoD* (Near Video-on-Demand) allows a user to receive a broadcast within a defined time after the client's wish has become known. This allows the use of broadcast media for NVoD services, when the programs offered are broadcasted cyclically. The broadcast distribution channels can be easily eavesdropped and need encryption methods to protect their contents.

Message or stock exchange services distribute their contents to clients in a targeted way, whereby the partition of information to be ordered is very coarse ("business", "art"). The distribution is then normally based on multicasting over different types of information networks. The distribution of such information within closed multicast groups is not practical due to the number of potential groups. Instead, topics have to be grouped, protected by additional methods, and then distributed to a larger number of receivers than the limited clientele. Encryption methods are useful in such a scenario.

To be able to implement the applications mentioned above, transmission channels from clients and non-clients can be eavesdropped. The consumers of a transmission medium may be clients of that provider, but not authorized to automatically receive all information contents. This is the case in MBone NVoD, message, and stock exchange services. Parts of data have to be allocated. In some cases, the mixing of data with different receiver groups is very strict. In the case of stock exchange services, we are normally talking about a distance of a few data bytes, in MBone about address ranges, in broadcast media about frequency ranges, and within those ranges, about time slots.

It is surprisingly easy to eavesdrop on all of these distribution mechanisms. Protection mechanisms are needed. In particular for business-relevant data, it may be of interest to a competitor to be able to intercept or to tamper with data. With the media introduced above, this is relatively difficult, but possible, when such manipulations are done in distribution stations (e.g., caches). However, the manipulator has to replace the data with meaningful data; otherwise the manipulation will be quickly detected.

It is also easy to feed additional, falsified data into several of the networks mentioned above. An authenticity proof of the sender for the legitimate client of a service is normally required for each data packet. On the other hand, the data volume should not increase much, the transmission time should not slow down, and the time for data interpretation should remain within narrow borders; otherwise the fairness principle would suffer, particularly for stock exchange data.

Encryption is one approach to limit the group of receivers. But: Conventional video CoDecs are resistant to data losses, so that the encrypted streams cannot be decoded with conventional encryption methods, if data errors or data losses occur. An attempt to infer parts from previously received data is dangerous in unidirectional distribution systems, because there is no way to verify the completed transmission of reference data.

A major problem in all digital data systems is the ease with which perfect copies can be produced. For this reason, a way should be found for legitimate clients to identify the original client when pirate copies of the original data are found. The use of digital watermarks would be very useful in such cases.

Modern wide area networks (WANs) normally use caches to reduce the data traffic and the latency for the client. One example is proxy caches on the Web. The cache owner has unlimited access to the data, so that contents providers have to make sure they can either trust the cache owner, or they have to protect themselves against data theft and reselling by a malicious cache owner. Other threats include, for example, attacks by clients of a pay TV provider, because such attackers have additional information and tools (decoder, chip card with secret key) at their disposal. We will briefly discuss the security problem and solutions using the example of pay TV systems.

Encryption in Pay TV Systems   A broadcasted pay TV program should be unusable for all unauthorized users. The classical method to make a message unusable or illegible is the use of encryption technologies introduced above.

Each encryption operation is controlled by a key and can be undone only with this key. Encryption is used in many places in pay TV systems. This is the reason why the processes on the program contents level have special names. For example, the encryption of TV program is called *scrambling* and the corresponding key is called the *control word*, or *CW* for short. Reimers describes a basic approach for conditional access in digital television (DVB) [Rei95].

Using a Special Security Module   Pay TV systems have to solve a particular problem, compared to classical systems in message encryption:

If two persons want to exchange messages in a confidential way, then both of them normally have an interest in not disclosing their secret key to third parties, so that no one except the two parties can read their messages.

The situation is different in pay TV systems. For example, a pirate could register himself or herself as a client of the provider and obtain the control word, or the key to decrypt the control word. If the pirate can read this key, which is a series of bits or numbers, then nothing can hinder him or her from simply copying this number sequence and selling it to others.

For this reason, keys with a long validity duration, which could be used commercially by a pirate, have to be stored in a security module in a form illegible for the client. Chip cards are the security modules most frequently used today. They are defined in an international standard (ISO7816), physically secure, and cheap to produce.

Access Control: System Key and Personal Key   To decrypt a pay TV program, each decoder or security module requires two different types of information:

1. A control word (CW), which depends on the program and is the same for all decoders. It should be updated regularly over trustworthy channels.
2. An individual user address for granting or revoking access capabilities.

Both types of information are changed by the program provider at certain intervals. Modern pay TV systems transmit both message types "over the air", i.e., together with the television signal.

A system-wide uniform key, the so-called *SK* system key, is required for confidential transmission of control words. To prevent receiver addresses from being duplicated, a personal key, *PK*, has to be used; this key is used in combination with the individual user address.

In practice, we distinguish pay TV systems by whether or not the two important keys, PK and SK, depend on one another in terms of cryptology. Cryptographically independent keys have to be linked by additional measures. Schwenk (1994) [Sch94] presents a detailed discussion of these processes.

Robustness   Practical systems have shown that every pay TV system can be attacked and successfully damaged. To develop a perfectly secure system, we first have to make different assumptions about what qualifies a system as perfectly secure. But these very assumptions are vulnerabilities. For example, it is normally assumed that secret keys cannot be read from chip cards. This holds true only provided that the keys have been personalized and produced correctly. A faulty chip card can compromise the security of the entire system.

Attacks on pay TV systems can be divided into non-technical attacks, scrambling system attacks, infinite life attacks, and key disclosure attacks.

Attacks on scrambling components depend strongly on the technical equipment of the attacker. The algorithms standardized within DVB are believed to be sufficiently secure. [Sch94] and [Rei95] contain detailed studies.

4.6.2 Information Services

In contrast to unidirectional distribution services, interactive information services work on the basis of handling direct requests by the system user. The user normally authenticates himself or herself to the system and can then access the system functions and the data contents. The communication may be eavesdropped and/or manipulated by unauthorized third parties. Protection mechanisms for confidentiality, integrity, and authenticity, as well as copyright, can be implemented in a user-specific way, because there is always exactly one communication relationship between the provider and the consumer. The following section describes one example: video archives.

Video Archives When considering video archives, we first have to determine whether or not the video data stored include confidential contents in the sense of the data privacy law, e.g., in police archives. If it is necessary to constantly access the data in real time, then a complete encryption of the archived data should be considered, to ensure that the data are protected, also in case of burglary or hardware theft. However, when the constant availability of the data in the system excludes a complete encryption and the related decryption delay, then the data should be kept in a closed system or a system properly shielded from the outside with corresponding access control and authentication of all users, to ensure sufficient protection.

Many public or private film archives, however, contain video data with non-confidential material which has been publicly distributed, e.g., on the radio. An encryption of such video data is not aimed at protecting the contents against eavesdropping, but rather represents a possibility of controlling access to the video material. Alone the gigantic quantities of film material, e.g., of the size of the order of several terabytes, would make it impossible or meaningless to fully encrypt the archived material. An encryption method used in such a case should have the following properties:

- The method should work at high speed, due to the enormous data volume, to allow encryption of a full archive within an acceptable time and the calculation of hardware cost.
- The encrypted video data should allow fast retrieval and other database operations, so that the protected data can be found within the repository and reused.
- The space requirement for video data should not increase when this data is encrypted, to avoid any resulting resorting and copying of the video material in the archive database. It is often meaningful for such systems to leave the video data unencrypted and to develop a sophisticated access strategy for the archive system instead.

4.6.3   Conference Systems

A *conference system* in this context is a computer-based application, where two or more persons exchange information in the form of several media at the same time. If video data are transmitted in addition, then we speak of a video conference system. One single communication relationship is called a *video conference*.

A video conference may have to transmit confidential information and thus impose the requirement that the conference participants authenticate themselves. One example of this kind of scenario is the working on a joint concept to gain a competitive edge over a competing company. Another example would be the transmission of less security-relevant data. Either scenario results in a desire to use a method allowing scalable security measures.

The most important difference between video conference and pay TV is the sender-receiver relationship. In a video conference, all participants are normally equal senders and receivers of video and audio data, i.e., a symmetric relationship exists. In contrast, in pay TV there is always only one sender, who cannot receive anything, apart from program orders, and many receivers, who cannot send anything, except program orders. This means that the relationship is asymmetric. Accordingly, asymmetric coding and encryption with the higher cost at the sender's end is normally acceptable in pay TV, while symmetric requirements have to be met in a video conference.

The number of participants in a video conference is normally much smaller than in pay TV systems and can be further divided according to the number of communication partners:

- There are exactly two participants. In this case, the two participants can address each other directly.
- There is a group of participants. This case requires some group management and a moderating authority to determine who belongs when to which group and how a group is to be addressed.
- The conference is based on broadcasting. This transmission to all is a special form of user group. However, this case is not identical with the removal of any security measures, because there may still be a wish to ensure that, in fact, all participants receive the messages, or that each receiver obtains the messages successfully.

Media-specific elements can be used to encrypt a video data transmission, i.e., we can look at the respective compression method from the security perspective.

One approach could utilize the properties of a compression method to reduce encryption costs. But it could well happen that the compression factor deteriorates as soon as encryption interferes with compression. The encryption should be based on a high coding level, because another source coding later on would be useless—a cryptographic algorithm transforms the data into a pseudo-random bit stream. The encryption cost increases in parallel with the redundancy remaining after compression in the video data stream, i.e., redundant data would have to be encrypted several times. The second aspect, which is decisive for a partial encryption of video data, in addition to redundancy, is the question of how well a compression method projects different meaning contents onto data structures. This projection can be used to separate the data into encrypted and non-encrypted parts.

Video conferences impose high requirements on the confidentiality of the transmitted information. An application offering video conference features cannot be designed in advance for the special requirements of a specific field of use. The significance of a video conference is normally determined later by the communicating parties and the respective conference topics. This means also that the motivation of outsiders to eavesdrop on the conference will be different in each individual case. An application intended for digital video conferences should be usable both for video data transmissions, where unencrypted public discussion threads are sent, and for confidential video conferences, e.g., for the management of international organizations.

In most cases, the protection of audio information is sufficient, while the visual information in the video data should be protected in confidential business applications, e.g., persons or text appearing in the video.

4.7 Final Remarks

This chapter introduced fundamental security requirements for multimedia systems and presented solutions based on a few examples. We do not claim complete covery of the issues concerned, but intended to give an insight into the issues and developments and to show that security is an important component of a multimedia system.

Documents, Hypertext, and Hypermedia

This chapter discusses documents in the context of multimedia. [App90] defines a document as a set of structured information which may be present in various media and may be generated or input at the time of presentation. A document is used by humans and is available for editing in a computer.

5.1 Documents

A *multimedia document* is characterized by information which is coded in at least one continuous (time-dependent) and one discrete (time-independent) medium. The integration of various media is possible because of close relationships between information units. This is also called *synchronization*. A multimedia document should be viewed in the environment of tools, data abstractions, basic concepts, and document architectures.

Continuous and discrete data are still viewed and treated in many different ways. A text within an editing program is treated as a type of programming language (type character), and a motion picture is manipulated in the same editing program only via library calls. The levels of view are different, and so are the manipulation options. The goal of *abstraction* of multimedia data is an integrated, uniform way of describing and handling all media. This means an essential reduction of the complexity with regard to setting up and maintaining such programs. Chapter 3, about programming, discusses various approaches in detail, so that this issue will not be discussed any further in this chapter. Abstractions of multimedia data serve as a basis for writing code for many different types of multimedia programs, in particular editors and other document-processing tools.

Fundamental *system concepts* use abstractions of multimedia data, they serve as a concept for information architectures, and they can be implemented by use of tools. In this respect, the terms *document architecture* and *information architecture* are synonymous. Essentially, system concepts include the variants shown in the context of programming in Chapter 3 for the use of object-orientation and the hypertext and hypermedia concepts described below.

5.1.1 Document Architectures

Exchange of documents means the communication of both content and structure. In addition to common communication protocols, it also requires the use of a *document architecture*. This includes standardized architectures, such as SGML (Standard Generalized Markup Language), as well as corporate developments, e.g., of DEC (DCA, Document Content Architecture), or IBM (MO:DCA, Mixed Object Document Content Architecture).

Such information architectures use data abstractions and their concepts for specification and implementation. A document architecture describes the interplay of models (see Figure 5-1).

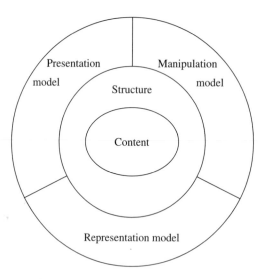

Figure 5-1   Architecture of documents and their components.

Figure 5-2 shows a multimedia information architecture characterized by the internal interplay of individual information units from discrete and continuous media.

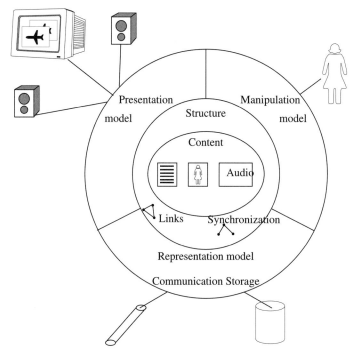

Figure 5-2 Architecture of multimedia documents and their components.

In the interplay of models, the manipulation describes operations that can be performed on multimedia information. Communication and storage define the protocols used to exchange this information between different computers and the format used to store data. The presentation of multimedia information collects relationships between individual parts of information, which have to be maintained in the presentation of this information (in the widest sense). Note that not every architecture includes all properties or models mentioned here.

5.1.2 Manipulating Multimedia Data

The user normally sees documents through specific tools used to *manipulate* multimedia data. Most of these tools include editors, graphics programs, and other *word processors*.

A document is normally subject to the processing process shown in Figure 5-3. The information present in a document is of a specific document type. This type can belong to the "business letter" or "internal memo" category. During the presentation, the same document can belong to another type, which influences essentially the final representation. The transformation of the actual information into its representation is subject to rules specific to the document architecture.

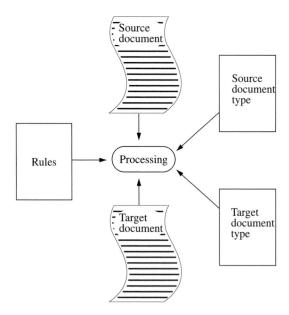

Figure 5-3   Processing a document, from information to presentation.

Based on the hypermedia or hypertext concepts, which are important for multimedia documents, the following section introduces the SGML document architecture in the context of multimedia.

5.2   Hypertext and Hypermedia

Today it is assumed that knowledge in the human brain—the association of individual thoughts and ideas—is stored in the form of a complex network [GS90]. These structures can be arranged hierarchically: Thoughts are associations of other thoughts and ideas. This is a different view of the spectrum of ideas presented below, in Chapter 7.

Writing reproduces knowledge stored in the human brain. People can use several media to communicate. Documents are one type medium used for this transfer of information, i.e., documents are used to exchange knowledge. When we read a document, we reconstruct some knowledge. In the ideal case, the transfer of knowledge originating from one author leads to the reproduction of the same ideas in the reader. The information loss is minimal. Figure 5-4 shows this communication process between an author and a reader.

The *linear* form of traditional, non-hypermedia documents does not support the reconstruction of knowledge, nor does it simplify its reproduction. Each piece of knowledge has to be artificially serialized before it can be actually exchanged, in order to transform it into a linear document. More specifically, structural information is integrated into the actual contents. In hypertext and hypermedia, the document allows a graph structure, which is thought to simplify the reading and writing of that document.

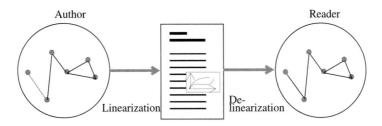

Figure 5-4   Information transfer between humans [GS90].

5.2.1   Hypertext, Hypermedia, and Multimedia

A book or an article in paper form has a pre-determined structure and is present in sequential form. However, we can read specific sections in a targeted way without having read previous sections. Authors normally assume sequential reading, so that many sections are based on knowledge previously acquired. Both fictional literature and movies always assume a purely sequential reception. Scientific literature can consist of independent chapters. However, in this context too, sequential reading is assumed.

Documentation in the widest sense often consists of a composition of relatively independent information units. A lexicon or the operating instructions manual of the Airbus, for instance, are created by several authors and always read sequentially in partial sections. In addition, this type of documentation always contains a large number of cross-references, leading to multiple browsing to different places during the reading process. In this case, an electronic aid, consisting of a concatenation of information, would be very useful.

Figure 5-5 shows an example of such a concatenation or linking. Each arrow specifies a relationship between logical information units (LDUs). A piece of text (top left in the figure) includes a reference to the climb properties of an aircraft. These properties are demonstrated in a video sequence (bottom left in the figure). At a different location in the same text, the sales subsidiaries located in Europe are listed (and the list is visualized in a graphical map, shown at the bottom right in the figure). More information about each sales point can be viewed by selecting that location in the graphical map. A special piece of information about the number of different aircrafts sold in the Paris subsidiary is shown in the form of a bar chart (top right in the figure). Internally, all information contained in this chart are present only in tabular form. The left bar refers to the aircraft, which can be seen in a video.

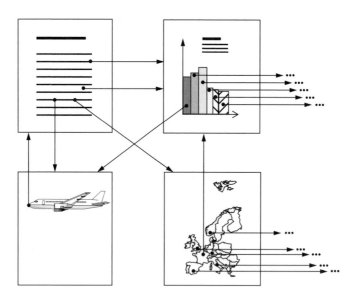

Figure 5-5   Hypertext data—example of linking of information from various media.

Non-linear Linking of Information   The most important property of hypertext and hypermedia is *non-linear* information linking. There is a reading sequence, but the reader also decides about the reading path. For example, when browsing in a lexicon, the reader can start with the term *hypertext* and then use the cross-reference *systems* to jump to a description of AppleTalk. Using this association, based on reference links, the author of the information normally determines the links.

As another example, consider this text about multimedia systems. The structure of this document actually consists of a set of chapters of equal rank, in addition to introductory and closing chapters, at least at first sight. In reality, Volume 1 Chapter 2 (Media and Data Streams) plays a dominant role: It should be read before the other chapters, because it includes a description of definitions and terms. All other chapters are relatively independent, and the reader can freely determine the reading path. This means that the structure is a tree, where in our example of this linear document, the reading path is not explained by the structure, but verbally. A hypertext structure is a *graph*, consisting of nodes and edges. The references pointing to other chapters and the literature references, for example, are also references or links, forming a graph of this document which is available in tree form.

- The *nodes* are actually information units, for example text elements, individual pictures, or audio or video LDUs. At the user interface, each information units is normally displayed in its own window.

• The *edges* form a relationship between different information units. They are called *reference* or *link*. A reference is normally a directed edge. Note that all linking elements contain information.

Anchors Browsing within a linearly sorted document is called *navigating* through a graph in a hypermedia document. At the user interface, the origin of references has to be marked, so that the user can jump from one information unit to another. These starting points for references are called *anchors*. One important factor at the user interface is the conception of this anchor: How can these anchors be properly represented?

• A *media-independent representation* can be realized with general graphic elements, like the ones commonly used for selection, e.g., *buttons*. The information about the target node should be included in such an element:

  If the target node is a piece of text, then an abbreviated, descriptive (verbose) summary of the contents could be represented. For a single image, the respective image contents could be displayed on the screen in the form of a miniature or "thumbnail". A visual representation of video contents could be implemented in the form of *moving icons* (micons). A micon is a reduced motion picture, representing a characteristic part of the video sequence of the target node (MIT Project Elastic Charles [Bra87]). If the contents of the target node consist of audio information, then the audio contents should be represented visually. For a music clip, for example, this could be a picture of the composer.

• For *text*, we could emphasize single words, paragraphs, or text sections of different lengths. A pointer can be positioned on a section emphasized in this way, so that the user could double-click the highlighted section to display the target node referred to by the pointer (see Figure 5-10 for an example).

• For *single images*, specific graphic objects or simply areas are defined as selection objects. A special marking could be a different color or hatching.

• For *motion pictures*, media-independent representations of anchors are the preferred method. We could also use areas that change over time. Normally, we would not use a local selection; instead, we would use a temporal selection, based on the entire displayed image.

• For *audio*, we would always have to use a media-independent solution. In this case, we would use a brief descriptive text or a single image in the size of an icon.

Figure 5-6 shows the relationship between multimedia, hypertext, and hypermedia.

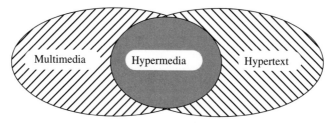

Figure 5-6   Hypertext, hypermedia and multimedia, and their relationships.

Hypertext System   A hypertext system is essentially characterized by non-linear link-age of information. References connect the nodes. The data of various nodes can be present in one medium or several media. In a pure text system, only the text sections are linked. The term *hypertext* means that several media can be linked, in addition to simple text.

Multimedia System   As described in Volume 1 Chapter 2 (Media and Data Streams), a multimedia system contains information encoded at least in one continuous and one discrete medium. For example, when text data are connected by a non-linear link, then this is not a multimedia system, but belongs to the hypertext category. A video confer-ence with simultaneous transmission of text and graphics from a conventional linear program for document editing is a multimedia application; but it has no connection to either hypertext or hypermedia.

Hypermedia System   A hypermedia system includes the non-linear linkage of infor-mation which is normally present in either a continuous or a discrete medium. For example, text and video data within a non-linear linkage structure belong to the hyper-media, multimedia, and hypertext categories.

Figure 5-6 shows that each hypermedia system belongs to the hypertext category and is a multimedia system at the same time. It forms the intersection set of both multi-media and hypertext.

As is the case with many definitions, the term *hypermedia* cannot be used in the strict sense. Therefore, we will use the terms *hypertext* and *hypermedia* interchangeably in the following sections.

5.2.2   Hypermedia Systems: Example and Typical Applications

Actually, it is not easy to imagine a real hypermedia system just by looking at this printed book. For this reason, we recommend that our readers should work with such a system to get a better understanding of the properties, benefits and drawbacks (e.g., by using an Internet browser to visit sites in the World Wide Web).

The following example of a lecture about hypertext prepared as a hypermedia document was adapted from [Nie90b] and [Nie90a]. It describes a part of a typical task using a hypermedia system. In this example, familiar objects are simulated for the reader of a hypertext document to suggest an environment which is as natural as possible (see Figure 5-7). For this reason, the example first shows a book from the outside, which can then be opened and browsed. The book designates the document. The title of the document is shown on the book cover.

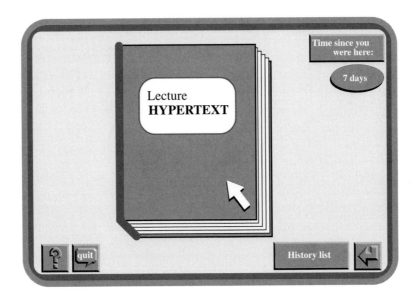

Figure 5-7 Hypermedia example —first screen introducing a lecture.

One possible piece of additional information would be when the reader has last opened the book. It refers to the entire document. The same information (when it is represented while the reader opens the book on the screen) refers then only to the node itself.

Regardless of the respective system state, a help function could be used to offer context-sensitive help topics. The help function describes the current state, their possible interactions and impact, and it offers the possibility of accessing general help information. A very popular hypertext application consists of this type of system-wide help functions. However, most of these applications use text as the sole or main medium. In Figure 5-7, the book is opened by moving the mouse pointer on the book and double-clicking the mouse button.

As shown in Figure 5-8, the opened book first offers a rough overview of the document in the form of a two-dimensional table of contents. In this example, there is no first chapter. In addition to connecting the nodes by edges (or connecting the information units by references), the physical arrangement of the nodes in relation to each other can intuitively convey additional information. For example, chapters closely related can be represented on the screen close to each other. The author can express this type of content relationships in the layout itself. Consider the following example of a document laid out in several sections: HTML, SGML, and hypertext. In this example, HTML and SGML could be close together, because both relate to document architectures. Hypertext could be used in both architectures.

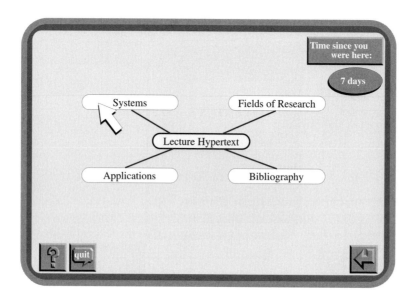

Figure 5-8   Hypermedia example—second screen showing the top level of the table of contents.

In its most general form, the table of contents is a graph, usually available in the form of a tree. The nodes previously visited could be marked in a special way, simplifying navigation. To keep things simple and easy, the example shows only a section of the full table of contents. The reader could become confused if too many nodes are represented together with their respective links in the table of contents. The maximum number of *nodes* for representation on a 14-inch screen in VGA resolution and a tree-type table of contents is approx. 30, when all nodes are represented at the same time. On the other hand, when too few nodes are displayed (e.g., only three each time), then this would lead to an unclear number of levels. The optimum number of represented nodes depends on the screen size, the number of references, and the linkage degree: Many nodes can be represented by means of trees, while few nodes should be represented when using complex graphs. Usually, tables of contents are structured in trees. The contents of the respective target node refines the table of contents. In this example, the reader selects *Systems*.

In the example in Figure 5-8, the hypertext lecture is organized into four sections: *Applications*, *Systems*, *Fields of Research*, and *Bibliography*. The structure of these sections can be represented in a refined version. In this case, the four sections can also be visualized in the form of buttons, which the user can select. In the example shown in Figure 5-9, there are *Requirements*, *User Interface Design*, and *Classification* buttons for *Systems*. This representation could hide a multi-level table of contents. However, this should not be the case here. Now, the user selects the User Interface information unit to obtain information about this topic. This calls up the screen shown in Figure 5-10.

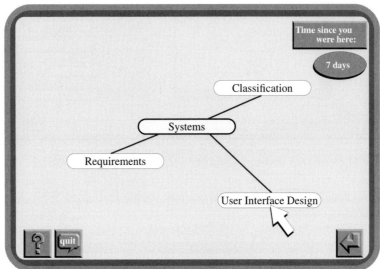

Figure 5-9 Hypermedia example—third screen showing the second level of the table of contents.

The example of the user interface shown in Figure 5-10 represents a typical information unit of the medium type text. Now, the book has been opened. At the same time, a screen with a general overview of the table of contents and the second level should also be visible. The selected path, i.e., *Systems*, *User Interface*, is especially marked in this example. This facilitates navigation for the reader. The displayed text is written to one page, forming the association with an opened book. Here, some text passages are highlighted as anchors: *Orientation*, *Overview Diagram*, *History Files*, and *Backtracking*. Each of these anchors hides further information. This situation could entice the user to browse quickly, without absorbing the information presented so far. Further information about the topic *Orientation* is available in the form of a motion picture. The user would like to obtain information about this issue, so that he or she selects the *Orientation* anchor shown in Figure 5-10.

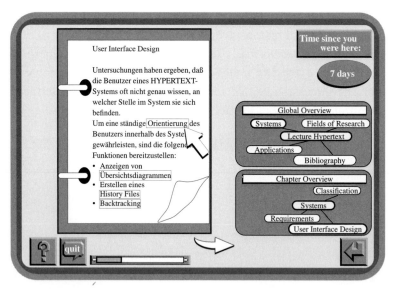

Figure 5-10   Hypermedia example—fourth screen showing GUI details.

This selection leads the user to the movie shown in Figure 5-11, which features examples related to *Orientation*.

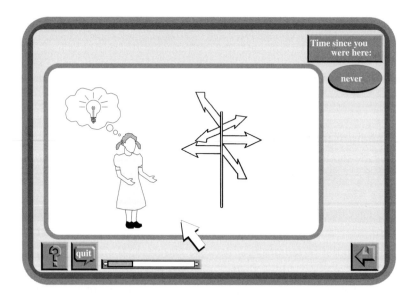

Figure 5-11   Hypermedia example—fifth screen showing GUI details.

There is an additional option available which displays a program about how to control the motion pictures on the screen. Like a video recorder, this displays a still image, which can be moved forward or backward at various speeds. This manipulation is shown on the screen. In addition, the user can jump to specific positions, e.g., to the beginning.

In contrast to the previous figures, the information about the last visit of this node has changed in this example: The reader has not read this information before. The reader has last visited all previous nodes seven days earlier (see Figure 5-8, Figure 5-9, or Figure 5-11).

Selecting the icon at the bottom right of the screen (arrow) takes the reader one step back to the previous node, e.g., to the User Interface. Looking at Figure 5-10, Figure 5-11, and Figure 5-12, we should mention the two icons underneath the opened book, and the scrollbar in the middle.

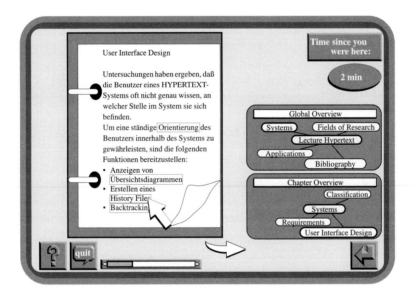

Figure 5-12   Hypermedia example—sixth screen showing GUI details.

In this example, the scrollbar indicates that the displayed page shows approx. 25% of the entire information available in this node about *Orientation*. Currently, the display shows the first section. More pages can be displayed by moving the scrollbar or by selecting the arrow shown on the right underneath the open book. Next, the user selects *History Files* on this page.

History Files means the path traversed so far during the current reading session. This path is also displayed together with additional information. In the example shown in Figure 5-13, the reader has visited the title page for five minutes or, more specifically, looked at the overview for two minutes and at the *Systems* section contents for four minutes. This overview shows all traversed nodes. By selecting a highlighted node, the user can jump to this node directly from such a list.

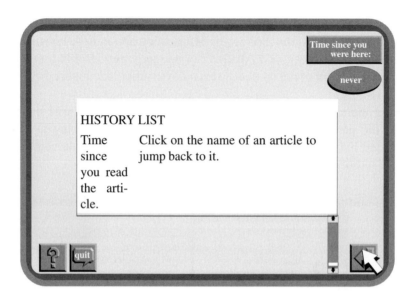

Figure 5-13   Hypermedia example – seventh screen showing the history of information visited so far.

A graphic allocation is normally easier to remember than a verbose description. For example, most users would easily remember that there was a picture of a red hat at the top right. This means that some alternative displays of traversed nodes also contain a set of miniaturized screen contents. However, this leads to unclear or messy screens in most cases.

This example of a short, virtual navigation through a hypertext lecture shows some characteristic properties of a hypertext system. Various systems use different concepts, functions, and user interface styles. The solution described here should be considered as an example only; it should not be regarded as an optimum implementation of hypertext concepts.

Other Applications   Lectures are not the only or even a typical application. In fact, hypertext has been used for the following applications:

• Hypertext is well established in some classical *computer-based applications*. In particular, this includes the help function of modern graphical interfaces. Most online documentation is implemented on the basis of hypertext and shipped on CD-ROMs.

- *Commercial applications* include repair and operating instructions. These applications also make extensive use of various media. For example, this technology could replace microfilms in the field of spare parts supplies in the future. A repair instructions manual could be represented by use of motion pictures. In this area, most users also expect some interaction in the form of slow forward and backward movements. Trade fair and product catalogs, together with other applications, form the basis of a large number of different applications in the advertising industry.
- *Intellectual applications* include organization of ideas, brainstorming, or text creation. For this type of process, the structure of the document currently being created is normally not more than a rough sketch which will gradually be refined and finalized.
- *Education and research* are areas with a large potential for improvement by use of continuous media. For example, audio is a useful and common medium to learn foreign languages. Many museums use audio and video for additional information about their exhibits.
- The *entertainment industry* has used hypertext for information or guiding systems for tourists and interactive science-fiction movies. This industry has also produced a new generation of computer games.

In summary, hypertext offers benefits in cases where the specific application does not dictate a strict linear document structure.

5.2.3 History

Hypertext has a relatively long history, although the first hypertext systems were introduced to the market only a few years ago. The integration of continuous media has also been demonstrated several years ago. This section provides a short overview of the history of hypertext and hypermedia, based on [Nie90].

Vannevar Bush is the author of the original hypertext concept, the linked information structure. He described the first hypertext system and called it *Memex* (MEMory EXtender).

Imagine all information stored on microfilm spread out on a table. With suitable projectors, we could display areas in a form similar to Windows systems. There would be an *associative index*, linking the different microfilm areas (these would be the references). Memex was never realized in a practical implementation; it always existed only on paper. Vannevar Bush developed the first ideas about this technology as early as 1932. In 1945, he published the first description in his article *As We May Think*.

During the period from 1962 to 1976, Doug Englebart developed a project to augment human capabilities at the Stanford Research Institute (SRI). This *Augment* project included *NLS* (*oN Line System*), which featured hypertext characteristics for the first time. NLS itself served as a common document repository for all documents created within this project. All scientists who worked on this project made extensive use of its reference or linking capabilities. Eventually, the project included approx. 100,000 entries.

The term *hypertext* was initially coined by Ted Nelson in 1965. His *Xanadu* system was intended to contain all information ever written. The concept of this system describes access both to local and remote data. Xanadu, with its global information contents, has not been implemented at the time of writing.

Staff at Brown University, Providence, have worked on hypertext systems since the mid-sixties, and the *Hypertext Editing System* was introduced there by a work group headed by Andries van Dam in 1967. This was the first practical hypertext system; it required 120 Kbytes of main memory, equal to the memory requirement of a small IBM/360 mainframe. The Hypertext Editing System was sold and then used to document the Apollo Mission. The successor project—*FRESS (File Retrieval and Editing System)*— was introduced in 1968. Both systems linked documents via references, while the user interface was implemented by text only. Since then, Brown University has performed successful research work in the field of hypertext and hypermedia.

Aspen Movie Map is probably the first real hypermedia system that additionally supports continuous media. It was developed by the *MIT Architecture Machine Group* under the cooperation of Andrew Lippman. Later this group and other groups formed the *MIT Media Lab* [Bra87]. This application can be used to simulate a virtual drive across the city of Aspen, Colorado, on the computer screen. In this application, the user can navigate to either of the four directions. A *joystick* is used to control the direction. The basic technology consists of a large number of single pictures stored on a video disk. For this purpose, four cameras are mounted on a cart and positioned at right angles to each other (viewing to the front, rear, right, and left). In a pilot demonstration, these carts drove through all major roads of the city and took single shots at an interval of every three meters. The images were then linked via implicit references, so that a ride across the city was simulated. The driving action itself was simulated by displaying a maximum of two pictures each, resulting in a speed of approx. 110 km/h. The display was shown on two screens: The first screen showed the road, while the second screen displayed a road map with the actual position. More recent projects deal with the combined use of video, single images, and text for repair instructions for bicycles and cars.

None of the hypertext systems described above has been taken to product implementation and seldom used outside the research groups. In 1982, Symbolics initiated the development of the *Symbolics Document Examiner*, and the first hypertext product was shipped in 1985. A major application was the documentation of the Symbolics Workstation, which comprised 8,000 pages at the time of writing. This project included approx. 10,000 nodes with approx. 23,000 links as pure hypertext. The project used a book as the metaphor on the screen and placed much attention on a simple and user-friendly interface.

Since 1985, many hypertext systems have been introduced on the market, including very successful ones. For example, *NoteCards* from Xerox and *Intermedia* from Brown University started as research projects and both led to product developments. The market leader introduced by Office Workstation Limited was initiated as a product development; it was the first product based on small computers (1986). Apple introduced *HyperCard* in 1987. It was pre-installed free of charge on all Macintosh computers and widely used since 1987. SEPIA of GMD-IPSI in Darmstadt, Germany, is a specialized system that supports the planning and argumentation of cooperating groups.

System Concepts Current hypertext and hypermedia systems differ in their fundamental concepts:

- *Application-independent systems* are not specific to a certain application. They are designed for general application to create and read documentation. One example for these applications is Apple's HyperCard product.
- *Application-specific systems* are designed for a specific use. For example, gIBIS offers explanations for political discussions. This system was designed as a decision tool. gIBIS includes three special node types and nine different reference types [CB88].

5.2.4 Systems: Architecture, Nodes, and References

The *architecture* of a hypertext system can be divided into three levels with a different functionality each [CG87]. We will describe each of these architectures in the following section.

Architecture The top or *presentation level* accommodates all functions relating to the user interface. This level is used to map nodes and references to the user interface. The user interface offers the visualization of one or several sections. Based on its structure and the display chosen by the user, this level determines the data to be displayed and how it should be represented. This level is also responsible for the control of all inputs.

The *Hypertext Abstract Machine* (*HAM*) is located between the presentation level (level One) and the storage level (level Two). This level takes database-like functions to store multimedia data within a local or distributed environment from the lower level. Note that the HAM level does not have to worry about the input and output of the upper level. HAM knows the structure of a document, and it disposes of knowledge about the references and their attributes. This means that the HAM level builds the data structure, or an object hierarchy, for document management.

Compared to the other two levels, the HAM level is the one least dependent on the system. This means that it is also best suitable for standardization [Nie90].

The *storage level* (also called *database level*) forms the lowest level. It includes all functions relating to the storage of data, i.e., secondary storage management. In this respect, the specific properties of the different sets of data from discrete and continuous media are important. This is also the level where capabilities of traditional database systems, i.e., persistence (data survives programs and processes), multi-user operation (synchronization, locking), and error recovery (transaction concept), are expected. The nodes and references of a hypertext document are handled like data objects, without any particular semantics. There are no specific functions relating to hypertext on this level.

Unfortunately, most current implementations of hypertext systems do not clearly separate these different levels. The reasons are normally a shorter development phase, a more efficient implementation, and shortcomings in most generally available multimedia interfaces for the lowest level.

Nodes A *node* is an information unit (LDU) in a hypertext document. The most important distinguishing criterion between different implementations is the maximum data quantity a node can accommodate.

- The *maximum data quantity* contained in a node can be limited to match the screen size. The metaphor of a note card, or a frame, was briefly introduced above in the HyperCard example. A motion picture sequence and an audio clip could be limited to a duration of — say — 20 seconds.

  This situation may force the author to distribute logically related text contents over several cards, although it is not desirable. This means that long audio and video clips would also have to be distributed over several cards, so that the close relationship of these sequences may be lost. On the other hand, a clear and intuitive environment is the major benefit.

- One alternative are window-based systems with a basically *unlimited data quantity* per node. The user interface supports several windows to facilitate user interaction, e.g., fast forward and backward movements. One such system is Intermedia. Intermedia does not limit the duration of continuous media with regard to the data volume its nodes can accommodate.

  This means that single nodes can have very different lengths and still appear equal-ranking. The presentation of additional information also uses two different methods at the user interface: First, there is a way to switch between the nodes, and second, a node uses the mechanisms known from window-based systems for *scrolling*.

A secondary criterion concerns the *time when a piece of information is created*. In general, the author can specify the entire contents of the nodes while creating a document. Alternatively, the author could specify that the information be generated at the presentation time. For example, a piece of information about a corporation could also include a reference or link to the current market price traded at the Frankfurt Stock Exchange. Videotext could then be used to request this information automatically and present it as part of the hypertext document.

References   *References* form the edges in a hypertext graph. Hypertext systems differ by various edge criteria. One of the first questions to ask here would be: *Which information is contained in a reference?*

- *Simple references* connect two nodes of a graph without containing any information themselves. They merely establish a relationship between those nodes.
- In contrast, *typified references* connect two nodes and include additional information. A *label* is assigned to each reference. This label is used to create comments to each reference (e.g., author and creation date).

We could well imagine additional semantics: In a teaching unit, continued reading of some details could depend on the result of a teaching test. The references could then contain a description how they can be activated, representing a dependence on the result of the teaching test. References can also be used to control access rights. Another possibility would be the typification of references according to their properties. For example, we could distinguish relationships by *target node as an example* and *target node as a detail*. These different semantics could then be expressed by various representations of anchors on the user interface.

Another property of references refers to the following question: *What does this reference mean*? References are often used jointly with very different meanings, making it more difficult to understand these references. The author of a hypertext should be aware of this problem and use unique references. We can distinguish the most frequent relationships as described below. This list of relationships expressed in references represents a few selected examples:

- *To be — A* is part of *B*. This represents a quantity relationship.
- *To present — A* is an example of *B*, or *A* demonstrates *B*. This case uses an example to state a fact.
- *To produce — A* produces *B*, or *B* is a result of *A*. This case can describe consequences from a fact in more detail.
- *To require* or *required by — A* requires *B*, *B* needs *A*. This relationship expresses an absolute necessity.
- *To own — A* owns *B*, or *A* is associated to *B*. This relationship expresses an ownership.
- *To include — A* includes *B*, or *A* consists of *B*, or *A* occurs in *B*. This relationship represents different meanings of an inclusion.
- *Similarity — A* is similar to *B*, *A* is different from *B*, *A* replaces *B*, *A* is the alternative to *B*. This relationship expresses similarities.

Another fundamental property of references can be described by the following question: *Who states a reference?* We distinguish as follows:

- *Implicit References* — A relationship between nodes can be created automatically by a hypertext system. The author specifies only the algorithms used to create the references. For example, the Intermedia system generates all references belonging to an index automatically. Similar things can be done for lexicons: cross-references are created automatically to the most important terms of each entry.

- *Explicit References* — All references are created by the author.

A reference can be created at different times, which leads us to the question: *When is the target of a reference stated?*

- In the classical case, a reference is created during the creation of the hypertext document, and both the origin and the target node are specified. When editing the document, the author specifies explicitly how the information units should be linked.

- A target node can be determined when the reference is used, i.e., while the document is read. The author specifies an algorithm to be used to create the references, while the references are determined when the user reads the context. The system calculates the target node.

One example for explicit references could be a train timetable, displaying the next trains to a destination station. A reference to the next train depends on the current time. This examples was taken from the *Glasgow Online* information system of the city of Glasgow [Har89].

In most systems, however, each reference has exactly one origin and one target node. On the other hand, we could ask the following question: *What direction does the reference have?* And: *What is the number of outgoing references?*

The direction is normally unidirectional, while the system itself supports backtracking. This means that we would always get back on track. The alternative would be bidirectional references, which means that we would have to highlight or mark both the target nodes and the anchors. When introducing bidirectional references, it could easily happen that several nodes refer to the same target nodes. This means that these references have to be explicitly distinguished at the target node. The same applies to references leading from one origin to several target nodes. Most systems support unidirectional references with only one target node each. This is easier to understand and to implement.

As our last question, we would have to deal with the appearance of an anchor on the user interface. More specifically, we can ask the following question: *How can a reference be represented?* Section 5.2 discusses several options available to represent references.

Tools A hypertext system consists of several required tools:

- One or more *editors* are used to edit information from various media. In addition, some kind of support is needed to create, manage, modify, and delete references.
- *Search tools* are used to find information, where various media have to be taken into account.
- A *browser* is used to obtain a short and clear representation of the nodes and edges. The description of nodes depends on the media. The user normally sees the structure in a graphical representation. Most browsers allow the user to selectively display visited parts or relevant information.
- When *navigating* through a document, suitable support should be provided to avoid the getting-lost-in-hyperspace phenomenon. This means that there should be some backtracking and a clear presentation of the entire structure with regard to the current position.

5.2.5 Closing Remarks on Hypertext Systems

The reading *order* of a hypertext document should be predefined according to the reading context. This means that the structure of a document can also change depending on the context [Hof91].

A textbook about the pancreas could offer an introduction into the functionality of this organ for undergraduate students. For this application, we would represent only a limited set of nodes, and most references would form a tree with a recommended reading path. The user can easily navigate through this document. For graduate courses, the students would be introduced to the endoscopy within their surgical studies. In this case, we could use text, images, video, and audio to show various possibilities for surgical interventions. In this context, the hypertext document would include a detailed description of a surgical intervention, in addition to an explanation of the basic terms. Other sections within the document would deal with research aspects, i.e., it could include references to a large number of other relevant work, and current research projects could be introduced. The user could easily navigate through the entire document.

Most current hypertext systems do not allow references to nodes outside their internal data structures. For example, it is not possible to maintain related electronic letters as one single document within a hypertext system, and use a mail client to send these letters at the same time. In this situation, some degree of *openness* would be required to be able to support references between information units of different applications. We would need standardized exchange formats and protocols.

A hypertext document is normally stored on a computer. With an appropriate *distribution* option, information units could reside on different computers. References can then work beyond computer boundaries. Based on the architecture introduced in this section, this requirement would mainly concern the storage level.

Other interesting research and development projects deal with the following aspects and issues:

- Size and concept of the information units. (What are *optimum* sizes? What factors determine these sizes?)
- Support of distributed documents to transfer information and/or reorganize the networks. (How can a document be maintained when its content is stored in a remote location?)
- Version management. (Which elements should be subject to version management? How could this versioning look like?)
- Authorization and access rights. (Which elements should be subject to authorization and protected by access rights? How could this management look like?)
- Cooperative work, joint document editing. (Which access types should be locked? How could such a management be implemented?)
- Virtual views of hypermedia documents. (Who determines virtual views? How could these views be managed?)
- Optimizing latencies for navigation through hypermedia [GCD02].

In closing our hypertext/hypermedia discussion, this section will briefly evaluate the most important properties. Part of this evaluation is based on the author's personal experiences and other ideas from discussions with experts: Many of the aspects we observed when working with such systems for the first time are very *positive*. Most systems can be used very easily, i.e., they are intuitive and do not require a user manual. The user will learn quickly and effectively how to find the desired information and how to manipulate data.

Many of the properties mentioned so far depend on the system. Most modern hypertext systems offer all of these properties.

The hypertext documents themselves are very different in nature. Some have a clear structure and are easy to read, while others have an unclear structure and are difficult to read. This means that hypertext-specific requirements are expected to be solved by the authors and creators of the information contained, which is not an easy task.

Hypermedia integrates various media elegantly and easily. All relationships between information units are implemented by use of references. Some systems provide additional support for the joint management of information by several persons.

On the other hand, some properties of this technology give rise to a more *critical* evaluation. The most common effect is "getting lost in hyperspace", i.e., a user can lose both the overview and the context while navigating through a document. When hypertext documents have an unclear structure and many references with different meanings, such a document can easily become a so-called *spaghetti book*. It is very difficult to turn a hypertext document back into sequential paper form without some loss of information. This means that, even for a simple document without audio and video information, we would have to rely on computer output. Some applications use their own window system. There is a lack of established standards for the exchange of information between the different hypertext systems available at the time of writing this book.

Several efforts have been initiated to elaborate hypermedia standards. Expansions of the SGML document architectures (see Section 5.3) include hypertext techniques. They will support the exchange of information with a heterogeneous hypertext-type document environment.

Other work has been proposed by the ISO/IEC JTC1 SC2/WG12 *Multimedia and Hypermedia Information Coding Expert Group* (*MHEG*). This work group deals with the *Coded Representation of Multimedia and Hypermedia Information* [MHE93]. The *Music Information Processing Standards* (*MIPS*) *Committee* was formed by the ANSI group X3V1.8M. In relation to hypertext, this group deals with HyTime and the *Standard Music Description Language* (*SMDL*).

In summary, we can see that hypertext is not equally suitable for all types of documents and applications. This technology is well suited in relation to lexicons. This field is based on independent information units that are easy to link by use of references. The use of a hypertext system is much faster, compared to browsing in a book.

In addition, audio and video media could be easily integrated in such a lexicon. For example, audio could be used to store music clips or animal sounds, while video could be used to create a brief representation of typical movements as part of a lexicon entry.

Another group of suitable applications for hypermedia is education. We could imagine courses with audiovisual support, adapting to the individual learning behavior of the students. Current work includes didactic aids to help instructors in preparing their courses. One example for such a system is the *Multibook* developed at Darmstadt University of Technology [SSFS99].

5.3 The SGML Document Architecture

The *Standard Generalized Markup Language* (*SGML*) [Org86] has been promoted mainly by US publishing companies. The authors provide text, i.e., contents. They use a uniform markup format to describe titles, tables, and other document elements, without actually describing the document's look (e.g., fonts or line spacing). The final layout is determined by the publisher.

The basic idea is that the author uses *tags* to mark specific text parts. SGML defines the look of these tags, but it does not define where they should occur, or what meaning they should have. Instead, user groups agree on the meaning of such tags. SGML offers a *frame* that can be used to describe the syntax in a way specific to a user group within an object-oriented system. Classes and objects, hierarchies of classes and objects, inheritance, and embedded methods (processing instructions) can be used in the specification. SGML defines the syntax but no semantics.

The following example shows the use of SGML in a text document, and we will briefly discuss a few important details below.

```
<title>Multimedia Systems</title>
<author>Felix Gatou</author>
<side>IBM</side>
<summary>This exceptional paper from Bernd ...
...
```

5.3.1   Using SGML

The handling process for an SGML document shown in Figure 5-14 splits the processing job into two processes. Only the formatter knows the meaning of the tags, and uses these tags to produce a formatted document. The parser uses the tags contained in the document in combination with the appropriate document type.

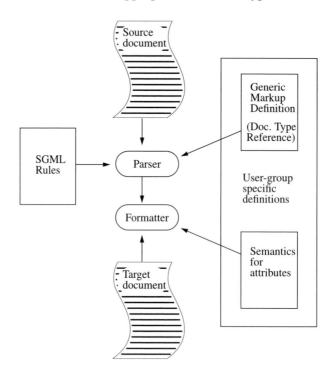

Figure 5-14   SGML document processing, from information to representation.

As mentioned above, tags can be used to define the structure of a document, which normally includes the association of some parts of the layout. It is based on the common context between the creator of the document and the formatting process, but not defined by SGML. There are various tag categories:

- *Descriptive markup tags* describe the actual structure in the following form:

```
<start-tag> or alternatively </end-tag>
```

One example is the definition of the beginning of a paragraph:

```
<paragraph> The text of this paragraph begins here...
```

- An *entity reference* points to another element, which then replaces the entity reference. This could also be interpreted as an abbreviation, which is later overwritten by copying the actual content in its place. The following example shows how we can use an entity reference to write a German word that contains an umlaut character:

```
&Ae;rger ... should read Ärger ...
```

- *Markup declarations* define the elements pointed to by an entity reference. The following example defines an umlaut:

```
<!ELEMENT Ae (...)>
```

A markup declaration can also be used to define rules for the structure (classes). The following example defines the structure of an article, *Paper*:

```
<!ELEMENT paper     (preamble, body, postamble)>
<!ELEMENT preamble (title, author, side)>
<!ELEMENT title     (#CDATA)>  -- character data
<!ELEMENT body      ( ... )>

 ...
```

- *Processing Instructions* are used to embed instructions for other programs into a piece of text, e.g., instructions for the formatter. Processing instructions can also be used to insert various media, e.g., images and video.

SGML uses a grammar for tags to define a syntax that has to be observed. It does not define the meaning of these tags. Figure 5-15 shows the information or document architecture of SGML. Using its tags, SGML has a representation model. Objects, classes, and inheritance can be used to define the structure.

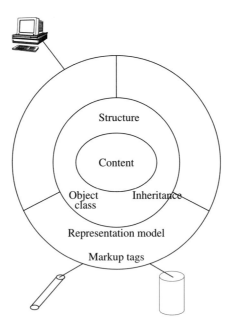

Figure 5-15   The SGML document architecture focuses on the representation model.

5.3.2   SGML and Multimedia

Currently, the SGML standard supports multimedia data only in the form of images. An image is embedded into an SGML document in *CGM* (*Computer Graphics Metafile*) form. The standard does not include specifications or recommendations for other media [Org86].

```
<!ATTLIST video   id      ID      #IMPLIED>
<!ATTLIST video   synch   synch   #IMPLIED>
<!ELEMENT video   (audio, movpic)>
<!ELEMENT audio   (#NDATA)> -- non-text media
<!ELEMENT movpic  (#NDATA)> -- non-text media
...
<!ELEMENT story   (preamble, body, postamble)> :
```

#NDATA can be used to set a reference that points to specific data. This data is normally external, i.e., stored in a separate file. The above example shows a video definition, consisting of audio and motion pictures.

Of course, multimedia information units have to be presented in an appropriate way, and the synchronization of components is very important. Efforts in this respect have been made for HyTime [Gol91] and MHEG [MHE93].

5.3.3   Final Remarks

Standardized document exchange is required with regard to communication. Both the sender and the receiver could be subject to a temporal and a spatial separation. In addition, most documents are subject to further automatic processing steps. This situation requires a common context. While the syntax is transmitted, the semantics has to be agreed upon separately in SGML. Document type definitions (DTDs) form the basis for these agreements.

While SGML will remain a fundamental standard in its current form [Org86], we can expect the development of expansions:

- A standardized layout semantics is required to simplify agreements between user groups. The *Document Style Semantics and Specification Language (DSSSL)* is an expansion for presentation. With regard to character sets, there should be some kind of information exchange about digital fonts.

- Extensive work has been made to develop a *Standard Page Description Language (SPDL)* based on Postscript.

- References should be embedded as non-text expansions for multimedia. This includes an expansion to describe music (*Standard Music Description Language—SMDL*) and HyTime.

5.4   Hypertext and the World Wide Web

The idea of the *World Wide Web* (*WWW*) was developed by Tim Berners-Lee, a physics scientist at CERN, the European Organization for Nuclear Research. The original idea was to allow the distributed representation of charts and images. For this purpose, it was necessary to develop an environment for the exchange of graphical elements. The *World Wide Web Organization* was formed at the beginning of 1994. This organization consisted initially of the CERN and the MIT (Massachusetts Institute of Technology), and the French INRIA (Institute Nationale de Recherche en Informatique et en Automatique) joined later. In 1994, the WWW Organization was renamed into *WWW Consortium* (*W3C*). Extensive information about the development of the Web is available online at http://www.w3.org/WWW/.

The original purpose of the World Wide Web was to be able to represent documents on different platforms and different user interfaces in one single computer network, including text-based and auditive interfaces. It was then planned to convert each document into Braille.

More recent developments tend to integrate all possibilities of modern publishing and layout into the WWW. Examples include the *Extended Markup Language* (*XML*) and *Cascading Style Sheets* (*CSS*), which will be described later. These developments will make the original goals more difficult.

5.4.1   Architecture of the World Wide Web

The WWW builds on a client-server architecture. The document residing on the server (e.g., text documents, images) can be retrieved from a client (browser). A client and a server use the *Hypertext Transfer Protocol* (*HTTP*), which builds on TCP/IP [Com95], to communicate. Figure 5-16 shows how clients and servers communicate over HTTP in the Web.

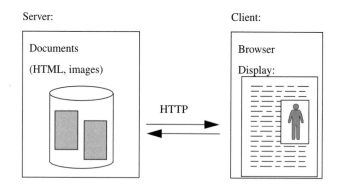

Figure 5-16   Communication between a server and a client.

5.4.2   The Hypertext Transfer Protocol (HTTP)

A WWW document can include text, icons, maps, and images. In addition, there is a possibility to integrate both audio and video clips, motion pictures and animations into a WWW document. These documents are written in the *Hypertext Markup Language* (*HTML*) and form a hypermedia system.

A *Uniform Resource Locator* (*URL*) states the exact address of a document in the Web and is used to specify distributed documents in the Web. A URL has the following form:

```
Protocol name://computer name:port/document name
```

The *protocol name* part specifies the protocol used (e.g., http, ftp), while *computer name* specifies the name or Internet address of the target computer where the document resides. A *port* states the port used to retrieve the document. The standard port 80 is used when no specific port is stated. The following example shows the address of a document:

```
http://www.kom.tu-darmstadt.de
```

The Hypertext Transfer Protocol (HTTP) is used to access hypermedia resources available at different locations. This simple protocol allows the exchange of hypertext documents between a browser requesting a document and a Web server offering the desired document. The communication between the client (browser) and the server to retrieve a document involves four steps (see Figure 5-17).

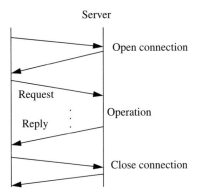

Figure 5-17   Communication between a client and a server over HTTP/1.0.

Both the request and the reply can be easy or detailed, and bth consist of the following elements:

- One start line,
- none or several header information lines, or

    - general header information (date, MIME version) and/or
    - request/reply header information (e.g., authorization, form, location) and/or
    - contents header information (`Allow`, `Expires`, `Content-Type`)

- one blank line, and
- an optional message, i.e., the content of the requested page.

Requests and replies differ in their start lines. In a request message, this line always begins with the request method, followed by the target address, and the version of the supported protocol:

```
Method/path/document.html HTTP/version
```

Table 5-1 describes the most important methods.

Method	Description
GET	Requests a Web document for reading.
HEAD	Requests a Web document to read the header.
POST	Adds data to a resource (e.g., News).
PUT	Requests a new document to be stored on the specified server.
DELETE	Deletes the specified document from the server.
LINK	Links two existing resources.
UNLINK	Removes a link between two resources.

Table 5-1   HTTP methods.

In contrast, a simple reply begins with the version of the supported protocol, followed by a status code and a verbose explanation of the status code:

```
HTTP/version status code reason phrase
```

The status code of a reply is a three-digit integer value. The first digit is the most important: it identifies one of the following reply categories:

- 1xx: Describes an information message.
- 2xx: Shows the success of the transaction:
    - 200 OK, request successful.
    - 201 OK, new resource created (for a POST method).
    - 204 OK, but no contents.
- 3xx: Redirects the client to another address.
- 4xx: Shows an error message on the client:
    - 400 Wrong request.
    - 401 The client failed to authenticate itself.
    - 403 Access to the document denied.
    - 404 The document was not found.
- 5xx: Shows an error message on the server:
    - 500 Internal error (in the server).
    - 501 The server is currently unavailable.

HTTP/1.0 has a series of difficulties and problems. For example, only one URL is sent for each TCP connection. This means that, if a document contains a large number of images and text, then a large number of accesses are required to transmit the entire page.

HTTP/1.1 (RFC 2086) was developed to increase the efficiency of HTTP. HTTP/1.1 allows the browser to execute several communication operations over one single connection. This has the benefit that the data volume transferred over the network can be reduced. Figure 5-18 shows the process when a client and a server communicate over HTTP/1.1.

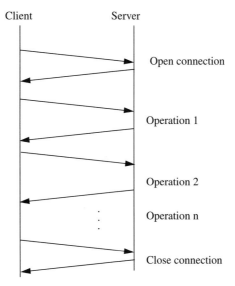

Figure 5-18   Communication between a client and a server over HTTP/1.1.

In addition, HTTP/1.1 supports caching. *Caching* is a technique used to avoid multiple retransmissions of requests and full responses, so that the required network bandwidth can be reduced.

5.5   The Hypertext Markup Language (HTML)

The *Hypertext Markup Language* (*HTML*) is a standardized language that can be easily interpreted and used to specify the look of specific text on the screen. HTML documents do not have a special file format; they are simple ASCII text documents that can be created in an arbitrary text editor. The representation of different HTML documents on different systems requires a browser, i.e., a program that understands HTML instructions (tags) and generates the appropriate page layout.
A browser displays a document in the following steps:

1. Get the requested document from the server.
2. Interpret the document's content.
3. Generate the local layout.
4. Display this layout locally on the client.

An example of a HTML document layout is presented in Figure 5-19.

Figure 5-19   Example of a HTML document layout.

5.5.1   The Structure of HTML Pages

An HTML document consists of three parts:

1. The first line is the only information source that defines the relation between HTML and SGML in an HTML document. This relation is defined by the `<!DOCTYPE>` tag, which describes the type of the text following the tag. This tag also states the HTML version used.
2. A descriptive header, containing the title and other meta information. This information is included between `<HEAD>`... `</HEAD>` tags.
3. The actual content of an HTML page as it appears in the browser is included between `<BODY>`... `</BODY>` tags or `<FRAMESET>`... `</FRAMESET>` tags.

The `<HTML>`... `</HTML>` tags include the second and third parts of an HTML document. This tag is optional, but it should always be used to simplify subsequent editing of that HTML document. The next lines show an example of a simple HTML document.

```
<HTML>
<HEAD>
<TITLE>KOM</TITLE>
</HEAD>
<BODY>
<P>Industrial process and system communication
<IMG SRC="KOM.jpg">
<P>Example text
</BODY>
```

5.5.2   Meta Information

In addition to information obtained by the user directly from the representation, an HTML document includes additional information about the document itself. This information is called *meta information*. It is one of the potential means to feed search engines in the World Wide Web with information about documents. HTML uses the <META> tag to add this information. The <META> tag takes two attributes: NAME and CONTENT. NAME specifies the type of meta information, e.g., author, date and legal or copyright information, while CONTENT specifies the document's content. Table 5-2 shows a series of typical examples for meta information.

Name	Content
Author	Author of the document.
Keywords	A list of words, separated by commas, which search engines should use for this document.
Generator	The name of the HTML editor used to create the document.
Classification	Classifies the document in a content category.

Table 5-2   Typical types of meta information.

5.5.3   Tags in HTML

HTML defines a number of tags. For example, the <A> tag defines a link to another page and the <IMG> tag defines an image embedded in an HTML page. The <EMBED> tag, which was later standardized and renamed to <OBJECT> tag by W3C, is used to embed objects, e.g., helper applications (plug-ins). Table 5-3 lists the most common HTML tags.

5.5.4   HTML Version Differences

HTML was further developed over time and adapted to the latest application requirements of the World Wide Web. The first generation was dominated by representation of text, so that the integration of audio and video into documents became a critical requirement only in the current HTML version. Table 5-4 shows some of the most important differences between the versions.

Tag Name	Function
<HTML> ... </HTML>	Declares an HTML page.
<HEAD> ... </HEAD>	Contains the header of the HTML page.
<TITLE> ... </TITLE>	Defines the page title.
<BODY> ... </BODY>	Contains the body of the HTML page.
<Hn> ... </Hn>	Defines a heading of level n.
<B> ... </B>	Highlights ... in bold.
<I> ... </I>	Highlights ... in italics.
<UL> ... </UL> or <OL> ... </OL>	Embraces an unordered list or a numbered list.
<LI>	Specifies the beginning of a list entry.
 	Sets a line break.
<P>	Begins a new paragraph.
<HR>	Adds a horizontal line.
<PRE> ... </PRE>	Specifies a preformatted text, which will not be reformatted by the browser.
<IMG SRC="address">	Loads the image specified by address.
<A HREF="URL"> ... </A>	Inserts a link with the description ...
<!-- ... -->	Specifies a comment.

Table 5-3   HTML tags.

Elements	HTML 1.0	HTML 2.0	HTML 3.0	HTML 4.0
Active maps and images		X	X	X
Equations			X	X
Forms		X	X	X
Hyperlinks	X	X	X	X
Images	X	X	X	X
Lists	X	X	X	X
Toolbars			X	X
Tables			X	X
Formulas			X	X
Objects (generalization of the EMBED tag)				X

Table 5-4   Differences between HTML versions.

5.5.5 Cascading Style Sheets

HTML defines layout properties within tags. The following example defines a title, shown in blue and centered:

```
<H1 ALIGN=center><FONT COLOR=blue>
Multimedia Documents
</FONT></H1>.
```

If there are more than one title, then this code would have to be written for each one. For this reason, it appears easier to state this information in one place (in the style sheet) and then use it several times. For example, the code in the style sheet would read as follows:

```
H1 {text-align: center; color: blue}
```

This code would appear in the document itself as follows:

```
<H1>Multimedia Document</H1>
```

Style sheets can be thought of as a type of templates including rules to declare HTML elements. This means that they separate between layout and content. Style sheets instruct the browser to use a predefined representation. Cascading style sheets (CSS) play an important role in the design of Web pages to determine the look of these pages in detail. Note that this does not the standards for predefined tags in HTML obsolete; we would merely expand or replace them.

Integration of Cascading Style Sheets into HTML Documents The style sheets used in a text are normally defined globally at the beginning of a page or stored in an external file. Either approach allows you to easily adapt the entire document. The <STYLE> tag is used to link an HTML document to a style sheet. There are several methods used to integrate cascading style sheets into an HTML document. The most commonly used methods are:

1. *Linkage to an external style sheet*: An external style sheet can be embedded into an HTML document by use of the <LINK> tag:

   ```
   <LINK REL=StyleSheet HREF="style.css" TYPE="text/css">
   ```

   The <LINK> tag is stated in the <HEAD> tag of a document. The optional TYPE attribute specifies the media type, e.g., text/css for cascading style sheet, and also enables the browser to ignore style sheet types it cannot support.

2. *Importing a Style Sheet*: A style sheet can also be imported by using the @import element.

   ```
   <STYLE TYPE="text/css">
   <!--
   @import url(http://www.html.help/style.css);-->
   </STYLE>
   ```

3. *Embedding a Style Sheet into a Document*: A style sheet can also be integrated into a document by using the STYLE element:

```
<STYLE TYPE="text/css" >
<!--
.tips { text-indent:1.5cm; color: red }
#myeffect { text-align: justify; border-style: dashed }
-->
</STYLE>
```

4. *Inline Style Sheet*: Styles do not have to be stated globally; they can be explicitly defined within a tag, like in the following example:

```
<P STYLE="color: red; font-family: 'Georgia', serif">
This paragraph is styled in red with the Georgia font,
if available.</P>
```

However, this method is not recommended, because it removes one of the major benefits of HTML, i.e., the separation of styles and contents.

Classes and IDs   Within the definition, the syntax of classes and identifiers (IDs) is different. An *ID* always begins with a # symbol, while a *class* begins with a dot, or includes a dot between the tag and the class name. The definition of an ID determines the style of the element with the pertaining ID, which may be used only once in a document. Classes can be used in different tags.

Nesting   When it reads several style definitions, the browser has to decide which one to use. This decision is based on the following rules:

1. Style sheets are evaluated from bottom to top, i.e., inner definitions have a higher priority than outer ones.
2. IDs rank before classes, and classes rank before pure HTML tags.
3. In case of doubt, or when there are equal-ranking definitions, the definition executed last will be used first.

5.5.6   Creating HTML Pages

The following guidelines should be observed when creating HTML documents:

- *Functional start page*: This page should introduce the spectrum of the issues dealt with on that Web site. Large images with long load times should be avoidedon the start page.
- *Effectiveness*: Anchor points of links should contain key words. Multiple links pointing to the same page should be avoided. For example: >>Click here for more information<< could be replaced by >>More Info<<.

- *Originality*:
    - Use a uniform layout for all pages.
    - Use a uniform background.
    - Use a uniform color for links.
    - Use the same icons for navigation.
- *Signature and date*: Visitors of a Web site are interested in the actuality and origin of the pages, so that it is recommended to sign the document and add the date when a page was last modified.

5.5.7 SGML and HTML

HTML is closely related to SGML. SGML (see Section 5.3) defines the syntax, but not the semantics. For books, we could use SGML to define a book document type describing, for example, that a chapter could be enclosed in `<CHAPTER> Text </CHAPTER>`. Such definitions are normally defined in a *Document Type Definition* (*DTD*).

A detailed description of DTDs would go beyond the scope of this book. It is important to know that there are various DTDs for different HTML language versions (see Table 5-5), and all of them use SGML mechanisms. However, DTDs define only the syntax, just like SGML, leaving the meaning of tags open, and they provide no statement about the formatting of HTML pages by the browser.

HTML2.0	"-//IETF//DTD HTML 2.0//EN"
HTML3.0	"-//IETF//DTD HTML 3.0//EN"
HTML3.2	"-//W3C//DTD HTML 3.2//EN"
HTML4.0 Strict DTD	"-//W3C//DTD HTML 4.0//EN"
HTML4.0 Transitional DTD	"-//W3C//DTD HTML 4.0 Transitional//EN"
HTML4.0 Frameset DTD	"-//W3C//DTD HTML 4.0 Frameset//EN"

Table 5-5   DTDs and HTML versions.

HTML 4.0 specifies three different DTDs: *HTML 4.0 Strict DTD* includes all elements and attributes not rejected by the WWW Consortium, or which do not appear in Frameset documents. *HTML 4.0 Transitional DTD* includes the Strict DTD and all elements and attributes rejected by the Consortium. *HTML 4.0 Frameset DTD* adds frames to the HTML 4.0 Transitional DTD.

5.5.8 Extended Markup Language (XML)

HTML is a specific application of SGML, which means that it uses predefined DTDs and is rather limited. For this reason, the WWW Consortium proposed a language draft by the name of *XML* (*eXtended Markup Language*) to allow users to define their own DTDs.

XML is not a markup language, but rather a meta language allowing the design of an own markup language. A regular markup language defines a way to describe information of a specific class of documents (e.g., HTML). XML can be used to define an own markup language for many document classes. XML is very important for the World Wide Web, because it removes two limitations of the Web:

- The World Wide Web no longer depends on one single inflexible document format (HTML).
- XML simplifies SGML and allows the definition of user-defined documents types for the Web.

The major differences between XML and HTML are:

- Information providers can use XML to define their own tags and attributes.
- The structure of a document can be linked in various levels of complexity.
- Each XML document includes an optional description of the underlying grammar, which can be used to validate the document structure.

XML is not backwards compatible to HTML. However, each document that meets the HTML specification can be easily converted into XML. XML is normally handled and implemented in connection with cascading style sheets.

5.5.9   Synchronized Multimedia Integration Language (SMIL)

Current multimedia presentations in the World Wide Web require extensive editing tools or programming knowledge. The *Synchronized Multimedia Integration Language* (*SMIL*) attempts to solve this problem. SMIL builds on XML and allows the execution of multimedia presentations in the World Wide Web by means of a simple text editor, without the need to write code. SMIL has the following properties:

- Synchronization primitives are easy to learn: two tags, i.e., `parallel` and `sequential`, represent the most important properties and strengths of SMIL.
- Hyperlinks: SMIL offers the same hyperlink functionality like HTML.
- Usability of media objects: URLs are used to reference media objects, which means that media objects are not embedded into a SMIL file, so that they can be used several times in parallel.
- Distributed load: Media objects can be distributed over a network.
- Language selection: Authors can state the language or languages to be used in a presentation.

5.6   Dynamic Documents

One of the most important properties of the World Wide Web is *interactivity*. Web documents include dynamic information, in addition to static information. One step towards this dynamics are *cascading style sheets* and *XML documents*. Note, however, that this dynamics refers only to the layout and not to the information contents. CGI scripts, Java, and JavaScript are options available to add dynamic contents to Web documents.

5.6.1   Common Gateway Interface (CGI)

Servers are suitable not only to distribute a large number of different documents, but also to execute programs. Many would like to use this option in the context of dynamic Web documents. On the other hand, it would not make sense to allow each user to run any arbitrary program on a server, or to even access that server. The *Common Gateway Interface (CGI)* was developed to solve this problem. CGI offers an interface to programs that run on a server, so that a user can interact with that program. However, this interaction is limited: The user can start a program on the server and wait for a response from the server.

CGI is used wherever dynamic WWW pages are needed. For example, visitor counters stating how many times a Web page has been visited are widely used today. A program running on the server is started over the CGI interface when that page is requested. The counter increments by one for each visit, and the current count is stored in a file on the server.

One of the most important applications for CGI are databases. In a database query, the resulting HTML page depends on the search terms added to a form. Figure 5-20 shows an example of how a CGI form is used.

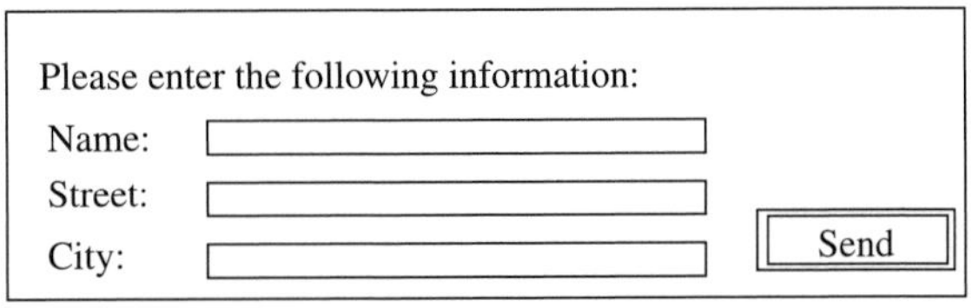

Figure 5-20   Example of a form to send information from a client to the server.

The HTML code for this form is:

```
...
<FORM ACTION="http://www.tu-darmstadt.de/cgi-bin/info"
        METHOD=POST>
<P>Please enter the following information:
<P>Name: <INPUT NAME="customer" SIZE=30>
<P>Street: <INPUT NAME="street" SIZE=30>
<P>City: <INPUT NAME="city" SIZE=30>
<INPUT TYPE=SUBMIT VALUE="Send">
</FORM>...
```

CGI does not depend on a specific programming language. Basically, CGI scripts can be written in C, C++, PERL, or another programming language. These languages are normally called *scripts*, because the programming languages most frequently used are Tcl and PERL. When a CGI script is executed, communication between a client and a server involves the following steps:

1. The client establishes a TCP connection to the server where the desired document resides.
2. The client requests that document, which includes dynamic information.
3. The server starts the script to generate this information and integrates the script output into an HTML document.
4. The server sends the complete response to the client.
5. The TCP connection is torn down.

CGI scripts allow very easy use of dynamic documents in the World Wide Web. Their drawback is that they have to be executed on the server. For example, a date information within an online purchase transaction must be validated on the server, which can lead to considerable delays in the data transfer.

One solution to this problem consists in the transmission of program code to the browser, and then let the browser execute this code. Figure 5-21 shows a schematic representation of how program code is executed in the browser.

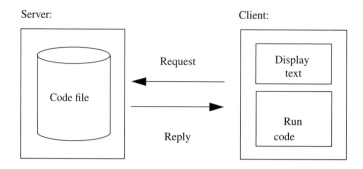

Figure 5-21   Executing program code in a browser.

Unfortunately, this method causes several problems:

- The program code has to be platform-independent so that each browser can use it on an arbitrary platform.
- The program should be prevented from running undesirable or destructive actions on the client machine. Security measures include some important requirements:
    - Protection against access to the file system and data stored on the client computer.
    - Protection against viruses on the client computer.
    - Protection against access to the browser settings on the client.
- Considering these security requirements, the programming language used for CGI scripts has to be robust and object-oriented and follow a modern paradigm.

One language offering such properties is Java, which will be described in the following section.

5.6.2 Java

Java is an object-oriented and interpreted programming language developed by Sun Microsystems. The development of Java was initiated in 1990 under the management of James Cosling (the original project was called *Oak*). Java has quickly developed into the major programming language for the World Wide Web. Java is independent both from the hardware and the operating system. The language includes components for international use (UNICODE). The program code is compiled into byte code and runs on the Java Virtual Machine, which is integrated in all major browsers. However, Java was not originally designed only for the Internet. In fact, Java can be used to write both small programs (so-called *Applets*, which run in browsers) and complex programs.

Major Properties of Java The most important properties of the Java programming language are:

- *Simplicity*: Java is easy to learn (especially for C/C++ programmers) and easy to implement. The number of language constructs is small.

- *Object-orientation*: The most important feature of object-orientation is data and its manipulation, and not procedures.
- *Interpretation*: During compilation, Java generates a byte code which is interpreted by the Java Virtual Machine on the client computer.
- *Platform-independence*: Java can run on each system that implements the Java Virtual Machine. The basic idea of Java is to write a program that can run on any machine without the need to port that program.
- *Portability*: There are no implementation-dependent language aspects in Java. Characters are always in Unicode format, and an integer is always 32 bit in size.

- *Distribution*: Java with its *java.net* class library offers various levels of network connectivity and distribution (*Java Remote Method Invocation—RMI*).

- *Robustness*: Java is strongly typified and allows sophisticated check mechanisms at the compilation time. The language was originally designed for consumer products and had to be very reliable.

- *Security*: Java basically assumes that no user can be trusted. For this reason, there is a restrictive limitation of the user areas, e.g., concerning storage on hard disks. However, it lets you sign Java Applets and then assign more freedom to these Applets.

- *Parallelism*: Parallel processes concern a program's capability to execute several tasks concurrently (e.g., computing data and graphics concurrently, or playing a video and audio file at the same time). Java offers an embedded support for threads, and these threads can be synchronized.

- *Dynamics*: Classes can be reloaded as needed.

Java, Hypermedia, and Multimedia A Java program has to be translated into *byte code* before it can run on an arbitrary platform. A Java program is implemented by the Java Virtual Machine integrated in the browser and called *Applet*. Applets are independent, high-performing programs, requiring storage space only during their use. An Applet terminates as soon the Web page containing that Applet is closed.

The pair of `<APPLET>`.... `</APPLET>` tags is used to embed an Applet into an HTML document. The `</APPLET>` tag takes the following attributes:

- `CODE` = `File.class` specifies the Applet code.
- `WIDTH` and `HEIGHT` define the height or width, respectively, of the screen area where the Applet runs.

The following attributes are optional:

- `CODEBASE` = defines a relative or absolute address for the Applet code, unless the Applet and the HTML document are located in the same directory.

- `ALT` is used to represent an optional text in a browser that does not support Java.

- `NAME` = Name of the Applets; this attribute is important when several Applets within the same HTML page want to communicate.

The `<PARAM>` tag is used within the `<APPLET>` tag to pass Applet-specific information (parameters) from an HTML page to an Applet. For example:

```
<APPLET CODE=Kom.class WIDTH=200 HEIGHT=200 >
<PARAM NAME=background VALUE="blue">
</APPLET>
```

5.6.3 Applets and Applications in Java

Although Java Applets are small applications and both Applets and applications are implemented by the Java API, Applets and applications differ in the way they are executed. Figure 5-22 shows the steps involved in the use of Java applets.

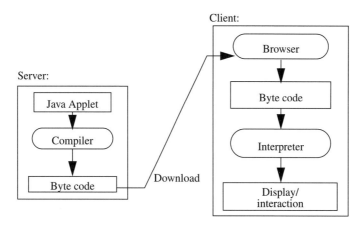

Figure 5-22 Steps involved in the use of Java Applets.

- *Code differences*: The most obvious difference between an Applet and an application consists in the static `main()` method, which is the main component of a Java application, but ignored in Applets.
- *Performance differences*: An Applet is generated to run in a browser. An Applet consisting of a 100-Kbyte byte code can require 4 MB, 8 MB, or even 16 MB of main memory storage, depending on the browser. A Java application is an independent program, so that it has to share resources, such as main memory, with other programs, because a Java application does not necessarily need a browser to run.
- *Security differences*: One of the most important aspects in Java is the implementation of security measures. Figure 5-23 shows the security restrictions of Java. The loading and executing of Applets from arbitrary servers in the Internet are subject to the following restrictions:
  - Applets cannot load system-specific libraries.
  - Applets loaded from the network cannot read or write files stored in a client machine.
  - Applets cannot start or execute programs on the client computer.
  - Applets cannot read all system properties of a client.
  - Applets can communicate and exchange data only with the server from which they have been loaded.
  - Applets can load HTML documents into a browser.

- Applets can communicate with other Applets or scripts within the same HTML page.
- Applets running locally are not subject to any of these restrictions, just like applications.

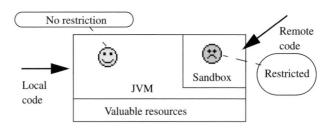

Figure 5-23   Security restrictions in Java.

Summary   Although Java applications are very similar to Applets, there are a few significant differences. Applications require the `main()` method; this is not the case with Applets. Java applications can access system-specific information, the local file system, and *native code* (e.g., C, C++). Applets downloaded from the Internet are not allowed to read the file system on the client computer.

Applets are subject to further security restrictions, while Java applications are more flexible and normally offer a better performance. These properties allow a wide range of options during the creation of an application.

5.6.4   JavaScript

While Java is a fully fledged object-oriented compiler programming language, JavaScript is an interpreted script language designed by Netscape. *JavaScript* offers a much smaller set of commands, but a similar syntax.

With JavaScript, the code is embedded directly into the HTML document and executed by the browser. This feature allows to respond to user requests without sending them to the server. JavaScript can be used to design interactive Web pages without the use of CGI scripts, widely extending the possibilities of HTML.

The pair of `<SCRIPT>...</SCRIPT>` tags is used to embed a script into HTML. This script can contain either a reference to a file that stores the script or program code. The tag should be used only in the header of an HTML document, and takes the following attributes:

- `SRC` = the Uniform Resource Identifier (URI) of the script, which is loaded over the network.
- `LANGUAGE` specifies the script language to be used. Common values are `JavaScript` or `VBScript`, where *VB* stands for *Visual Basic*.

Scripts can

- validate forms (data type, date);
- generate HTML pages;
- change the browser environment (color of links, status bar);
- load new HTML documents; and
- interact with Java Applets (LiveConnect).

5.6.5   ActiveX

ActiveX is a technology developed by Microsoft Corporation, building on components and adapting the following for the Web:

- *Component Object Model* (*COM*), and
- *Object Linking and Embedding* (*OLE*).

ActiveX builds mainly on *OLE controls*. An OLE control is a reusable software component from different vendors, adding special functionality to Web pages. OLE controls contain well-defined external interfaces. ActiveX components can be written in various programming languages, e.g., C, C++, or Visual Basic. The use of ActiveX controls (equal to OLE controls) in HTML pages requires a script language, such as JavaScript or Visual Basic Script.

5.6.6   Plug-Ins

A *plug-in* is a software module that can be easily integrated in a browser. Plug-ins extend a browser's capability to display a large number of interactive multimedia applications. Plug-ins dispose of a large set of functions and properties to increase the functionality and compatibility of a browser. Plug-ins are available for many different purposes, for example:

- Multimedia viewers, e.g., Live3D, Macromedia Shockwave, and Adobe Acrobat.
- Applications like personal information managers and games.

Plug-ins normally include a setup program, so that they are easy to install on a computer. When it has to process data requiring a plug-in, the browser performs several steps: It loads the appropriate plug-in and allows the plug-in to execute the files either within the browser or in a separate window. The plug-in remains active until the file it runs is closed.

5.6.7   LiveConnect: Example of an interaction between Java, JavaScript, and HTML

LiveConnect enables a browser to support communication between JavaScript and Java, VRML, or plug-ins. The example in Figure 5-24 shows how we can use LiveConnect to determine the screen size. JavaScript calls Java AWT directly to determine the screen resolution.

```
<HTML>
<HEAD><SCRIPT LANGUAGE="JavaScript">
var tool = java.awt.Toolkit;
var screenSize = new java.awt.Dimension
(tool.getDefaultToolkit().getScreenSize());
var myWidth = screenSize.width;
var myHeight = screenSize.height;
alert('Screen resolution is: '+myWidth+'x'+myHeight);
</SCRIPT>
<HEAD>
Here is the body of the HTML-Document.
</HTML>
```

Figure 5-24 Example for an interaction between JavaScript and Java.

5.6.8 Closing Remarks

Java is a powerful object-oriented programming language that can be used to generate platform-independent applications. Java programs can be integrated in a browser or run as independent applications. JavaScript is a script language used to write code that can be embedded directly into an HTML document. JavaScript is easy to learn, and it supports communication between Web browsers, plug-ins, and Applets.

Design

Commercially successful multimedia products that use the possibilities offered by new media are normally developed by designers. This chapter deals with issues regarding the design goals to be achieved by each medium, and the design tools available to achieve these goals.

The primary work area for designers is *visual communication*. Visual communication deals with the (very old) development of alphabets from sign language, among other developments. In addition, it forms the basis for written communication, its most important role being the typographic design.

The design of multimedia products involves new requirements to graphic design, originating mainly from the availability of continuous media on computers, or by different temporal changes (*dynamics*) and *interaction*. Chapter 7 discusses interaction issues in detail in connection with user interfaces. This chapter concentrates on graphic design, especially in the fields of *typography* and *layout*, and the *production of images*.

6.1 Design-specific Properties of Images

Images can be classified over a spectrum ranging from "abstract" to "concrete". An *abstraction* does not consider "random" details of an object. Instead, the important properties of an object are well elaborated and generalized into a larger set of objects. This means that abstract/concrete is not a property with absolute validity for a representation; it should always be seen in comparison with other representations.

In visual art, the *abstract/concrete* (or objective) opposite pair belongs to the fixed description inventory. One criterion for an objective representation is actually whether or not the viewer accepts it as such, or whether or not he or she can understand the distribution of colors on a surface by an (arbitrarily subjective) projection of physical objects [Goo73].

Objective images are based on the projection of a spatial fact. This does not necessarily mean that the representation is naturalistic, i.e., shape, color, and surface structure of physical objects do not have to be experienced in a specific illumination or shown from a specific angle. Moreover, the image does not have to be determined by a mapping process, similar to the human vision (see Figure 6-1).

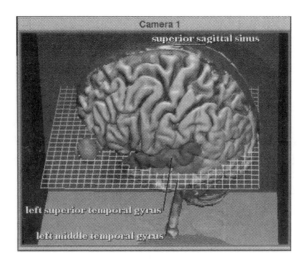

Figure 6-1   Example of an objective, non-naturalistic image from the electronic medical atlas VOXEL-MAN.

In contrast, *abstract images* are not intended to map physical objects. In fact, some images do not map anything, but are a pure interplay of colors and shapes for their own sake. Other images represent rather associatively abstract definitions and qualities (e.g., human emotions).

Another classification criterion are the *spatial and temporal dimensions* of the graphic representation. For example, we can distinguish between two- and three-dimensional representations, and between static and motion pictures. These criteria overlap with the classification of images on a scale ranging from abstract to concrete, because the selection of a movement state and the angle of vision themselves represent an abstraction.

Another way to classify images results from the *directness of the representation* (see Figure 6-2). The real communicative goal of metaphoric, indirect images is normally not the representation of a concrete object. Such images serve to transport information about another—normally abstract—object. To achieve this, both objects must have a few relevant properties in common.

Although the classification criteria introduced above are relevant for the use of images and the meaning of the design in multimedia products, we will discuss images by their functions, divided into three classes: *visualizations*, *symbols*, and *illustrations*.

Figure 6-2 Example from a lecture about the development of hypertext: Fortune Cookie, a boat that cuts through a smooth water surface, is used as a metaphor for an uncertain but promising future and an attempt to position the discipline in the future.

6.2 Visualizations

Visualizations—also called *info graphics*—serve to map facts. Normally, extensive information is to be transformed in a form to facilitate the interpretation, search and comparison operations for the viewer. Such mappings have to meet specific requirements. Theories of graphic representations [Pal81] [KR95] [Kam97] demand from an image to establish relations between graphic objects, which have some properties in common with the relations between the visualized information (or the mapped objects).

This requirement leads to a restriction of the expressive power of visualizations (e.g., versus verbose descriptions) [SO95]: When using graphic tools it appears to be meaningful to make absolute statements. For example, a thematic map of a geographic region could show that a hazardous material, A, was found in region X in a concentration of n milligrams per cubic meter of soil. This could be emphasized on the map by showing the area concerned in a lighter or darker shade.

A problem arises when such an observation is not an exact measurement, but an estimate or forecast, saying something like: "The concentration ranges from a minimum of n to a maximum of m milligrams", or "... below the neighboring area". Although we could try to find some relationship between such graphic statements, we would have to introduce a new graphic vocabulary and agree about new meanings. For example, the filled rectangles in the geographic area concerned could represent the minimum concentration, while additional empty rectangles could describe the maximum concentration. In addition, relationships between values could be expressed by new symbols. On the other hand, new definitions mean that the representation would move further and further apart from a visualization. In fact, the intuitive, immediate understanding of a visualization is based on the fact that the information is conveyed by means of few agreements which, in contrast to speech, are neither more arbitrary nor more discrete [RKKB98].

6.2.1   Objective Visualizations

One important type of visualizations is the *objective* visualization. This type of visualization is based on a spatial fact, like all objective representations. The position of the rollers inside a photocopying device, or the rooms inside a building, or the relative position and movement of the parties involved in a traffic accident, are three examples for such visualizations. This means that the distribution of color over an image's surface can normally be used to derive the distribution of real objects over a three-dimensional space. Objective visualizations are often shown in more or less *schematic* detail; this depends on the desired statements about the shape, the surface structure, and the distribution of the real objects.

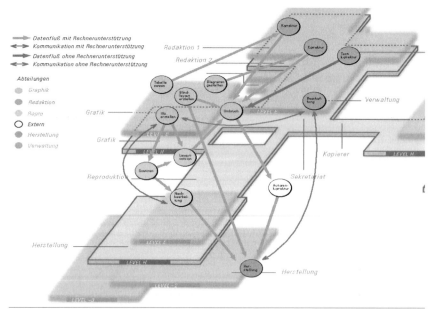

Figure 6-3   Representation of the workflow and networking within a company; the background shows a plan of the corporate building.

Well-known types of objective visualizations are geographic maps, city maps, underground maps, and floor plans or cross-sectional and explosion drawings (see Figure 6-3). The use of motion pictures is relatively common in objective visualizations.

Objective visualizations can also include *abstract data*. The color of the image pixels (dots) is normally different from the color and illumination of the object itself to reproduce some abstract information, i.e., a value for a variable, which changes depending on the position within that space. Examples are the harmful substance concentration in a region, or the temperature distribution over the surface of a work piece.

6.2.2 Abstract Visualizations

Abstract visualizations are drawn in the form of *diagrams*. A diagram or chart represents purely abstract, relational data. Diagrams do not contain geometric information, which is of graphic nature by definition. This means that we cannot derive the distribution of the graphic objects in an image from the "geometric" distribution of the visualized information. For this reason, the first thing we should find when designing diagrams is the fundamental form of representation. Well-known forms are bar charts, pie charts, network charts, or line charts, and representations based on coordinate systems.

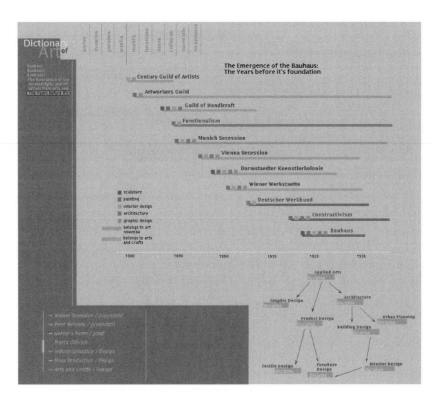

Figure 6-4 Use of diagrams as navigation tools in a multimedia art lexicon; from [KR95].

More generally speaking, diagrams or charts use graphic means, such as color, shape, size, relative position of graphic objects, or connections between them, to convey facts. These basic means of expression, which are also the basis for the chart forms mentioned above, can be combined in almost any way, so that more and more variants of intermediate shapes and new types emerge in practice [Har96].

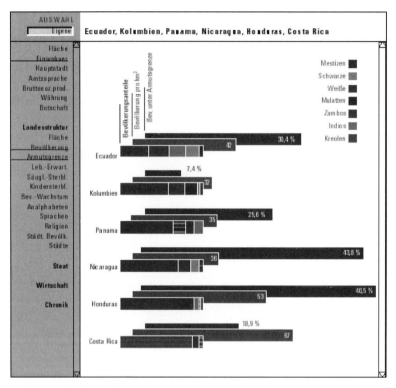

Figure 6-5 Example for a dynamic visualization, converting quantitative information into bar charts.

Motion pictures are less common for the visualization of purely abstract data, but when they are used, their representation is normally interactive.

6.2.3 Producing Visualizations

Many visualizations are complex and their production is costly, particularly when using the so-called "scientific visualization". Recent progress in the field of computer graphics allows *automation* of the *executive* part of a production to some extent. This is of particular interest in cases where concrete data, which change constantly, can be "filled" automatically into a form of visualization suitable for a specific combination of data types.

The work of an *info graphic designer* requires a high amount of special qualification in the field of graphic design. Visualizations are less subject to fashion trends or changes than other graphic design products. Info graphics include typographic elements, in addition to graphic and (more seldom) pictorial elements, so that the requirements resulting from the integration of their styles into the overall design are particularly demanding. These factors should be taken into account when a multimedia product is produced by a job-sharing team.

6.2.4 Good and Bad Visualizations

Other types of images, such as symbols and illustrations, can belong partly to the objective and the subjective category, e.g., some are considered *ugly* or *less impressive*. This situation happens when they do not meet their tasks properly. In fact, visualizations can be totally wrong ("unexpressive" in the popular terminology). This is the case when the established graphic relations and objects lack important properties of the data relations they represent. We would also use the term "bad" when a visualization includes data communicating properties that are actually not there.

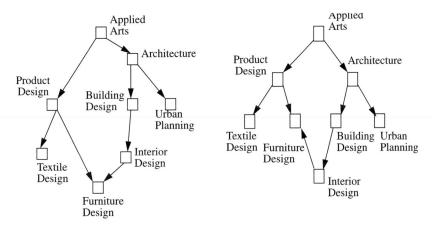

Figure 6-6 Example for a misleading visualization.

The example shown in Figure 6-6 visualizes the connections between partial section, partial area, and partial discipline [KR95]. More specifically:

• *Furniture Design* appears as a generic term of *Interior Design*.
• When looking closer we can see that the two abstraction ladders, connecting *Applied Arts* and *Furniture Design*, are different in length.
• The right side of Figure 6-6 shows that the direction of the arrows (from top to bottom) is not consistent.

- This example implies a symmetry that does not really exist (nodes in levels on a non-weighted tree).
- The implicitly visualized "transitivity" with regard to the relationships between the node is not complete.

Another source for bad visualizations are *interferences*, disturbing the purely formal or graphical comparison of sizes, lengths, or colors. This is mainly the case in charts. Representations where the addition of some perspective or volume has an impact on the way how the size of graphic objects is perceived are found relatively often [Har96]. Such representations suggest faulty associations; like in the example illustrated in Figure 6-7.

Figure 6-7   Distorted perspective makes it difficult to compare exact bar sizes in this bar chart.

6.3   Symbols: Logos, Icons, and Pictograms

Logos, icons, and pictograms should generally not be used to explain an object, but merely to identify it, i.e., provide a visual label for the object. Pictograms are usually the only form where identification works for a schematic, objective representation.

In *logos*, the mapping of a real object takes a totally different character, if such a mapping is used at all. The mapped object becomes a *symbol* for another object. For example, the image of a globe could represent an entire product range of maps offered by a company. In this case, the picture of a globe is not the goal of the representation, but a means to a specific end, i.e., an *indirect mapping* in the sense introduced above.

Particularly when the object to be identified has a certain degree of abstractness, the association is often produced over purely formal, graphical properties of the image, and not through another object. For example, an organization could be represented by a set of points (many points, many employees), or the logo of a service provider could be an open hand. The interlinking of shapes could reflect the interplay of components; graphic formulas for movements could illustrate a dynamic process. To take this principle a step further, we could use purely conventionalizing graphic symbols (e.g., arrows), and in the field of graphic art, we could use purely typographic symbols.

The quality of a symbol depends primarily on the unambiguity, originality, uniqueness, and simplicity of the graphic object. Additional qualities are shape and appearance, which are often represented in opposite pairs [Kur94], e.g., dynamic/static, strict/loose, soft/hard, traditional/modern.

Icons behave in many ways like logos—an excessively naturalistic, true-to-detail representation contradicts the actual purpose. The printer icon in the icon bar of a popular software program should represent a generic printer, i.e., it should not include visual properties of a specific printer type or model. Icons lend themselves to observe how reduced mappings coagulate and form conventionalizing shapes. Returning to our printer example, we can often observe that symbols representing matrix printers are still used for printer icons. It appears that this symbol has gained a certain independence over time.

In most cases, we would need not single icons, but an entire series of icons, as shown in Figure 6-8. The major problem is the development of a coherent shape language, rich enough to provide a symbol for each operation.

Figure 6-8   Series of icons for an editor desktop at dpa (Deutsche Presseagentur).

6.4   Illustrations

Illustrations generally serve to direct the viewer's attention to a text, to decorate that text, or to loosen up this text, but they are always strongly related to a written piece of text. An illustration is normally *objective* and has an *indirect character*, where the relationship between the mapped object and the contents does not have to be metaphoric. An illustration uses the entire spectrum of rhetoric figures, as can be well observed in the strategies established in writing, where they assist the designer in finding ideas.

An illustration often exceeds the boundary of pure representation. It can visualize an analogy to another field, elaborate a new aspect, or state an ironic comment.

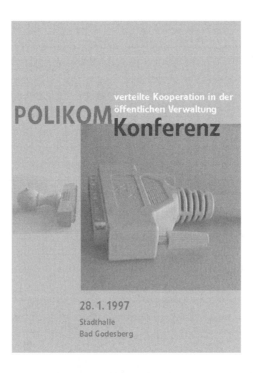

Figure 6-9   Advertising a conference about the introduction of electronic media for corporate management. This illustration selects a technical connection as a metaphor for this introduction, indicating the challenge of the POLIKOM project, i.e., the difference between the "management" and "technology".

The character of an illustration is more subjective than that of visualizations or symbols, always in search for original imageries. This leads to an enormous stylistic multitude, originating from the use of all image production techniques described below. The *esthetic orientation* is particularly important: Illustrations impress primarily in that they create a mood or trigger certain associations. The *individuality* of various illustration styles reflects also in the fact that an illustration is normally contracted and specified by an *art director*. The illustration style is coordinated with the esthetic strategy of the multimedia product by the illustrator's choice and not by the illustrator's presumably flexible adaptation to the stylistic requirements of the respective contract.

6.5   Image Production Techniques

So far, we have described *design* mainly as a production of static or motion pictures, including the set of functions the different types of images could meet. This section briefly introduces the design techniques available to create graphic representations.

In theory, each technique can be used to produce any realizable image. In practice, however, the different range of techniques involves different types of color application or coloration of entire image regions, leading to a *microstructure* which is *characteristic* for each technique. In drawing and painting, the microstructure (or the so-called *ductus*) of an image is determined by the background, drawing material, solvent and, of course, the artist's motoricity. In drawings produced in computer-supported drawing programs, the available operations (e.g., fill surface uniformly with color, or define the course) are the primary factors determining the microstructure of an image. This applies equally to animation in the form of cartoons.

The designer influences the result by manipulating a real or virtual scene used to produce images in a *projection process* in photos, movies and videos alike. This means that there is no direct manipulation of the image surface. The options available to the designer to manipulate images are limited to the pure selection of *subject*, *image section* and *capture time*, at least with some types of photos. In *studio photography*, for example, the artist can also change the shooting angle, the illumination, and the arrangement of the photographed objects. *Computer graphics* and *animation* let the artist additionally manipulate the object shape and the surface structure. In many cases, the work of a photographer concentrates on removing undesirable, distracting details, e.g., shadows and artefacts, dirt or distortions, and to obtain a typical photographic view of the object. In contrast, explicit efforts are necessary in computer graphics and animation to enrich the image with details.

The drawing and painting arts normally have a subjective-expressive character, while photos appear more neutral and objective, and computer graphics and animation always have some idealized-artificial touch [HR89].

There is often some specialization to one of the available techniques, because each technique demands a very specialized qualification.

6.6 Typography

In addition to the production of images, the second task in graphics design is the visual transformation of the text, i.e., the typographic design and the separation of the print or screen page.

The primary information to be conveyed origins here from an author and not from a designer. The basic components used by the designer in his or her work, i.e., the text and the characters of the alphabet, are given. The author's contribution is always understood as a "function" of the primary text message as a structure of this message or as a comment to that message. In addition, this contribution is bound to the conventions of the Latin typeface and to the rules of legibility, i.e., two factors beyond the designer's influence. This makes communication a secondary and typography an *applied* instead of a *free* discipline.

This does not mean that there is only one single solution to each typographic problem. In a broader sense, *typography* includes the overall design of a publication or multimedia product as an esthetic object, i.e., for decisions regarding a specific font, a specific design pattern, or a specific page layout. These decisions are comparatively free or esthetic and together called *macro typography*, in contrast to *micro typography*, the latter dealing with the details of *typeface* and *type setting* [Hoc87].

Although detail typography knows fixed rules, these rules present themselves as insider knowledge. A good example are the problems of orthotypography, such as the use of correct or wrong quotation marks, or differences between dashes and hyphens. Other examples are the characteristics of print fonts and the difference between real and false italics and capitals, which are normally known only to experts.

Questions regarding font attributes for the different set of elements and the correct choice of margins are rather difficult to answer, because there is normally a wide range of possible solutions. The purpose of margins is to visually convert the natural hierarchical structure of a text, i.e., building words, paragraphs and sections from words. In this respect, typography uses constructions, such as lines and columns, to fill the available space meaningfully. Figure 6-10 shows a "typographically correct" representation of a fictitious cookbook.

Figure 6-10   "Correct" design.

Figure 6-11 shows potential errors in the microtypographic design of a multimedia cookbook. For reasons of clarity, this example shows a series of dramatic errors in the detail typography, which would hopefully not happen in practice.

Figure 6-11   Example for potential errors in microtypographic design.

6.6.1   Layout

The most important task of *macro typography* (or "layout") is to define the structure of documents with regard to the distribution of their elements (text blocks, images, graphical elements) over the surface and to define optional text attributes and formatting parameters.

Most typographic functions beyond the pure support of linear or selective reading or searching are implemented by macrotypographic means; [WF97] includes an overview. This could mean that a text should be formatted as a footnote or marginalia to emphasize that it could be skipped without losing the coherence of the text as a whole. Another example is the clear separation of sections in connection with especially formatted headlines, where headlines can be marked as an alternative reading start point.

In contrast to detail typography, macro typography can also contribute to the interpretation of text. The information that two pieces of text origin from different sources, or that one text is a comment, an introduction, or an expansion to another text, is normally expressed by combining language and macrotypographic means [RK97].

Figure 6-12 and Figure 6-13 show two macrotypographically faulty versions of our previous "cookbook" example. In the example in Figure 6-12, all elements are treated equally, with the result that the page appears like a recipe with no ingredients and no description; instead, it is divided into five steps. In addition, the first photo seems to be referring to the first step of the recipe only.

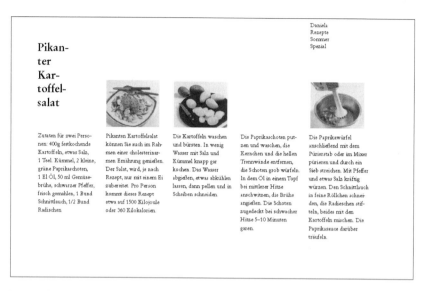

Figure 6-12   Example for errors in the macrotypographic design.

Figure 6-13 gives the misleading impression that we see a description of five different dishes without particular relationship and without pre-given reading sequence.

Figure 6-13   Example for a misleading description.

All these misinterpretations refer to the structure of a document and not to its content. This confirms the fact that the communication of the document structure is the most important object in macro typography.

A layout should also integrate material from different image production processes. In most cases, this appears to be an esthetically difficult or demanding problem due to the different appearance of the images. Here, there is a wealth of separation and combination strategies. For example, a strong formal straight-jacket, e.g., the distribution of images over equal-sized raster fields, could be an effective integrating measure. Another possibility could be the creation of several levels by overlaying heterogeneous images.

6.7 Esthetics

In graphic design, esthetics is inseparably connected with the corresponding style history of this discipline. In graphic design, just like in applied art, the range of freedom in the development of new esthetic effects is limited, so that most work can basically be classified into existing esthetic principles. [FOS98] classify the typographic work of this century very clearly and impressively into four groups, while Leu identifies twelve different style groups in his stylistics work proposed in 1993 [Leu93] (not to claim completeness). Note that there is still no consent about the extent a classification can satisfy the stylistic multitude in graphic and typographic design. Therefore, it appears to be justified to use the same or similar categories to describe this multitude. This means that traditions have been maintained in this field.

The *tradition* that forms the basis of current graphic design goes back to the beginning of the letterpress. A design that places this tradition in the foreground orients its vocabulary to historical reproduction techniques. One typical example is the choice of fonts, which is limited to renaissance, baroque, or classicistic Antiqua fonts. Another typical example is working with one-color images on white background, which are often available as vector drawings, just like ornaments. A design oriented to tradition does not want to expand this limited vocabulary, but produce a perfect balance within its borders (e.g., between the weight of a font and the illustration, or between printed and unprinted surfaces). In addition, we normally prefer a perfect overall design, nstead of introducing a novelty.

Functional design places the structure of a text message in the foreground and aspires clarity and neutrality. At the same time, functional design normally connects certain style elements, which can be explained from the formation of the functional design as a counter-movement to a specific traditional design practice. For example, functional design includes the use of sans-serif (and seldom serif) fonts, asymmetric orientation of the material (often controlled by a design raster), and the preference for photographs when images are used for illustration (see Figure 6-14). Functional design is subject to a certain change. For example, "extremely cool" and strong fonts like Helvetica had been typical representatives of a functional style and have recently been replaced by other sans-serif fonts, e.g., Syntax, Frutiger, or Meta.

Figure 6-14   A catalog of events as an example for functional layout.

In a design targeted to the *strength of expression*, modern currents play the most important role and encourage the quick advent or disappearance of new styles. In this context, visual effects have a much stronger meaning than, for example, a clear representation of the document structure. In fact, the text often serves only as a basic material for the construction of graphic shapes or textures, where textures often occur in a formal esthetic calculus [RKKB98].

Figure 6-15   Poster of a scientific congress as an example for expressive design.

To increase or revive the attractiveness of the familiar character system of the Latin typeface, *expressive design* uses distancing means, such as typeface interference or distortion: Text mutates into a graphical or even pictorial element. In many cases, the design is not intended to create harmony but *tension* or *imbalance*, like in the example shown in Figure 6-15. These goals and means often put expressive design in opposition to the laws of readability. This means that its primary activity is in the field of media products, where raising attention and a holistic impression are more important than the structure and easily understandable preparation of complex contents.

Note that the use of different formulas of expressiveness, but also the traditional, functional, or expressive basic attitude turn increasingly from an ideological issue into an issue of the available repertoire (see also [FOS98]).

User Interfaces

Multimedia would be meaningless if the applications would not use the media available at the interface for input and output. Media determine *how* and how *well* human-computer interaction is supported. On the first computers, either the user or the computer had to enter various addresses by setting switches or entering commands. The medium "text" was used to allow users and computers to interact. The only computer input was punched cards and paper was the only output form. And text was also the only means for screen displays. Later applications offered text menus, which facilitated inputs for the user, but they still had to adapt to the computer.

The most important novelty was the development of graphical user interfaces (GUIs). From the technical perspective, a GUI is defined by its capability to control each screen pixel during the display and interaction, as opposed to the coarse character raster of ASCII terminals. However, this is only the prerequisite for the more relevant property of GUIs, namely the use of graphical or typographic means to present data and operations. This means that visualization is only one side of a GUI: the other side is the graphical interaction (point and click).

GUIs and the use of a mouse as an important input device, facilitate the human-computer interaction considerably. GUIs have put user friendliness in the foreground and made it one of the most important properties of a good user interface. On the other hand, it is not always easy to define the meaning of user friendliness and how it can be achieved, as can be often observed in many commercial applications. A number of measures contribute to a user-friendly user interface, but they cannot be easily combined. A particular problem is normally the large number of conflicting requirements a GUI should meet. On the one hand, the user interface should be intuitive and easy to learn; on the other hand, both occasional users and experts should be able to use it efficiently.

In many cases, the design of a user interface fails easily due to an unclear definition of its target group.

The example of a very clear (and not new) representation in Figure 7-1 shows Napoleon's march to Moscow and back. The figure shows troop strengths, temperatures, and the path.

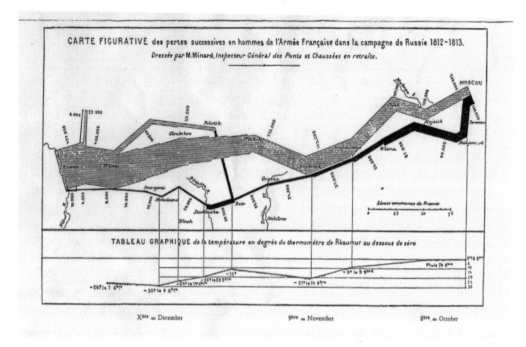

Figure 7-1   Schematic representation of Napoleon's march.

This chapter introduces a series of general aspects for the design of multimedia user interfaces (see also [Shn97] and http://www.aw.com/DTUI).

We will use an example to explain the conflicts in the design of user-friendly user interfaces discussed above, where various principles and their benefits and drawbacks will be described. One of the principles, which has become a quasi standard, i.e., direct manipulation, will be described later in more detail, followed by an overview of existing user interface components, so-called *widgets*. The chapter ends with an outlook on non-standardized interaction forms, i.e., human-computer interactions not based on mouse and keyboard.

7.1   Example: Remote-controlled Video Camera

We use this example to ask a number of important questions with regard to the design of user interfaces. First we will look at an application used by an engineer to monitor a CIM manufacturing process at a remote location by means of a *remote-controlled video camera*.

The camera is connected to a computer working as the *camera server*. The camera server sends commands, such as *focus*, *zoom*, and *position*, over this serial interface to the camera. The actual control of the camera is done by the application, which runs on a *camera client* (at a remote location). This computer is located at the engineer's place of work and displays the video image captured by the camera.

The user working at the camera client wants to reposition the camera, for example to better study other details of a faulty production line. The user uses the user interface at his or her camera client to send the *position*, *focus*, and *zoom* commands. The user can follow the operations as they are executed on his or her video window. This requires the design of a suitable multimedia *user interface to control the camera*.

The first and most important question in the design of a user interface for camera control concerns the states a user can activate and the operations to do this. Is the camera's position permanent, so that only up/down, right/left panning and zooming have to be executed? Does the camera have to be tilted around the shooting axis? Or should the camera arbitrarily move? Figure 7-2 shows an example with relative and absolute positioning of the camera.

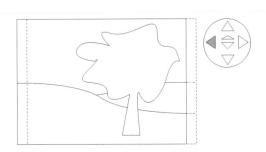 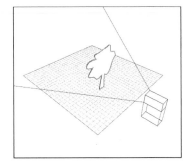

Figure 7-2 Relative positioning of the camera by using buttons (left) and absolute positioning by using an overview of the scene, which contains the camera itself as an object (right).

Subsequently, a decision can be taken as to whether or not there should be an absolute or relative positioning. If the designer decides in favor of the relative positioning, then we will have to answer the question whether or not the movements should be implemented as closed movement units with a specific unit interval. Interaction mechanisms to actuate and stop a continuous movement could be used alternatively.

If the principle of the absolute positioning is selected, then additional auxiliary objects are required, e.g., an overview window showing the camera as a graphical object that the user can grip or move.

Depending on the relative or absolute positioning and on technical side conditions, the suitable input device (mouse, keyboard, or joystick) can be selected. A physical input device is often accompanied by a virtual one, e.g., buttons displayed on the screen, which can be clicked (see Section 7.5). If the presentation of the camera image is also the main means of input, then we speak of an (articulatory) more direct manipulation (we will explain the term "direct manipulation" further below). Think of a tree in the upper right corner of the video window. The user points the cursor on this object (the tree in this example) and double-clicks that object. This causes the camera to be positioned so that the tree forms the center of the video window. The algorithm used to control the camera has to automatically derive the positioning commands from the relative position of the cursor when the object is activated in the video window and the selected focus.

As an alternative, the relative position of the cursor can determine the direction of the camera movement versus the center of the video window. With the cursor positioned on the left-hand side of the window center, the camera pans to the left. The camera stops as soon as the user releases the mouse button. The camera can move at different speeds. The following mechanisms can be used to specify the range of speeds in the user interface: If the mouse used has several buttons, then these buttons could be coupled with a different speed each for a camera movement. The left mouse button would be responsible for a slow and accurate movement, while the right button could be used for quick pan of the camera.

The distance of the cursor from the window center could also determine the speed, instead of using several mouse buttons, where the movement should become faster as the distance of the cursor to the center increases.

Direct manipulation is an issue directly related to the transmission of 3D movement options to the 2D projection surface of the screen. For example, how can we implement forward and backward movements and zooming of the camera? It would certainly be difficult to combine this goal with the paradigm of direct manipulation, because the third dimension is contained in the camera image only implicitly. This means that forward and backward movements can be implemented only by direct, more symbolic operations, using buttons or various modes. In addition, some systems allow for automatic and multi-user control (e.g., [LKF+02], [RHGL02])

7.2 Usability

7.2.1 Goals of Usability

The use and operation of an application should be *easy to learn* for various types of users, although learning an application easily is not the most important element of a user interface. In fact, the term "usability" emphasizes the use; or we might just as well call it a learning interface. In many cases, a thorough introduction phase is normally useful, especially for professional users who are willing to make more efforts for the sake of increased efficiency later on.

The term *effectiveness*, oriented to experienced users who know both the task and the system, deals with the number of operations required to achieve a specific goal.

Terms like *learnable*, *simple*, and *consistent*, relating to inexperienced users, are based on different criteria: How many cognitive operations are required to achieve a specific goal? To what extent can the user predict the effects of his or her operations? What kind of help is available to the user by the way an operation is implemented, if the user has to first find that operation, or select one out of several similar operations, when the user does not necessarily know how he or she can apply such an operation to one or several objects, or if he or she wants to parameterize it?

To turn inexperienced users into experienced ones quickly, it is important to have operating instructions that are easy to memorize. This requirement is supported by the *intuitive association* with known knowledge. One important prerequisite is that developers of user interfaces can put themselves into the user's situation.

7.2.2 Solving Usability Problems

One of the traditional fundamental questions in the design of GUIs is whether the object of an operation or the operation itself should be selected first (i.e., *object-action* or *action-object*). In either case, the first selection limits the second, and the second selection is facilitated (once the user has selected the object, he or she merely has to select from the actions available for that object, and vice-versa).

If the user opts for the *object-action* selection, then the action is normally selected in a very direct and implicit way, i.e., by clicking, double-clicking or drag and drop. It is very easy to use one single function in this way, but there are normally several functions available as graphical operations. This leads to the problem that these operations have to be unique. Some of the possibilities to achieve this are:

• Create uniqueness via prompts or the Control key;

Problem: tedious mainly because the user is just starting the operation.

• Create uniqueness via the context;

Problem: The context is either defined by the system, which limits the functionality; or the system has to try to predict the context from the user actions, i.e., it could make false assumptions.

• Select an object via special handles;

Problem: Distracts the user from the actual object, especially with text, where the handles are normally very small.

• Uniqueness via different modes, which are persistent, in contrast to all other options;

Problem: Users are often not aware of the current mode, and frequent toggling between modes is tiresome.

• Various mouse buttons, double-click;

Problem: No other function can be assigned to the same button or double-click.

Another classical problem concerns the *pre-structuring* of the interaction in *several windows*: It is seldom that all data and functions can be accommodated within one surface to make them visible all the time. In fact, data and functions are normally grouped by tasks and distributed over various windows (or similar user interface elements). We will then have to ask the question: Which properties do these windows have and what are the relationships among these windows? Are they static or do they remain open until the user takes an action, e.g., pressing the mouse button? Are these windows cascading or tiled over the screen?

The problem becomes more serious if the user can open more windows from one window, instead of allowing a fixed number of windows with a fixed relationship between them. This leads us to the immediate question whether or not the new window should depend on the previous window, from where it was opened, i.e., whether or not it should be automatically closed with the previous window.

The general problem behind these detail questions is: How does the system recognize a *shift of attention*; how does it know whether or not this is long-term or short-term; and how can it be taken back? For example, if we can be sure that the request for a new information is nothing more than a short excursion, we would ideally use a pop-up window, that disappears immediately after. But what if we cannot be sure whether or not the user wants to continue from this information? In this case, we would want to open another persistent window.

The lack of consistent rules, the necessity to weigh a large number of alternatives against each other, is characteristic for the design of user interfaces. However, there are a few principles in this difficult situation that have been widely accepted. We will discuss these principles briefly below. We know one principle from our camera control example: *direct manipulation*.

7.3   Direct Manipulation

Graphical data processing has increasingly used interactive techniques to create and manipulate two- and three-dimensional graphic objects since the beginning of the sixties. The *Sketchpad* of Sutherland [Sut63] was one of the first graphic systems using several input devices, including a light pen, and it was one of the first to support control buttons and function keys to manipulate objects. Sketchpad was a pioneer in interactive computer graphics and for interactive work on computer systems. Due to the high hardware requirements of graphic systems, it took almost twenty years to make this interaction form available to a large user community and to give it a name that is still be used today: *direct manipulation*. The term was coined by Ben Shneiderman (1982, 1983) and describes user interfaces that meet the following requirements:

- Objects that users can interact with should be permanently visible.
- User actions on these objects should be fast, incremental, and easily reversible.
- System responses to user actions should be visible immediately.
- User interactions should replace complex commands.

7.3.1   Characteristics of Direct Manipulation

User interfaces based on these principles are be characterized by a high user acceptance, according to Shneiderman. Especially new computer users are be enthusiastic and challenged to discover the entire functionality of their systems [Shn97]. Shneiderman mentions several reasons, printed in italics in the list below, which were later modified in [HHN86]:

- *Beginners can learn the basic functionality of such systems easily; a demonstration by experienced users is often sufficient.* The functionality can always be learned easily when the user interface becomes integral part of the range of tasks, and if the user is familiar with this area. In addition, the demonstration of the functionality in the form of a dynamic example represents generally a superior method to convey knowledge and is by no means a particularity of direct manipulation. Actions on such interfaces can be followed more easily by onlookers than entering commands on the keyboard.
- *Experts can work very efficiently with these systems in various tasks and even expand their functionality.* However, a series of studies has shown that experts can work faster by use of command languages than by means of direct manipulation. This means that the execution speed is not the only relevant factor for the use of direct manipulation. The same applies to expandability: for example, macros have been around for some time.
- *The operation concepts are easy to understand and can be memorized even by occasional users.* Each action semantically relating to the task is forgotten more

slowly. This property applies to many well-designed user interfaces and is not specific to direct manipulation.

- *Error messages are needed to a lesser degree.* From a critical perspective, this aspect should be formulated differently: The fact that the results from user actions are visible immediately, certain error types can no longer occur, and new errors emerge instead. Especially semantically faulty actions are hard to discover and can have disastrous effects, although they are permitted from the purely operational view. In addition, direct manipulation lends itself to the so-called do-nothing strategy, leading to the undesirable suppression of a series of errors.

- *Users can see immediately whether or not their actions take them closer to their goals.* If this is not the case, then they can react immediately and correct their approach.

- *Users have to worry less about faulty system operations, because these systems are intuitive and users can undo actions easily.* The option to undo an action is desirable in most cases. In addition, immediate feedback messages are useful for other user interfaces. These functions were put in the foreground of direct manipulation.

- *These systems give users a feeling of being in control, because the approach can be planned and the system behavior is predictable.* The above statements are difficult to prove and are mainly based on subjective user responses. Several studies conducted in this respect have led to different results.

7.3.2   Forms of Directness

We can distinguish various forms of directness in user interfaces [HHN86].

- *Semantic directness* describes the relationship between a user's goals and the meaning of objects and functions offered by the user interface to the user to achieve these goals. In this connection, it is important not only that user interfaces offer the functionality needed to achieve the goals, but that this functionality can be used quickly and effectively.

  For example, if the goal is to delete a word in a text, then an interface demanding that the word be first selected before the delete operation can be used is less direct compared to an interface that lets you use a pen to cross out the word to be deleted.

- *Articulatory directness* describes the relationship between the meanings of the components of a user interface and the physical actions a user has to take to activate these components or interact with them. This means that, when being manipulated by a user, components should always behave in the way implied by their appearance.

This is the case, for example, if the user can use the mouse to move a shape that is a section of a larger shape. A less direct method would be the use of scrollbars to move that shape. The latter method always leads to poorer articulatory directness, because the moving direction of the mouse is opposite to the desired movement of the shape.

[ZF88] discusses these aspects and integrates them in their general layer model of human-computer interaction, resulting in two additional forms of directness:

- Aspects of temporal control structures of the interaction and the input syntax are used to evaluate a user interface with regard to *operational directness*. Systems should respond immediately to user inputs and not dictate specific flows of action, like in the above example where the user wants to delete a word. Using a pen to cross out that word has more operational directness than selecting the word and activating the delete function.
- *Formal directness* refers to intuitive user interface outputs and the familiar handling of elements offered by the user interface. For example, the user can click the mouse button to select an element, or drag a document on a printer pictogram, or use WYSIWYG (What You See Is What You Get) applications for document editing.

In summary, these forms of directness can be seen as a measurement stating the difference between goals, expectations, and methods of users and user interfaces. The smaller the distance between the two, the more direct is the user interface.

7.3.3 Discussion of Direct Manipulation

The majority of current user interfaces follows the paradigm of *direct manipulation*. This form has been accepted in the market since the introduction of the STAR system [SIK+82]. Various studies [ZF88] discuss the question of objective benefits offered by direct manipulation, compared to other interaction forms, but the results are different. In fact, the results range from "ineffective" and "similar" to "superior", depending on the set of tasks and user groups involved in the study.

Major problems of direct manipulation include the efficient realization of recurring operations, the ability to distinguish graphical representations, and the necessity to make precise inputs (demanding high concentration from users). Another major problem is the approach to map processes and objects users are familiar with in the form of interface components naturally, and to communicate the value-adding features of the technology in the same natural and familiar way. This means that metaphors fail in many places. Direct manipulation is not a universal solution; we will have to find a number of trade-offs, depending on several aspects, including motorial aspects or the selected input device.

The most important benefit of direct manipulation, if properly used, is that it encourages easy learning and consistent user actions. Most interactions are normally done by use of a mouse, so that they are limited to point-and-click or point-and-drag operations. Consistency should not be an end in itself, because this could lead to losses in the interaction efficiency [Gru89]. A consistent user interface that facilitates the familiarization and learning process, but hinders the work of experienced users is not a well-designed interface. After all, we want to develop *user interfaces* rather than *learning interfaces*, says Grudin.

Many developers of user interfaces neglect the statements of Shneiderman, considering them rather as a set of orientation rules, and concentrate more on concrete quality criteria for interaction design [FWC84]. These quality criteria include aspects influenced by the experience and knowledge of users and the properties of physical input devices. For example, this includes the time required to complete a task, the accuracy of the result, and subjective perceptions while using a user interface. Other criteria are the time required to learn and memorize a functionality. Important factors include low stress for the short-term memory (for the individual steps required), good long-term memory (for the sequence of these individual steps), and fatigue (both from monotonous tasks and motorial actions, also leading to more error-prone work). In addition, factors like limits of the functionality, complexity, and naturalness of the interactions, i.e., the transfer of every-day knowledge and experience, should be observed. These latter points are not tied to consistency, as suggested by direct manipulation, because inconsistent user interfaces could appear naturally to the user [Gru89]. Its inconsistency is not detected when the interface behaves as expected by the user. And users themselves do not always act in a consistent way. It is believed that user interfaces should offer various forms of partial consistency in different work contexts rather than total consistency, a goal hard to achieve.

7.4 Guidelines for User-friendly User Interfaces

A detailed discussion of the principle of "direct manipulation" shows that it is difficult to define a set of general rules for the design of user interfaces. The design guidelines described below should also be seen in a relative context.

- *Logically relating functions* should be grouped, and their design should show the connection between these functions. Two such functions in telephone networks are "call divert" and "call forward". Both functions require the input of a telephone number or subscriber, and they are mutually exclusive. This means that it appears meaningful to assign a common number field to both functions and to disable the button representing one function when the user selects the other (these buttons are called *radio buttons*).

- *Graphical symbols* or short motion picture sequences are normally more effective than a textual input and output. Carefully designed icons facilitate their use.
- Requirements should be met both for *occasional* and *professional users*. One simple solution to the problem discussed above, i.e., different sets of requirements for different user types, is a user-specific configuration. In addition, we could offer alternative operations leading to the same results. For example, most popular applications allow the more time-consuming use of layered menus and additionally keyboard shortcuts for the same functions.
- A well-designed user interface should not require the use of operating instructions in paper form during routine use and rarely during the learning phase. Electronic tutorials and a *context-sensitive help* function based on hypermedia techniques are most useful, where the extent and depth would depend on the application.
- One of the most important design principles is to communicate the system state to the user *at any given time* and to immediately respond to his or her actions. The appearance of the cursor could change for this purpose, e.g., an *hourglass* could be used instead of an arrow for a lengthy process. Actions that cannot be activated by the user should be disabled, and any operation on a disabled function should be ignored. To mention another example, many items in menu bars are grayed out to indicate that they are disabled, while all selectable functions appear black.

More time-consuming work in an application should appear to the user as such, e.g., by using a progress bar in relation to the entire process. For example, when the user formats a disk or transmits a number of packets over the network, a filling progress bar could indicate the time left to completion. The actual meaning of this technique is to inform the user about the state of ongoing work. Another useful technique is used to show the user that the operation he or she *selected* is in progress before it is actually started to avoid the function from needlessly being repeated. These techniques ensure that the system or application does not appear in an undefined state.

7.5 Components of Graphical User Interfaces

The functionality of an application presents itself to users in many aspects, including the number of functions available. How these functions are represented depends usually on how they are activated. A series of components—so-called *widgets*—have been developed for GUIs to present functionality to the user [Mye90]. This section briefly describes the most important GUI components.

Buttons Probably the simplest technique to activate functions are buttons, also called *command buttons*, *action buttons*, or *push buttons*, depending on their purpose. A *button* is a textual or icon representation of exactly one function of an application. Users can click the mouse on such a button to activate the function represented by that button.

Many user interfaces allow the user to abort the operation after they clicked the button, if they change their minds. The user simply moves the mouse cursor away from the button and releases the mouse button. Buttons are often designed so that they protrude from the user interface to suggest a type of interaction similar to pressing a key, and the response from the user interface to an activated button looks similar. For buttons that appear as a framed box or rectangle on the screen, the system response is normally shown in inverse. Figure 7-3 shows several types of buttons.

Figure 7-3   Different representations of buttons.

Most buttons in current user interfaces are used mainly in special areas of an application, i.e., in so-called *toolbars* or *toolboxes*, and some interfaces let users modify or expand the icons appearing in a toolbar. Most toolboxes let the user toggle between two modes, while toolbars include functions accessible from other components. In summary, buttons support a more effective interaction.

Menus   Most modern user interfaces arrange the majority of application functions in menus. *Menus* are linearly or hierarchically structured lists of functions, and these lists are normally invisible and arranged under a main menu item. When the user clicks the mouse on one of these main menu items, the options available under this item become visible. The user can then select one of the options available from the list of functions. The list of functions under a main menu item normally closes automatically, while the main menu bar remains visible (see Figure 7-4).

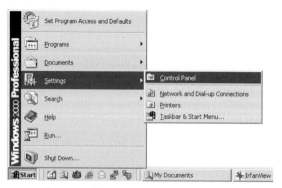

Figure 7-4   Pull-down, pull-up, and pop-up menus.

We distinguish between *pull-down*, *pull-up* or *pop-up* menus, depending on the position of the menu bar. While the menu items appear underneath or above the menu bar in the first two variants, the main menu item is often overlaid or covered when opening a pop-up menu. In addition, pop-up menus have the particularity that they do not necessarily rely on textual descriptions of a menu title. Some user interfaces let you create a pop-up menu for each data object. The data object itself assumes the role of the main menu item. This allows more efficient interactions, because the functionality is always context-specific and available where needed. The user does not have to move the cursor to the menu bar, which normally contains all menu items supported by that application.

Menus have the major benefit that most of the functions of an application can be hidden behind menu items, taking very little space on the screen. This means that the user interface does not appear overloaded, which would be the case if we were to make all functions permanently visible and use a large number of buttons (see Figure 7-5). Inexperienced users can learn the functionality of an application step by step by simply opening and closing the menus.

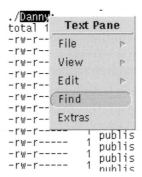

Figure 7-5   Pull-up and pop-up menus.

While the above feature is useful for beginners, it can quickly turn into a drawback for experienced users, because it takes more time than necessary to open and close menu items to activate a function. Most experienced users find menus a drawback. For this reason, there is a number of methods to activate functions hidden behind menu items, without opening that menu item. Two examples are *keyboard shortcuts* and *toolbars*. More and more experienced users rely on these features. Most continue using rarely needed menu items from the menu bar, while using keyboard shortcuts or icons for all frequently used functions. The reason is that it normally takes some time to memorize keyboard shortcuts and toolbar icons.

Clipboard   The basic functions of GUIs include moving, duplicating and deleting of data objects. The STAR system [SIK+82] offers function keys that switch the interface into a corresponding mode. User interfaces like that of Apple's Macintosh system [Gui86] or Microsoft Windows use the non-mode abstract concept of a *clipboard* for such purposes. The clipboard is operated by three functions: cut, copy, and paste.

- The *cut* function moves a selected data object into the clipboard.

- The *copy* function creates a copy of the selected data object in the clipboard.

- The *paste* function copies the contents of the clipboard to the cursor position.

Navigation   The screen area is normally limited so that a large volume of information is not fully visible, i.e., the screen displays a section of that information. Applications are designed to allow users to define such sections and to modify them in several detail levels. *Scrolling* is the most frequent navigation form in modern user interfaces, although it is not the only approach. Plaisant, Carr and Shneiderman [PCS95] propose a taxonomy of alternative approaches, e.g., *fish-eye views*.

A *scrollbar* is the most common component used in GUIs to support scrolling. Scrollbars come in different flavors, differing both in their components and in their influences on the information section to be represented [Mye90].

Scrollbars were originally used in the mid seventies in the Bravo system, which included a series of other important components for the development of GUIs. Bravo did not have visible scrollbars, but showed them to the user by changing the look of the mouse cursor when positioned within a scrollable screen area. The scrolling functionality, i.e., move the visible section up or down by one screen size, was assigned to the mouse buttons. Smalltalk-80 was the first programming environment to use scrollbars as visible components [Gol84]. The environment showed an area on the side of a section consisting of two components: a so-called *container*, which symbolized the entire information, and a *thumb* that marked the part of this information currently visible. The user could move the thumb within the container to change the section. The thumb was moved either directly with the mouse or by clicking into a container area outside the thumb position. The latter option enabled browse or jump movements. In contrast to Bravo and its successor STAR, this option moved the section itself instead of the information shown in that section, i.e., moving the thumb in one direction resulted in a movement of the information shown in the section in opposite direction.

Both the division of a scrollbar into these two components and the effect on the movement of a section are still used in most modern user interfaces, although the names and the way how the components are represented vary from one system to another. For example, some use elevators or knobs instead of thumbs, and some user interfaces show the thumb always in a fixed size, while others adapt the thumb dynamically in relation to the section versus the entire information quantity. Figure 7-6 shows examples of scrollbars used in different user interfaces.

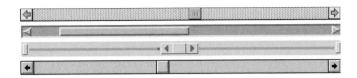

Figure 7-6 Examples of scrollbars from different user interfaces.

The Macintosh user interface added *scroll buttons* to scrollbars. These scroll buttons allowed users to move a section in finer-grained levels, e.g., line by line in text representations. Before the Macintosh was introduced, this was either difficult or not available. Most modern user interfaces use the term *scrollbar* to include both scrollbars and scroll buttons, and scroll buttons can appear in different places within a scrollbar, e.g., at the ends of the container or on the thumb itself.

Although scrollbars have proven and established themselves as a navigation component over the years, they have been criticized in a number of aspects. For example, one critical argument is that scrollbars are not suitable for navigation over two dimensions. In general, scrollbars allow *movement in one dimension*, either horizontal or vertical. This means that two scrollbars are required for two-dimensional navigation. A user who wants to scroll diagonally has to split this movement into its horizontal and vertical parts and implement them by use of two different scrollbars. The drawback is that the navigation slows down, and it becomes more difficult for the user to maintain an overview of the entire information quantity as he or she has to use two scrollbars to move a section. [Kap95] compares several navigation techniques, where scrollbars performed worst among all criteria studied. For example, using scrollbars to move a section was found unnatural and strange, compared to the direct movement of information shown within a section. The best results were obtained from direct moving of information shown in the section and defining a section in an overview over the entire information quantity. The latter is particularly helpful for users who know the entire information quantity, i.e., users who memorized its visual structure. Kaptelinin's observations were confirmed by [Joh95].

[FWC84] established the requirement for interactive GUIs that the movement of the input device should match the system's feedback on the screen. Scrollbars meet this requirement only in an abstract way. Although the thumb follows the mouse movement, it is actually not the user's intention to move this thumb. As soon as they have activated it, they concentrate on the information shown in the section and find that it moves opposite to the mouse movement. In addition, the speed of movement of the information shown in the section does generally not match the mouse movement. Instead, the transformation from the input movement to the output movement is determined by the ratio of the volume of section information to the volume of the entire information. Users cannot recognize in advance how exactly a thumb movement would influence the information shown in a section. This still depends largely on the computer and operating system performance.

Dialog Boxes   One of the most commonly used forms of interaction between applications and users are dialog boxes. A *dialog box* informs the user about a system state or process, or warns of possible consequences, or expects simple decisions about the next processing step.

In general, *simple dialog boxes* consist of not more than two to five components: a descriptive text, an input field or a list, and a couple of buttons, where the user will activate exactly one at the end of the dialog. Therefore, a simple dialog box has always *exactly one result*. More complex inputs are similar to simple dialog boxes, but they combine a series of additional components and lead to a complex result.

The simplest form of dialog used by an application is to inform users by displaying *messages*. A message normally consists of an informative text, e.g., telling the user that a process has been completed. In contrast to passive information, which is normally displayed in the status bar, messages in dialog boxes require the user to confirm the message to remove the box before they can continue. This means that every message displayed in a dialog box is acknowledged by the user; it cannot be covered by other GUI components, as is the case in status bars, or overlooked inadvertently.

A particular form of messages is a *warning* message used by an application to warn the user of an undesirable result. This dialog form has a two-fold purpose: it warns the user and allows the user to either continue or abort the currently active process. Conventional warning messages normally include two buttons with a confirming and a rejecting text, respectively.

Dialog boxes where an application asks a *simple question* that require a Yes or No answer do not differ from warning dialog boxes, with regard to the type of interaction.

An expansion of the dialog boxes introduced above leads to dialog boxes offering the user more than two response options. Most of these dialog boxes have *complex questions*, offering several response options. However, the number of possible answers is normally limited to three to five. Complex dialog responses are represented in lists and handled similarly to screen sections, as discussed above. Most response options in a question dialog box are implemented by buttons, where each button represents exactly one answer, and the user has to click the desired button.

Dialog boxes that offer the user *several response options* to select one or several should include a list component with scrollbar, in addition to a descriptive text, especially when they concern sizes that cannot be fully displayed in the dialog box. In addition, they generally include two buttons—one to terminate the selection and another one to abort the process.

In addition, dialog boxes are often used to prompt the user to *input values* in the form of text or numbers. Common forms of these dialogs consist of an input prompt, an editable field, and buttons to confirm and abort the process.

More complex settings (than those introduced above), e.g., to *set several parameters* or *define object properties*, are often implemented in so-called *option sheets* or *property sheets*. This type of dialog boxes can contain some of the components introduced above. This section briefly describes check boxes and radio buttons.

A *check box* can be used to manipulate a value that can take two states; it is normally described by a short text. Modern GUIs represent such options by a check box to the left and a short description to the right of that box. When the user clicks a check box the GUI fills this check box with a tick mark. The user can click the same check box again to deselect that option. Check boxes are normally used when alternatives are not mutually exclusive, or may be applied simultaneously, such as type styles: a type can be both bold and italic at the same time. Check boxes never initiate or conclude an action, they are only used to set choices.

Similarly to the check box, *radio buttons* can be clicked to select an option. The main difference is that instead of allowing a user to specify multiple answers to one question, the radio button element ensures that one and only one selection is chosen from among the group of buttons. Radio buttons are normally represented by a round or diamond-shape button and a brief description next to each button. When a user clicks a radio button, the round or diamond field is filled to indicate that the option represented by that button is selected. When a user clicks another radio button, the system removes the previous selection, as radio buttons are mutually exclusive.

Windows One of the most important components of conventional user interfaces is the window. *Windows* are generally specific to applications, serving then as a representation pane on the computer screen. An application can normally use overlapping or tiled windows, so that the available screen surface can be optimally used by displaying several windows at the same time [BR86].

Users can manipulate windows in many different ways. Common functions include free size scaling, minimizing and maximizing in horizontal and vertical directions, arranging windows as icons, changing the relative position to other windows, moving windows on the screen, and closing. Modern GUIs support components for each of these functions, including buttons, menus and *handles*. For example, a user can drag handles to move, manipulate, resize, or reposition a window.

On the other hand, windows can cause a number of problems. For example, studies have disclosed that users spend up to 30% of their work time to organize windows on the screen, i.e., to position windows in relation to other windows, and to scale them according to their needs. Some critics argue that windows should allow flexible and dynamic adaptation and never overlap. Window actions, such as minimizing them to icons or free scaling, were found to be tiresome actions, e.g., moving the mouse with the mouse button pressed, or finding and clicking a button to maximize or close a window.

7.6 GUI and the Audio Medium

Audio is a medium that can be used on the user interface of a computer to control applications. The use of audio for this purpose requires a speech analysis, which can be speaker-dependent or speaker-independent.

Existing audio input and output devices (e.g., headphones, microphones or loudspeakers) can be connected to the computer, and signal processors installed in the computer are used to digitize data, and for compression and decompression, if required.

Audio output lends itself to use two or more converters to introduce a *spatial representation dimension*. The best known techniques are stereophony, artificial-head stereophony, and quadraphony, where the latter two are further developments of the first. *Stereophony* assigns spatial positions to audio sources, e.g., a fixed location can be assigned to each participant in a conference. The motion picture of participant L is displayed on the left side of the screen, and only the left loudspeaker is used to transmit the pertaining sound. Assume that participant M_1 is in the center; only the left loudspeaker is used to transmit M_1. Participant M_2 is visually and acoustically located in the center, and participant R is to the right of M_2. In this example, the conference system always activates the video window of the participant speaking loudest (assuming that the strongest acoustic signal is determined as an integral value over a duration of five seconds, so that brief and undesired loud signals are compensated). The windows of the other participants show the motion pictures displayed last as single images. Volume 1 Chapter 3 describes audio techniques in detail.

In *monophony*, all audio sources have the same spatial position, which means that humans can understand only the loudest audio signal at a time. You can easily simulate that effect by holding your hand to one ear. Stereophony allows humans with bilateral hearing ability to understand a lower audio source, when this source is located at a different position than the loud source. Note that the extraction of lower signals within a loud environment and not the aware spatial localization of audio sources is the most important benefit of bilateral hearing.

A GUI system based on windows allows the user to position windows individually on the screen. [LPC90] ported this paradigm to audio: The application defines a position for various sources, and the user can change the position of the audio signals (*audio windows*) as needed, but the number of audio windows is limited. The user can normally have windows for synchronized sources open, such as in our conference example. Practical experiences have shown that, otherwise, not more than two audio windows should be open at the same time.

As an expansion to [LPC90], the user can also set the relative sound volume and tone, in addition to the spatial positioning of audio windows. This expansion offers another possibility to differentiate between several audio windows.

The concept of audio windows allows the user to control audio parameters, including spatial positioning, regardless of the active application. Current multimedia applications that use audio normally determine their spatial positioning themselves, and the user has no way to change this.

7.7 Innovative Forms of Interaction

All of the design possibilities and principles discussed in this chapter build on the paradigm of a GUI. This input and output form is not always ideal, and it does not use all communication channels available to humans. Innovative multimedia-enabling GUIs reach far beyond the classical input and output possibilities, i.e., using keyboard and mouse for input and viewing the output on the screen. The past years have seen a series of new forms of interaction, together with the development of new GUI components. This section briefly introduces the most important representatives.

7.7.1 Virtual Reality

Virtual reality represents an alternative form of human-computer interaction. As the term suggests, the technique creates an artificial reality for the user of a computer system, where the user can "immerse" into that reality by means of special peripherals.

Currently the characteristics of this artificial reality are limited to the visual dimension, supported by spatial-acoustic features. The other senses of humans are addressed to a limited extent or not at all. The most popular interfaces to this virtual computer world include a *data glove* and *VR goggles*. A user can put on such a data glove, which can optionally be expanded to a *data suit*, equipped with sensors to detect the position and orientation of the hand or fingers. The data sensed through the glove can be combined with gesticulation to let the software derive actions, e.g., instructions to change a position, open a menu, or grip virtual objects. A virtual pendant of the user's hand with a data glove and a computer-generated actual image of the virtual reality is displayed permanently and in real time for the user through VR goggles, containing small monitors (for each eye). This makes the user think and feel that he or she is part of that virtual reality, able to interact in it.

7.7.2 Computer-augmented Reality

Computer-augmented reality can be seen as a counter-movement to virtual reality. In a computer-augmented reality, users remain in their physical environment, do not immerse into a second—virtual—reality, and their interaction with the computer is oriented to daily movement routines. The enabling information technology is pushed into the background to the widest possible extent, i.e., hidden from the user's perception, so that users can concentrate on their tasks. But the enabling information technology is omni-present, i.e., built into many physical objects (*ubiquitous computing*). The key technologies for this form of human-computer interaction are sensory analysis and detection of gestures.

Pen computing is an area that demonstrates a large amount of overlapping with computer-augmented reality. *Pen computing* means that a computer is operated mainly by use of a pen. So-called pen computers can have various sizes, from handheld devices to devices the size of a wall. The common feature of all of these devices is the external reduction onto an interactive screen. A user uses a special pen to write on this surface, which means that this surface is both input and output medium at the same time. Certain inputs can be detected as gestures and cause the software to trigger actions.

The *human speech* is considered an integral part of a modern GUI, similar to and as an expansion of pen computing. Special software can be used to synthesize speech and use it for system feedback, especially in cases where the user does not see the screen. The detection of speech has also made considerable progress on the input side. For example, it is no longer necessary to pause after each spoken word, as *discrete speech recognition* required for a long time. This means that *continuous speech recognition* does no longer hinder humans in their fluent speaking. In fact, the new speech recognition technology can analyze and interpret fluently spoken text, e.g., as in a dictation.

Expansion by Multimedia   Speaking may be more adequate than writing: Changes and comments to a document available in electronic form can be more effective (i.e., faster) verbally, as opposed to editing electronic text. Reading and hearing are no real alternatives, but complement each other (like human language textbooks). Using graphics or text to describe movement sequences is normally much more complicated than watching a motion picture sequence. Imagine a textbook about tennis: The individual ball techniques and typical errors could be represented much better and more intuitively in a video, as opposed to single still images.

Time as a *representation dimension* is assumed to be the most important expansion of a GUI. Data is not displayed statically, but dynamically. This dynamics consists of a sequence of static elements (representation values) that, together and in the appropriate speed, create an illusion of *continuity* for the human viewer.

For *audio*, the continuity of data is achieved by reconstructing an analog signal. This signal is continuous, while the digital values are present in the computer both in temporal and value-discrete form.

Audio and video improve the flow of information between humans and machines [LM90]. Figure 7-7 shows the process of an information transmission according to [Wat87]: An *idea* or thought (representing the information) in the human brain is converted into an idea spectrum. The human sender uses this idea spectrum to communicate with other people (receivers).

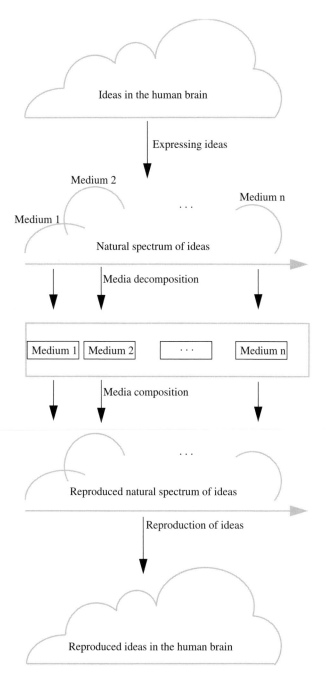

Figure 7-7 Multimedia increases the information bandwidth; adapted from [Wat87].

From the physical perspective, various media are used for inter-human exchange of information, including *gestures* and *mimics* as important information carriers (e.g., [LN02]). The idea spectrum reconstructed on the receiver side is then converted into the actual idea. Using an idea spectrum for the expressive process is a natural ability of humans and coined by people's experiences in their environment. The conversion of ideas into an idea spectrum and into media on the one hand, and of media into an idea spectrum and into an idea on the other hand, is normally subconscious and does not take much intellectual effort. Speaking a foreign language is one example for an aware (de)composition into/from media.

When using lesser media, a virtual media transformation is necessary to convert an idea spectrum into media. Information available in one medium has to be described by means of other media and reconstructed accordingly at the receiver. If only text and single images are available, then a motion picture sequence, for example showing a dance, would have to be described by these media. Humans will then have to do with such a reduced number and type of media. The use of audio and video, in addition to the media available on a computer, facilitate the transformation of information. This also means that less information will be lost during the transmission, and the user can select the suitable media when communicating with the computer. This means that appropriate applications are required.

Multimedia Learning

T he use of technology for learning purposes has a long history: learning machines, "programmed teaching" in book form, first implemented on mainframes and later in learning software for the PC. The development of PCs and networked multimedia systems laid the foundation necessary to develop multimedia learning software and improve the way humans learn. This chapter discusses several possibilities and side conditions for multimedia learning on the computer [Has95] [IK97] [Sch97]. Our discussion focuses on learning as a process to acquire knowledge, as depicted in Figure 8-1).

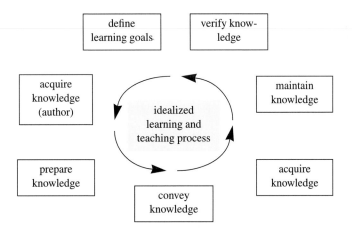

Figure 8-1 Idealized learning and teaching process from the perspective of the authors/tutors.

8.1   Learning Software

The generic term *learning software* can be differentiated in *learning program* (i.e., learning software that controls the learning progress) and *learning environment* (i.e., the learning software has provider character, while the student controls the learning process directly). Computer-supported learning includes all forms of learning software applications to control or facilitate learning [OW98]. Multimedia learning software can facilitate learning in several ways:

- *Multicodality*: Various symbol systems (codes) can be used to present information. For example, content can be represented as image, pictogram, video sequence, number, or verbose description. This opens up a large number of learning areas for computer-supported teaching, but learning contents should always be represented adequately for those contents.
- *Multimodality*: The information offered can address various human senses. For example, a piece of information can be perceived only visually, or only acoustically, or over several senses at the same time. Multimedia learning software can be tailored to the media preferences of the student.
- *Dynamics*: In multimedia learning software, information can be presented both statically (discrete medium, i.e., still image or text) and dynamically (continuous medium, i.e., video, animation or audio). For example, animation and simulation software can show processes, while video allows a more realistic representation for many learning areas.
- *Interactivity*: The possibility for the student to interact with the learning software, i.e., to edit tasks, make decisions, and obtain individual feedback, is one of the major benefits of multimedia learning, compared to traditional textbooks or films.

8.2   The Role of the Computer

Computers for learning purposes can assume various roles [BHLM92]:

- *The computer is the learning object.* Learning concerns the computer itself, including issues like architecture and functionality of the computer, operation, programming, applications, economic or social impact of the use of computers.
- *The computer is the learning tool.* Similar to other learning tools, such as a pocket calculator, the computer and suitable standard or proprietary software (drawing programs, databases, word processors) are used by the tutor or student, for example to create learning material, edit tasks, or search information in the Internet.
- *The computer is the learning medium.* The computer serves as a carrier of the learning content, i.e., it assumes one or more teaching functions, such as presenting information, motivating, controlling activities and achievements, printing feedback.

The following section sees the computer mainly in its role as a learning medium. Note, however, that the boundaries to other applications are fluid, depending on the learning software.

8.3 Types of Learning Software

The computer assumes different teaching functions, depending on the type of learning software used. The types of learning software in the following list are often mixed in practice, for example, a learning environment could also include a test component.

8.3.1 Learning Software Programs

- *Drill and tutorial programs*: Drill and tutorial programs serve to strengthen (previously acquired) knowledge by review exercises and practical application to ensure successful learning. There is a large number of such programs for almost all knowledge disciplines and all types of students, from vocabulary book over electronic review collections to mathematical tutorials.

- *Test software*: Test software is used to run and evaluate learning controls, where computers are used instead of paper or oral tests to edit the tasks. This type of software to verify and evaluate the performance is suitable particularly for knowledge disciplines that can be reviewed in closed questions, e.g., multiple-choice exercises or intentionally incomplete answers (e.g., driver's license tests). A computer-supported test can relieve the tutor from routine performance verification or serve as a control in autodidactic learning. Better testing allows adaptive test systems, and enables us to determine the type, degree of difficulty, and number of test tasks dynamically, depending on the current test progress.

- *Tutorial systems*: Tutorial systems, often called *computer-based training* (*CBT*), assume all teaching functions. The learning software conveys a specific knowledge discipline, lets the student edit tasks, outputs feedback about the learning progress, and determines the further learning path in relation to the student's answers. *Intelligent tutorial systems* (*ITS*) use separate modeling of the knowledge, the student, and the didactic strategies in an attempt to better individualize the learning process. Tutorial systems are widely used (e.g., foreign language courses or product training) and suitable mainly for autodidactic studies.

8.3.2 Learning Environments

- *Animations and simulations*: Animation and simulation software can be used to show facts and processes dynamically, which would otherwise be too big, too small, too fast, too slow, too dangerous, too expensive, or unavailable in the real world for another reason. Simulation allows students to influence the process, recognize the underlying relationships, and review their comprehension. To increase the learning effectiveness, the software should be prepared in a learning context and subsequently evaluated. You can simulate either concrete systems (e.g., a specific machine), or use a simulation kit to build and simulate systems from readily available elements (e.g., electric circuits from batteries, wires, and lamps). Social and economic relationships are suitable for simulation-based learning.

• *Problem-solving environments*: Problem-solving environments offer the student maximum freedom in the design of his or her learning process. The software or the tutor confronts the student with a complex task, or the student selects such a task directly to solve it on his or her own. From the technical perspective, problem-solving environments are based on expert systems, databases, hypertext or hypermedia systems. Learning environments generally serve to train people in action strategies and problem solution abilities. The transition of the process to the computer as a learning tool (e.g., for information research in the World Wide Web) is fluid in these systems.

• *Learning games and edutainment*: This form of learning software uses the computer for playful acquisition of knowledge. For example, learning contents are presented in a motivating and entertaining way, including competitive elements or comic figures. Depending on the design, there are fluid transitions to all other types of learning software.

8.4   Learning Theories

The learning software types introduced above are very different, because they build on different learning theories. Three fundamental paradigms are *behaviorism* (approx. 1920-1960), *cognitivism* (approx. 1960-1990), and *constructivism* (from 1990). The years stated designate only the "heyday" of these theories, i.e., all approaches can coexist.

8.4.1   Behaviorism

Behaviorism is based on observable changes in behavior. It focuses on a new behavioral pattern being repeated until it becomes automatic. The theory of behaviorism concentrates on the study of overt behaviors that can be observed and measured. It views the mind as a "black box" in the sense that response to stimulus can be observed quantitatively, while ignoring the possibility of thought processes occurring in the mind. Some key players in the development of the behaviorist theory were *Ivan P. Pavlov* and *Burrhus F. Skinner*. Pavlov is best known for his work in classical conditioning or stimulus substitution. Like Pavlov, Skinner believed in the stimulus-response pattern of conditioned behavior. His theory dealt with changes in observable behavior, ignoring the possibility of any processes occurring in the mind. Skinner's work differs from that of his predecessors (classical conditioning), in that he studied operant behavior (voluntary behaviors used in operating on the environment). Learning programs with the following principles were developed on the basis of this theory [KFK96]:

- The learning objectives should be formulated clearly and objectively so that matching feedback can be generated.
- The learner should be able to determine the learning speed, i.e., the tasks should be prepared to ensure a high probability that the learner will solve them correctly, and the learning path should lead from easy to increasingly difficult tasks.
- There should be an immediate feedback to each of the learner's answers.
- Particularly good answers should be rewarded.

The behavioristic learning theory has influenced mainly programmed instruction in the sixties, but tutorial systems that attempt to teach knowledge in small units are still developed today. The behavioristic stance is not suitable for teaching of complex relationships, but rather for simple and structured knowledge areas (e.g., vocabulary tests or learning body movements).

In summary, behaviorism deals with the control of behavior and not with aware cognitive processes. The learning process is seen as a simple conditioned reflex. There is always one and only one correct answer to each task. Errors are not detected and dealt with, but gradually "eradicated" by appropriate feedback. Behavioristic learning programs are less suitable for the understanding and learning of complex relationships and processes. In its function as the tutor, the computer decides what the learner should learn in which sequence and what way. The computer gives positive or negative stimuli (feedback), depending on the learner's behavior, and strengthens or suppresses certain behavioral patterns [KFK96].

8.4.2 Cognitivism

Cognitivism is based on the thought process behind the behavior. Changes in behavior are observed, and used as indicators as to what is happening inside the learner's mind. One of the major players in the development of cognitivism is *Jean Piaget*, who developed the major aspects of his theory as early as the 1920's. Piaget's ideas did not impact North America until the 1960's after *Miller* and *Bruner* founded the Harvard Center for Cognitive studies.

Cognitive science began a shift from behavioristic practices which emphasized external behavior, to a concern with the internal mental processes of the mind and how they could be utilized in promoting effective learning. The design models that had been developed in the behaviorist tradition were not simply tossed out, but instead the "task analysis" and "learner analysis" parts of the models were embellished. The new models addressed component processes of learning, such as knowledge coding and representation, information storage and retrieval as well as the incorporation and integration of new knowledge with previous information [And93].

Learning programs based on cognitive theory are much more flexible than "drill-and-practice" programs. The computer acts as the tutor, observing the learner and helping him or her to find one or more correct solutions to a problem by applying the correct methods and processes. Such programs let the learner set specific levels (e.g., beginner or advanced) during the course of the program. Using the underlying learning model, the computer selects the sequence of single learning units and forms to represent the information. In contrast to the rigid behavioristic program courses, this supports a flexible and dynamic course of the learning process [KFK96]. Adaptive learning systems and intelligent tutorial systems are based on cognitivism.

8.4.3 Constructivism

Constructivism is based on the premise that we all construct our own perspective of the world, through individual experiences and schemas. Constructivism focuses on preparing the learner to solve problems in ambiguous situations. *Bartlett* (1932) pioneered in what became the constructivist approach. Constructivists believe that "learners construct their own reality or at least interpret it based upon their perceptions of experiences, so an individual's knowledge is a function of one's prior experiences, mental structures, and beliefs that are used to interpret objects and events. What someone knows is grounded in perception of the physical and social experiences which are comprehended by the mind [Kos96].

Constructivism is based on the following assumptions: Knowledge is constructed from experience. Learning is a personal interpretation of the world, and an active process in which meaning is developed on the basis of experience. Conceptual growth comes from the negotiation of meaning, the sharing of multiple perspectives, and the changing of our internal representations through collaborative learning. And finally, learning should be situated in realistic settings; testing should be integrated with the task and not as a separate activity [DJ91].

Programs based on constructivism are *simulations* and *micro worlds*. These programs do not force a predefined set of tasks, which means that the user has to develop problem-solving strategies for totally new problems. The course of such a program depends entirely on the user. The computer assumes the task of a cooperating advisor, which is not infallible or perfect, but disposes of a wealth of information and hardly makes errors [KFK96].

Table 8-1 summarizes and compares the three learning theories discussed above.

	Behaviorism	Cognitivism	Constructivism
Thinking or the human brain is...	a black box	an information-processing process	a closed information system
Knowledge is...	acquired and stored	processed and stored	constructed and stored
Knowledge is...	a correct input/output relation	a patching internal processing process	dealing with a situation
Learning is ..	to build stimulus/respnse chains	to build cognitive structures	to acquire experiences
The learning objective is...	to find one (single) correct answer	to adapt correct methods to find a solution	to handle complex situations
The computer is...	an authoritative tutor	an observing and assisting tutor	a cooperating adviser
The program sequence is...	rigidly defined	dynamically created, depending on the learning model	freely defined, autonomous
Problems and solutions are...	predefined; only one correct answer	predefined; several solutions are possible	constructed separately: first the problem, then a solution
Learning program type	Computer Aided Instruction (CAI), "drill and practice" programs	Computer Based Training (CBT), (intelligent) tutoring systems	simulations, micro worlds

Table 8-1   Comparison of the three learning theories.

8.4.4 Integrating the Learning Theories

Readers will probably ask themselves: Which learning paradigm is the "correct" one? Unfortunately, there is no simple answer: Given that we will most likely never "see" an atom, we will never "see" learning either. Therefore our learning models are mental pictures that enable us to understand that which we will never see. Does the development of learning theories follow a similar pattern as the atomic theory?

The behaviorist learning theory centered around that which was observable, not considering that there was anything occurring inside the mind. Using overt behavior as a starting point, people began to realize that there is something happening inside the organism that should be considered, since it seemed to affect the overt behavior. Hence, cognitivism was born.

The constructivist learning theory tells us that each organism is constantly in flux, and although the old models work to a certain degree, other factors must also be considered. Constructivism builds upon behaviorism and cognitivism in the sense that it accepts multiple perspectives and maintains that learning is a personal interpretation of the world. Many believe that behavioral strategies can be part of a constructivist learning situation, if that learner chooses and finds that type of learning suitable to their experiences and learning style.

Cognitive approaches have a place in constructivism also, since constructivism recognizes the concept of schema and building upon prior knowledge and experience.

In summary, none of the learning theories introduced above can claim generality, and none is absolutely right or absolutely wrong. The "right" learning theory depends perhaps on the learning situation, and the "right" learning software will most likely be the best suitable for the learner and the task, as summarized in Table 8-1 [OW98].

8.5   Trends and Current Developments

Since the computer has been used for many years for learning purposes, we can observe a gradual shift in the field of research and development in many ways:

- Learning software is increasingly less seen as a tutor replacement, focusing instead on the learners and their learning processes. Software has become an information provider and learning tool.
- Learning software, particularly in the form of learning environments, involves the learner more, focusing on the communication and cooperation with other learners as well as tutors, teachers, and experts.
- Learning software is increasingly seen from the stance of flexible and life-long learning, both in the personal environment and on the job.
- There is a shift from learning software to its tuning with other elements of the learning process, such as the learning method and media preparation of the learning content.

8.6   Learning with Hypermedia

A *hypertext* is a structure with (small) information units (so-called *nodes*), consisting of text and graphic elements, which are not present in sequential order, but instead organized like a network and connected by links (see also Chapter 5). *Hypermedia* expands hypertext as it replaces text by media and other forms of representation, such as images, animation, audio or video [OW98]. The best known and most popular implementation of hypertext or hypermedia is the *World Wide Web*.

Nodes can be accessed in an arbitrary sequence by selecting one of the links they contain. This process is called *navigation*. Navigation in hypermedia documents can take several forms: *directed* or *undirected*, *systematic* or *controlled*. *Browsing* is the common navigation method, corresponding to (directed or undirected) skimming of documents. The reader sees the content of a node and selects the link pointing there. In a systematic search process, the reader specifies search words and gets a set of nodes containing information about these words. For example, virtual guided tours are a form of controlled navigation [OW98].

Learning with hypermedia can offer a number of benefits. The non-linear structure of these media allows the intuitive representation of complex relationships between knowledge structures. Hypermedia-enabled learning environments encourage explorative learning and ask the readers to actively use their abilities, instead of passively responding to external stimuli. Users can explore fields of knowledge and concentrate on their own interests, strengths and weaknesses, as long as the information units are organized meaningfully. With equal prerequisites and well-designed links between the information units, we can represent the content of a field of knowledge in an easily understandable and comprehensible way. Embedding dynamic (i.e., multimedia) elements (e.g., animation, video or audio) is helpful in presenting contents and processes much more intuitively, compared to conventional textbooks. In addition, hypermedia systems are very useful in the field of distributed information processing.

Like all good things, hypermedia has a few drawbacks. Most of them are dealt with generally in Chapter 5, so that this section will concentrate on this issue in relation to the *learning process*. Separation of an interrelated field of knowledge into small information units can mean that the reader gets lost in the wealth of information. The unlimited freedom of navigation can lead to undifferentiated browsing habits, to reduced concentration and finally to inefficient learning. Learning contents have to be especially prepared for this medium to achieve optimum presentation results. The combination of static and dynamic media has to follow the didactic goal and protect the user from overstimulation or cognitive stress. At the same time, the designer should be careful to achieve a meaningful linkage of all nodes involved to allow easy and intuitive navigation. The potential risk to get lost in hyperspace increases as the complexity of contents increases. And finally, self-controlled learning requires a lot of discipline and self-critical attitude, regardless of the systems used [Dan97] [OW98] [Has95].

Hypermedia poses high requirements to both the authors and the readers of such systems. Unless these requirements are carefully observed, the use of such a medium can easily turn from a helpful into a complicated tool. Designers of multimedia systems have to pay utmost attention to the semantics and optimal coordination of the range of different representation forms (e.g., static forms like text and images, or dynamic forms like audio, video and animation). Although multimedia can be fun and increase the user's motivation, overlapping (static and dynamic) representation forms do not automatically contribute to a better understanding. In fact, they could lead to overstimulation, hindering successful learning [Has95].

In summary we can state that hypermedia offer great benefits, despite some potential risks. Well-designed hypermedia systems support targeted, creative learning and concentrated acquisition of information.

8.7   Adaptive Learning Systems

Adaptive learning systems are learning programs capable of adapting themselves to the individual abilities of the learner, e.g., previous knowledge, interests, weaknesses or preferences with regard to forms of representation. Adaptive learning programs do not have a predefined learning path, and they are flexible in the choice of how information is represented. One variant of adaptive learning systems are *adaptable systems* where the user can set various system parameters to adapt the program to some extent [KFK96] [OW98]. This section briefly discusses the difference between *adaptivity* and *adaptability*.

- *Adaptable systems* allow the user to control these adjustments, often providing guidance or specialized help to the user. A classical example for an adaptable system is the desktop environment on a UNIX machine. The user can modify specific configuration files to adapt their work environment to their preferences, e.g., setting a different background color, resize screen windows or arrange icons.

- *Adaptive systems* monitor the user's activity pattern and automatically adjust the interface or content provided by the system to accommodate such user differences as well as changes in user skills, knowledge and preferences. Adaptive systems can be contrasted with "training wheels" systems, which simplify an interface by disabling or removing components not typically used by novices. Adaptive systems generally retain the full power of the system, but hide rarely used components, much as lesser used controls on a television or VCR are often hidden behind a flip-down panel. These controls are made visible to the user when they reach the appropriate level of expertise, or the user can explicitly enable them through preferences" setting, normally saved to a user profile.

The following sections introduce two types of adaptive systems: *Intelligent Tutorial Systems* (*ITS*) and *Adaptive Hypermedia Systems* (*AHS*). ITS have been used for some time in various fields where knowledge is clearly structured (e.g., programming languages) [KFK96[[OW98]. AHS have been introduced a few years ago and are increasingly used in the field of teaching and learning. They combine new multimedia techniques with ITS concepts and practices.

8.7.1   Intelligent Tutorial Systems (ITS)

Intelligent tutorial systems (*ITS*) are based on the findings from research efforts in the field of artificial intelligence (AI). An ITS is a program that builds a student model from the learner's behavior, which is used to control the program course (e.g., selection of the learning units, the forms of representation, and the type of feedback in case of errors). The system creates a tailored learning path which has to be followed by the user to reach a certain learning objective.

In addition to the student model, an ITS also contains a didactic component. This component is used to implement and apply the selected teaching principles or the selected learning theory, respectively. Similar to a teacher, it determines the tutoring or learning strategy and the type of error handling best suited for the user. This can mean, for example, that user *A* will be interrupted and corrected as soon as he or she follows a wrong solution path. In contrast, user *B* is left to discover his or her wrong approach, because he or she may win specific knowledge from it.

This means that an ITS is capable of creating an individual curriculum and check users' responses and solutions for correctness. In addition, they are capable of responding and correcting unexpected reactions of the learner or unexpected questions.

Figure 8-2 shows the basic architecture resulting from the above mentioned characteristics of an ITS. The components of this architecture assume the following functions: the *knowledge domain* is the specific information source of the system, supplying the content to be conveyed, and it can solve tasks and check solutions. The *student model* stores the actual knowledge of the learner. The *didactic component* selects a matching teaching strategy, plans the learning path, and defines the type of error handling. Finally, the *user interface* is responsible for the dialog with the learner [OW98].

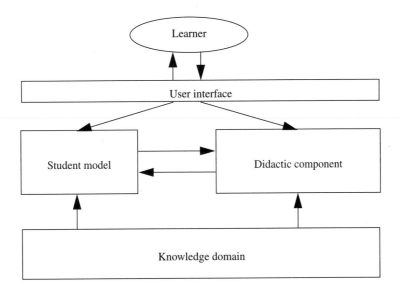

Figure 8-2   Structure of an intelligent tutorial system (ITS).

8.7.2   Adaptive Hypermedia Systems (AHS)

Adaptive hypermedia systems combine two different approaches:

- First, adaptive systems which use a model about objectives, desires and preferences to adapt themselves to the user.
- Second, hypermedia systems which are used mainly as explorative systems, offering tools so that the user can find information independently in a complex network.

The basic problem with the second approach has been mentioned in the previous section: the information space is very large and often has a poor structure. Systems taking the needs of a specific user group into account are normally hard to use for other user groups [BKV98].

Adaptive hypermedia systems solve this problem by adaptive interaction with the user. This means that the system stores certain information about the user and his or her interaction with the system in a *user profile* or *user model*. It then uses this information to adapt itself to that user. For example, an adaptive hypermedia system can assist the user with navigation help or prepare information based on criteria defined by the user or select information units according to the user's objectives and add comments to these objectives. [BKV98] define adaptive hypermedia systems as systems that meet at least the following three criteria:

- The information is prepared in the form of hypertext or hypermedia.
- The system includes a user model that reflects certain user characteristics.
- The system adapts the interaction with the user to the characteristics contained in the user model.

In addition, adaptive hypermedia systems can be classified based on the following criteria [BKV98]:

- *Application of an AHS*: An AHS can be used for various applications, e.g., educational systems, online information systems, online help systems, information retrieval systems, institution-specific systems ,and personalized view systems.
- *Adaptation basis of an AHS*: Identification of the user characteristics stored in the user model or in the user profile as a basis for adaptivity.
- *Adapting components*: Identification of the parts or functions of an AHS to be adapted to the user (e.g., adaptation of the content to the user's knowledge or control of the navigation).
- *Goals of adaptivity*: Identification of the goals to be achieved by adaptivity and what problems this could solve.

Some AHS are partly based on ITS and can optionally contain a tutorial component. The functionality of an AHS can be similar to that of an ITS, e.g., controlled navigation through the knowledge space, acquisition of problem-solving skills, but it is generally less restrictive. The user of an ITS learns (in the sense of acquiring problem-solving skills), while the AHS offers the additional option to browse the knowledge space [OW98] [KFK96]. The knowledge space can be much larger than in conventional tutorial systems (theoretically, it could be unlimited; think of the World Wide Web). Figure 8-3 describes the basic architecture of an AHS.

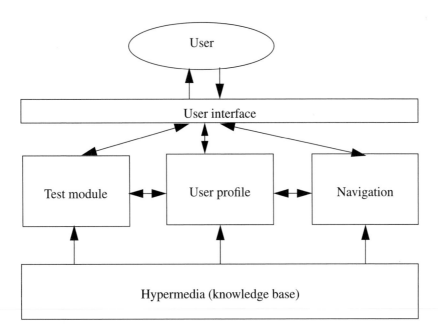

Figure 8-3   Structure of an adaptive hypermedia system (AHS).

8.8   AHS Systems — an Overview

This section introduces a few practical AHS, starting with systems that can be classified into the educational or learning program category, followed by some AHS who meet similar functions.

8.8.1   Adaptive Educational and Learning Systems

ELM-ART   ELM-ART [SW96] is an intelligent interactive learning system to support learning programming in LISP. ELM-ART demonstrates how interactivity and adaptivity can be implemented in WWW-based tutoring systems. The knowledge-based component of the system uses a combination of an overlay model and an episodic user model. It also supports adaptive navigation as individualized diagnosis and help on problem-solving tasks. Adaptive navigation support is achieved by annotating links in different colors, indicating the status of the sections concerned (e.g., green for completed and red for pending tasks). Additionally, the system selects the next best step in the curriculum on demand. Results of an empirical study show different effects of these techniques on different types of users during the first lessons of the programming course.

Hypadapter   Hypadapter [HBG98] is a system for explorative learning and programming in LISP. The system supports the user by adaptive presentation and navigation, including personal user preferences (short or long explanations, many or few examples). Stereotypes are used to initialize user models, and the user can modify specific parts of a model. The system also supports a bookmark function.

HBLE   The HBLE (Hypermedia-Based Learning Environment) project was proposed for the development of applications and technologies to create, manage and evaluate WWW-based tutorial events in universities (especially in mathematics) [Nyk97]. The learner is offered several functions based on a user model: controlled learning (defined curriculum), support of navigation specific to the user's learning goal and personalized views of the material (adaptive presentation). The user model reflects the learner's state of knowledge and is based on so-called *prerequisite graphs*.

SQL Web-Tutor   SQL Web-Tutor is an adaptive web-based educational hypermedia system for studying the SQL database language [PB97]. SQL Web-Tutor adapts it's behavior to user's knowledge, goals, needs and to teacher's strategies. It uses the knowledge-based approach for adaptation, which is based on knowledge about the user and the domain being learned. The user works with a regular web browser that communicates with a web server running SQL Web-Tutor. While working the student sequentially receives web pages with presentations of SQL concepts and commands, examples of the language use, tests and tasks. They can also enter their own examples and play with them in a special "SQL environment" as well as play with examples provided by the system.

Each page contains links to other pages of the course: a concept can have links to other concepts—it's prerequisites and consequences, to similar concepts, to generalizations, and to special cases, and so on. Navigating through such links, the user learns the domain. The system can essentially assist the user and even take the control over the navigation using the knowledge about user and the domain. It uses visual adaptive annotation and direct guidance techniques to provide adaptive navigation support. Each hyper-node may have a different educational state for a given user at different times.

8.8.2   Other Adaptive Hypermedia Systems

This section describes a few other adaptive hypermedia systems for various functions, e.g., online help systems or adaptive navigation support.

Metadoc   Metadoc [BE98] is a system that adapts the presentation of hypertext contents to the user. For this purpose, the system maintains a user model reflecting the user's knowledge. The information stored in the user model is used to represent the hypertext content in short form or with additional explanations. This type of adaptive presentation is also called *stretchtext*.

Although the system adapts the degree of detail of the represented content automatically, the user can interact and change the representation. For each information fragment there is a (short) visible place holder. The system determines which fragments should be "stretched" (i.e., shown) and which fragments should be "shrunk" (i.e., only the place holder is shown). This decision only determines the initial presentation of the fragment. The user can stretch or shrink fragments through mouse clicks. The system uses these user actions to better predict which fragments to stretch or shrink in subsequent page requests.

Metadoc uses the four stereotypes common in UNIX: *novice*, *beginner*, *intermediate*, and *expert*, because the system is mainly used for technical documentation [Chi86]. A new user to the Metadoc system has to begin by entering some information about their computer experiences (e.g., knowledge of specific UNIX concepts); alternatively, the systems uses a default user model. The user can change this user model and state the topics that should be handled in more/less detail. In addition, the system supports an implicit modeling, i.e., when a user requests additional information about a specific topic, the system assumes that the user is not familiar with that topic.

Metadoc uses an adaptive presentation in various degrees of detail and stereotypes. A drawback of Metadoc is that the system does not know *work modes* and *learning objectives*. Presumably, this may be due to the system's primary use for technical documentation.

HYPERFLEX   HYPERFLEX [KFC98] is a prototype for an adaptive hypertext system, creating mainly navigational suggestions based on the goals and preferences of the user. The approach of this prototype is based on the observation that associations between knowledge units play a major role for the human memory. The units (or nodes) used as a basis of the hypertext used are organized in a *semantic network*. The semantic relationships between units are defined in *association matrices*. The values written to these matrices show the relevance of a unit with regard to another unit (the higher the value the bigger the relevance between the topics). HYPERFLEX lets users specify a topic they are interested in or an objective they follow, or both. The system then calculates and presents proposals in a list ordered by priorities. The user can select an entry from this list or reorder the topics within the list. This causes the system to update the values of the appropriate association matrix, adapting it to the user.

HYPERFLEX can also be used as an authoring tool. The system supports learning objectives and adaptive navigation, but no adaptive presentation, because it cannot handle different degrees of detail or several possible representations of the same information. Another drawback of HYPERFLEX is that it does not support stereotypes, work modes or text in a hierarchical notation of levels of difficulty.

ifWeb   ifWeb [AT97] is a prototype of an intelligent agent, supporting the user in the navigation based on a user model. Navigation is supported by classifying the documents andlinks by relevance.

UMIE   UMIE [BKS97] is a prototype for adaptive presentation or preparation and filtering of different types of information, organized in a hierarchical knowledge structure. UMIE maintains a user model reflecting the interests of a user in various topics. The system uses stereotypes.

AVANTI   AVANTI (AdaptiVe and Adaptable INteractions for Multimedia Telecommunications ApplIcations) is a project sponsored by the European Union for a heterogeneous user group. It offers personalized multimedia information about a region over the WWW [FKS97]. The system defines and maintains a user model containing information about the characteristics and preferences of users. This information is used to select specific parts from the data repository, and then prepare, compile and finally present this data. The system's capability to adapt includes technical user equipment (i.e., fast/ slow Internet access or powerful/less powerful computer).

Comments on Learning Software   The above discussion of learning software represents only a small part from the wealth of learning programs available today. Our discussion focused on systems featuring interesting properties with regard to multimedia learning. To the time of writing, no system combined all desirable properties.

The following sections discuss telelearning and computer-supported cooperative learning, two interesting developments, and the VITAL learning environment.

8.9   Telelearning

Telelearning involves learning processes which overcome distance. Multimedia technologies allow important expansions of the traditional forms of distance learning. Telelearning supports learning processes where the tutor and the student do not have to be in the same location, opening new chances for handicapped, commuters or people living in areas far away from educational institutions. Applications for telelearning include courses in schools, universities, and further education and professional training.

Telelearning is often characterized by a high amount of self-study, where the learner acquires knowledge from various sources, e.g., the World Wide Web. Depending on the concept, telelearning is expanded by teletutoring or teleteaching [OW98]:

* *Teletutoring*: The learner is assisted by a tutor regarding questions about the material or learning process, as needed. The learner can communicate with the tutor in various ways: asynchronous, e.g., by e-mail, or synchronous, e.g., in an audio or video conference.

- *Teleteaching*: A lecture or course session is transmitted to several locations over an audio/video connection. This is normally a unidirectional communication, where feedback to the tutor can be asynchronous, e.g., by e-mail or electronic message boards, or synchronous, e.g., in an audio or video conference. One of the best known practical implementations is the system operated by the University of Mannheim, Germany, to transmit lectures by Professor W. Effelsberg, since the beginning of the nineties [GEE97].

8.10 Computer-supported Cooperative Learning

Practical experiences gained from various learning software products have disclosed a series of limits and drawbacks [BWPSW98] [OW98], including the following:

- The interactivity offered by learning software is limited.
- The extent in which the learning path can be personalized is normally limited to few navigation paths defined by the tutor.
- Learning software can provide feedback on contents only for relatively simple, structured fields of knowledge.

Communication and cooperation with other learners within a team can provide the required extent of interactivity, personalization, and feedback. In addition, the requirement for team capabilities and self-organized learning suggests a need to introduce cooperative learning methods. In today's dynamic world of work, a great deal of knowledge is not available from books, but develops on the job, distributed over several persons within an organization. Modern computers with their ability to support communication can overcome the isolation of individuals, connecting them with other learners, tutors and teachers. In this respect, *computer-supported cooperative learning* (*CSCL*) offers several dimensions:

- *Synchronous and asynchronous cooperative learning*: The people involved in the learning process participate in the learning process concurrently (video conference) or at different times (discussion by e-mail).
- *Local and remote distribution of learners*: The people involved in the learning process can be in the same location (course room) or in distant locations (tele-learning).
- *Individual and group learning phases*: Cooperative learning can consist of individual or group learning phases, with or without teachers or tutors.

Effective cooperative learning requires a structured situation and the willingness to cooperate, as well as technical tools, e.g., electronic conference rooms or audio/video and data conference systems [SGHH94]. The major drawback, i.e., lack of personal presence, has to be compensated (e.g., by social protocols, group awareness), particularly in distributed environments.

8.11 eLearning Standards

Multimedia learning always means more effort and costs for the authors. The generation of multimedia learning material requires considerably more time and more technical resources. These costs are acceptable only if the generated material is used in more than one context. Therefore, the learning material has to be designed and realized to be exchangeable. Cooperations were established to define standards for the interoperability of eLearning and multimedia learning. In the following, the main cooperations are listed and the metadata standard LOM (Learning Object Metadata) is elaborated in more detail.

8.11.1 Standards Organizations

Four main organizations defined requirements for multimedia learning.

- *IMS (Instructional Management System) Global Learning Consortium*: The members come from every sector of the global eLearning community, both commercial and academic. They develop open technical specifications for interoperable learning technology.
- *Aviation Industry CBT Committee (AICC)*: The roots are in the aviation industry, but now they understand themselves as an international association of technology-based training professionals.
- *Institute of Electrical and Electronic Engineers (IEEE) Learning Technology Standards Committee (LTSC)*: Its aim is to develop accredited technical standards, recommended practices and guidelines for learning technology. The membership is open to everybody who is interested.
- *Alliance of Remote Instructional Authoring and Distribution Networks for Europe (ARIADNE)*: The European cooperation consists mostly of universities and other research institutes. The aim is to "enable better quality learning through the development of learning objects, tools and methodologies that enable a "share and reuse" approach for education and training" (http://www.ariadne-eu.org).

In order to coordinate the activities of these groups the Department of Defense of the USA initiated in 1997 the *Advanced Distributed Learning (ADL) Initiative*. One product of this group is the specification SCORM (Shareable Content Object Reference Model). It is a model which demonstrates how such learning content can be exchanged between learning environments without adaptation.

SCORM was first published as "Shareable Courseware Object Reference Model" in January 2000 (version 1.0). Since then, the number of specifications has undergone constant expansion through a cooperative effort of industry, the American government, and academic institutions. SCORM 1.1 was published in January 2001 under its current name, "Shareable Content Object Reference Model". The replacement of Courseware with Content emphasizes the fact that SCORM can now implement different levels of content (entire courses or parts thereof).

The current version of SCORM (version 1.2) is a multiple-section document. Each section is called a "book", whereby each of the books represents a different set of specifications provided by other standards committees.

Book 1 (SCORM Overview) contains an overview of the ADL-initiative, the motivation for SCORM, and a summary of the technical specifications occurring in the remaining books.

Book 2 (SCORM Content Aggregation Model) contains a specification for the creation of metadata for the courses, contents, and media elements. This includes the IMS Learning Resources Metadata Information Model and the IMS Content Packaging Specification. With the aid of these specifications it is possible to meet the requirement for interoperability between different learning environments.

Book 3 (SCORM Run-Time Environment) contains AICC specifications related to the run-time environment, including, amongst others, an API, a communication model for content to learning system, and instructions for the publication and tracking of contents. This complies with the requirement for the reusability and discoverability of the contents.

The upcoming version 1.3 will have a Sequencing Schema, in order to describe how learning content could be sequenced in an interoperable manner. Changes will be made to SCORM 1.2 Meta-data, based on XML binding of LOM of IEEE LTSC. XML binding defines how the SCORM 1.2 Meta-data Information model is interpreted and bound into XML.

LOM is introduced in the following section.

8.11.2 The Metadata Scheme LOM

One of the most promising approaches for metadata describing learning resources is developed by the IEEE Working Group P1484.12, the "Learning Object Metadata (LOM)" scheme. In June 2002 the draft version 6.4 became the international standard ISO/IEC 11404. IMS has provided XML bindings. LOM is mainly influenced by the work of IMS and the ARIADNE Consortium. There are already editors available, e.g., the LOM editor developed by Darmstadt University of Technology [Ste02] (see Figure 8-4), and companies have started to offer free software, e.g., Microsoft's LRN 3.0 Toolkit (http://www.microsoft.com/elearn).

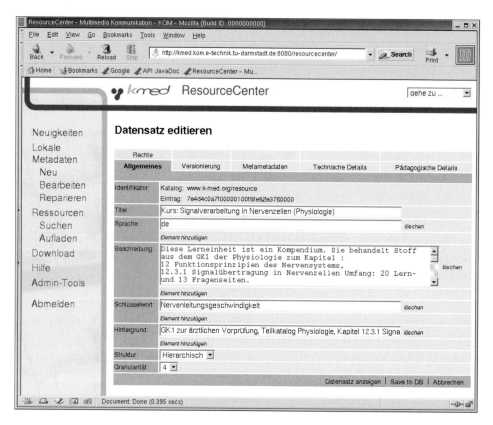

Figure 8-4   Screenshot of the LOM editor by Darmstadt University of Technology

The LOM scheme uses almost every category of Dublin Core (http://dublincore.org), a basic metadata standard and extends it with categories and attributes tailored to the needs of learners and authors searching the Web for material.

The LOM approach specifies the syntax and semantics of Learning Object Metadata. A Learning Object is defined as any entity, digital or non-digital, which can be used, re-used or referenced during technology-supported learning. Examples of technology-supported learning applications include computer-based training systems, interactive learning environments, intelligent computer-aided instruction systems, distance learning systems, web-based learning systems and collaborative learning environments. Examples of Learning Objects include multimedia content, instructional content, instructional software and software tools, referenced during technology supported learning. In a wider sense, Learning Objects could even include learning objectives, persons, organisations, or events. The IEEE LOM standard should conform to, integrate with, or refer to existing open standards and existing work in related areas.

In the LOM specification (http://ltsc.ieee.org/doc/wg12/), the following points are mentioned as the purpose of this standard:

- To enable learners or instructors to search, evaluate, acquire, and utilise Learning Objects.
- To enable the sharing and exchange of Learning Objects across any technology supported learning system.
- To enable the development of learning objects in units that can be combined and decomposed in meaningful ways.
- To enable computer agents to automatically and dynamically compose personalised lessons for an individual learner.
- To complement the direct work on standards that are focused on enabling multiple Learning Objects to work together within an open distributed learning environment.
- To enable, where desired, the documentation and recognition of the completion of existing or new learning & performance objectives associated with Learning Objects.
- To enable a strong and growing economy for Learning Objects that supports and sustains all forms of distribution: non-profit, not-for-profit and for profit.
- To enable education, training and learning organisations, both government, public and private, to express educational content and performance standards in a format that is independent of the content itself.
- To provide researchers with standards that support the collection and sharing of comparable data concerning the applicability and effectiveness of Learning Objects.
- To define a standard that is simple yet extensible to multiple domains and jurisdictions so as to be most easily and broadly adopted and applied.
- To support necessary security and authentication for the distribution and use of Learning Objects."

The definition of LOM divides the more than 60 descriptors of a learning object into nine categories as can be seen in Table 8-2.

LOM categories	Meaning
General	all context-independent features of the resource
LifeCycle	features linked to the lifecycle of the resource
MetaMetaData	features of the description itself (rather than those of the resource being described)
Technical	technical features of the resource
Educational	educational and pedagogic features of the resource
Rights	conditions of use of the resource
Relation	features of the resource that link it to other resources
Annotation	allows for comments on the educational use of the resource
Classification	description of a characteristic of the resource by entries in classifications

Table 8-2 The base scheme of LOM

Taken all together, these categories form what is called the "Base Scheme". As an example the detailed structure of the educational categories are presented in Figure 8-5.

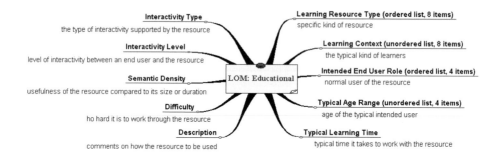

Figure 8-5 LOM category Educational

Some elements like the Description element of the General category allow free text as values, while for other elements the values are restricted to a limited vocabulary.

8.11.2.1 Structures of Learning Material based on LOM

Supporting search machines is not the limitation of metadata. Metadata schemata providing several granularity levels allow for well defined structures of composed learning material. This way, sections, chapters and complete courses can be reused as well as more atomic learning modules. For more details the reader is referred to [HSDK+03].

8.11.2.2 Critical Discussion of LOM

Following Dublin Core, all categories are optional in the LOM scheme. The reason for this is simple. If someone wants to use all categories and attributes from LOM, he has to fill out at least 60 fields. Entries like author, creation date or probably keywords can be filled in automatically by an authoring system. But then there are still many entries left, which the author has to fill himself. The time needed to describe all the properties of a resource is considered as an obstacle to a wide distribution and usage of a metadata scheme. Another problem with the use of a general scheme like LOM is related to special attributes for example the difficulty level (category educational), which should be an integer between 0 and 4. It seems to be almost impossible to find a value for difficulty which is valid in diverse societies and institutions all over the world, even if you can specify a target group with values of other attributes. Furthermore, the difficulty level of a resource depends on the existing knowledge of the user and especially the context in which the resource is used. There are other examples which demonstrate that some of the attributes can only be used in closed systems or special cases. The limited possibilities of a single LOM description to make statements about a resource concerning, for example, the difficulty is that these are important but also very complex educational statements. Using modular learning resources to build individual lessons automatically requires more information than the description of a single resource can provide. Ideas to enhance the category Relation by adding more semantic and didactic relations are developed. Another critical point about the educational category is the fact that it is suitable for traditional learning methods, based on the ideas of a book or a lecture, but not sufficient for constructivist methods like case based learning. But also categories with no educational background have this problem. Also the Rights category does not provide enough information to manage a resource within a commercial scenario.

The reason is that LOM is reducing the needs from all the areas of eLearning to a common denominator. It cannot and it is not meant to provide all information for every scenario. All categories are optional and the Base Scheme is supposed to easily be extended to fit particular needs. LOM is just the common starting point of a growing user community including companies and scientific projects, to share and reuse their existing learning materials and knowledge.

8.12 Closing Remarks

We can currently observe a high degree of euphoria in schools and companies about the possibilities offered by multimedia learning on the computer. It can be expected that educational organizations, publishing companies, software vendors, and media producers will increasingly develop and distribute multimedia learning software.

The use of multimedia system offers an enormous didactic potential, considering the integration of image, sound, and interactivity. For example, multimedia learning environments let you represent the human heart in a live video and in the form of black-and-white functional line drawings directly from the operating room. Depending on the context (i.e., target group or learning objective), both forms of representation are justified. The *potential* pedagogic and didactic benefit of multimedia learning environments is that they allow this wide spectrum of representation forms.

On the other hand, this great potential depends on the implementation of a large number of variables relating to the learning process. And finally, learning is always connected to building or rebuilding behavior, cognitive structures, schemas of action, or experiences. This means that the learner will have to invest considerable time and commitment. After all, learning has never been easy, regardless of the tools available and the amount of "self" in self-learning systems [OW98].

Multimedia Applications

Applications are required for users to be able to interact with multimedia data. This means that applications are of central significance for users of multimedia systems, e.g., a person in search for some information from a kiosk system, or an artist who wants to create a presentation combining music, video, and animation. In all cases, users and data need an application to interact and create, modify and view this data. On the other hand, there is no general or universal approach to classify the large number of existing applications. This chapter introduces a representative set of this wealth and variety of multimedia applications.

One successful theoretical method to classify applications uses the analogy of a *food chain* as a structuring aid (see Figure 9-1). A series of transforms have to be followed, where specific types of applications are used to enable users to interact with multimedia data. First, elements (objects, data contents) from the real world have to be transported into the electronic virtual world (e.g., by scanning photos). This step is called *media preparation*. Once these elements are available in digitized form, i.e., when they can be electronically accessed, they can be modified on the *media preparation* level. This level is also used to add new data which have no counterpart in the real world (e.g., text entered in a computer), separately for each medium. Next, the *media integration* level is used to relate multimedia data originating from many different media (e.g., combining an electronic lexicon with video and audio information). When the multimedia data has been created, we have to deal with the way they can be brought to the user. This is the *media transmission* level. Finally, a user can consume multimedia data in many different ways, where the *media usage* level is represented as the sink.

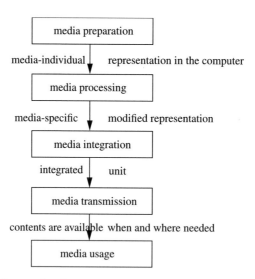

Figure 9-1   Multimedia applications structured as a "food chain".

9.1   Media Preparation

The transition of elements or information from the physical world into the electronic data world requires some kind of a physical "bridge". Such a bridge is normally implemented by special devices, assuming the role of a switching unit between the physical and the virtual worlds. More specifically, information flows over that bridge in two directions, because some hardware is needed to represent multimedia information in the real world. The following sections deal with these two directions, i.e., the transport of information into and from the computer. Each medium uses special input and output devices and appropriate software to implement the transformation of media.

Audio Information   Different types of microphones are the conventional option to transport audible information (speech, music, noise) into the computer (see also Volume 1 Chapter 3). A stronger representation of the spatial sound versus the conventional stereo sound can be reached by using *multi-channel systems* (front-left, center, front-right, rear-right, rear-right, and *subwoofer*). Systems capable of handling speech can be used to recognize and digitize speech information, and virtual reality (VR) applications use VR head sets with built-in microphones and loudspeakers to support sound interaction.

Video Information   Digital cameras are increasingly used to digitize visual information streams. A digital camera can capture both still and motion pictures and store them immediately in digital form. For a digital camera to capture and output images, critical factors are the image resolution, i.e., the number of pixels, the color depth and, above all, the number of single images per second. Monitors in various sizes and resolutions are normally used to output video information, e.g., *media walls* and *beamers*, in addition to standard desktop monitors. Virtual reality technologies use a *head-mounted display* (*HMD*), built into a helmet, which users wear on their heads. In addition, so-called *surround displays* envelop users within their environment, instead of presenting a "flat" information surface. Stereoscopic effects and an adequate response to head movements can be achieved by adding special goggles and head movement sensors to these systems.

Text, Graphic, and Still Image Information   Most information objects in our daily lives are still in paper form, e.g., printed text, hand-written notes, and drawings. To digitize this information we need a scanner. A *scanner* is a device that samples the light points of an object and uses them to create a digital image. When sampling a real object, a scanner always reduces the resolution of that object to a certain extent. *OCR* (*Optical Character Recognition*) programs can be used for information including both drawings or images and text to recognize and store the semantic part of the information in digital form.

2D and 3D Motion Information   There may be situations where we want to digitize both the image of an object and its dynamic properties. For example, to record the movement patterns of a natural human to produce an animation of an artificial human, a user may want to control the representation in a virtual reality room. A so-called *tracker* is a device that allows you to register and record movements and behavior patterns of objects (position, orientation, acceleration). These trackers use electromagnetic markings on objects, ultrasound, or optical methods.

9.2   Media Editing

With the desired media readily digitized and stored in the computer, users normally want to change and adapt them or create new media objects. There are specialized applications for each media type for media editing.

Word Processing   Word processing programs are used to write and modify text. In contrast to the typewriter, a word processor offers the users many different ways to manipulate the content and visual design of a text document. The most important feature of a word processor is that the user can change the content over and over again; text can be arbitrarily deleted, copied, and inserted in different places. The user can change the arrangement and organization of a document easily and quickly, and freely select a layout. The user can select a font type, size and style (e.g., bold or italic), change the line spacing and page format, and use text effects (e.g., shades or patterns). On the other hand, this freedom of choice means that the user is often held responsible both for the content and for the layout of a document. In general, the large number of layout options should be carefully selected and balanced.

Image Editing   Image editing programs offer many options to modify the contents of images. Most functions correspond to the options users are familiar with from working with real images in paper form. For example, an image editor lets you use colors, brushes or various pens, as well as tools to cut, crop and glue image parts. Most modern editors let you modify additional image properties. For example, image sections can be copied an unlimited number of times, and image parts can be skewed, scaled or mirrored. In addition, you can change the color palette to convert an image from color to black and white. Most image editors include artistic tools, e.g., to add perspective to images. On the other hand, one major drawback of conventional image editing software is that a computer treats each image as a table consisting of picture elements (pixels), determined only by their location of x-y coordinate and by their color. For an image editing program, it does not make any difference whether a specific pixel belongs to the background or to a text inside an image, i.e., all pixels are equal. This means that an image editor does not support object-oriented editing, e.g., moving text within an image. To solve this problem, modern image editors use several layers, which can be overlaid or arbitrarily hidden and displayed, similar to color layers. For example, images on one layer can be freely moved to allow a certain degree of quasi object-oriented work.

Graphic Editing   In contrast to images, graphics are nor surfaces consisting of pixels, but of a group of objects. There are various object types, e.g., circles, rectangles, and lines, which can be individually positioned and modified. Of course, images can be embedded as objects. Sophisticated graphic programs include recognition modules capable of recognizing structures in images and transform them into objects. For example, a circle in an image can be converted into a circle object. The major benefit of graphics is that you can change the arrangement of objects much easier than in images, because it is easy to identify and change the properties of objects, e.g., their coordinates.

Animations   Animations use images and graphics as graphical 2D or 3D objects. The additional dimension introduced by animations is *time*, which can also be changed (4D editing). For example, objects can appear and disappear over time, or move on different freely selectable paths and rotated around all axes. Additional functions are available to modify shapes, colors, and other properties. One of the more important aspects of creating movies is the programs' ability to move an object from one location to another, filling in the sections between frames thus creating a smooth animation. This process is called *tweening*. Objects may also be tweened along a set path by linking a normal layer to a motion guide layer for the object to follow along.

Image *morphing*, i.e., the construction of an image sequence depicting a gradual transition between two images, has been extensively investigated. For images generated from 3D models, there is an alternative to morphing the images themselves: 3D morphing generates intermediate 3D models, the *morphs*, directly from the given models; the morphs are then rendered to produce an image sequence depicting the transformation.

Audio Editing   Applications to edit audio data can be roughly classified in two subcategories: *sound applications* take data in the form of sound, noise or speech, while *music applications* use the composition of a song and the allocation of instruments to specific tones. Sound data represents a continuous data stream, from which a user can remove, copy and insert parts, but changing the internal structure of those parts is a major problem. For example, a specific instrument in a sound file cannot simply be controlled to be less loud or entirely mute. Similar to a graphic editing program, a music editor lets you easily modify single structural elements, because a user can access the internal structure (e.g., notes, instruments, volume, or pitch).

Video Editing   Video editing programs use motion picture scenes as their data source. A user can cut, delete and rearrange scenes similarly to working with physical film material. In addition, you can overlay the transitions between scenes with different fade-over effects, or edit sound and video tracks separately.

A special feature of modern video editing programs is *non-linear editing*. This means that a user can specify partial sections from several video sources and use a type of time table to put them together to form a video sequence, without having to copy previous versions of the planned sequence. The playback of this video sequence is then controlled based on table entries. For example, this allows a user to easily create various versions of a video sequence that require little storage space.

9.3   Media Integration

The use of multimedia technology is aimed at combining various continuous and discrete media. For this combination, special applications are available, allowing this integration normally in the form of a multimedia document.

Multimedia Editors   Multimedia editors offer the functionality required to edit and integrate multimedia documents and their components (e.g., structured text, multi-font text, images, graphics, video or digitized sound). Most applications of this type use the WYSIWYG (What You See Is What You Get) principle, allowing fast and reliable editing of a document's presentation. The following properties are important for multimedia editors:

- *Standardized document structure*: The functionality of an application depends largely on the structure of the multimedia document. To ensure that documents can be exchanged, for example within computer-supported cooperative work (CSCW), it is important to select a standardized format for document storage.
- *Integration of media editors*: Each medium has its own structure, so that multimedia editors use a series of special media add-ons supported within an integrated GUI. The components (menus, icons, buttons, text) of that GUI should be uniform

and consistent. In addition, it should support the transfer of data from one media type to another type.

- *Multi-window interface*: Users often need to edit several multimedia data types at the same time. For this purpose, an editing window is opened for each of the objects to be edited. This means that the GUI should support multiple active windows for different media types.

Hypermedia/Hypertext Editors   Hypermedia/hypertext documents consist of multimedia data and non-linear links between information. The data is structured and stored in a database or a standard format. Note that this data may be stored in more than one location, i.e., information could be distributed over several locations. For the user to view these hypermedia documents, it is necessary to integrate a network service into the links, similarly to the World Wide Web.

Authoring Tools   Imagine an application that controls a multimedia presentation. This application has to have a dynamic behavior and be capable of responding to specific user inputs. To implement such an application that meets these dynamic requirements, we would have to program several processes. This type of application can be written either in a programming language or implemented by use of an authoring system (e.g., [BKC01]).

An *authoring system* is a set of software tools embedded in an authoring environment. A person who creates applications for media integration, e.g., a presentation, is called an *author*. When using an authoring system to create a multimedia application, the underlying process involves several steps (see Figure 9-2).

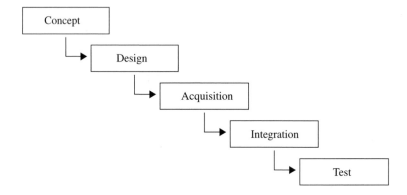

Figure 9-2   The phases of a design process.

- *Conception*: This step defines the target groups, the type (e.g., presentation or interaction), the purpose (e.g., inform, entertain, or teach), and the general context of the application.

- *Design*: This step defines the style and exact content of the application. The specifications should be described in detail to prevent interruptions in the subsequent steps, i.e., acquisition and integration. The authoring system can support the design documentation by storing information required for the next editing steps, e.g., structuring the application, creating storyboards and flow charts, sorting pages, and other descriptions.

- *Acquisition of contents*: This step collects and enters content into the authoring system. In general, this includes the creation of images, video sequences, and sound tracks. If all materials needed are available in digitized form, then the user does not need applications for media preparation. These digitized media can be imported directly into the internal format of the authoring system by use of a conversion tool. In contrast, if the author has to create new content, then most authoring systems offer tools for this purpose (text generation, image and graphic editing, audio and video editing). However, many of these programs reach only a limited part of the functionality available in specialized applications.

- *Integration*: This step integrates the application into a multimedia presentation. Beyond the design of pages and user guidance, this often requires the implementation of functions to add more interaction behavior to the application. Most authoring systems include their own languages, partly offering the complexity and flexibility of programming languages.

- *Test*: This step is used to test the new application. Sophisticated authoring systems offer additional functions, e.g., gradual testing or verifying links within the application.

9.4 Media Transmission

Media transmission refers to applications that use tele-services (e.g., video conferences or e-mail) to transport the set of different media over a network to multimedia end users, or exchange such media between users (see also "Multimedia Systems" Chapters 5, 6, and 7). The major benefit of tele-services in multimedia applications is that users can exchange information and interface with remote data or devices, although they are located in different locations. The (current) drawback is that the response time of a tele-service is longer than the processing time of a local multimedia application. For example, the time from the request to the start of a video conference is normally longer when it is initiated from a video server instead from a secondary storage on the local computer. For this reason, a trade-off has to be found between the choice of a location and short processing times.

Tele-services are provided by communication systems based on audio and video data. These systems can be divided into two categories: interactive services and distribution services.

9.4.1   Interactive Services

Interactive services include the exchange of control information between remote stations to control the presentation of continuous media streams. Communication between the sender and the receiver can be *synchronous*, which means that the data is exchanged within a defined time, or *asynchronous*, which means that the data can arrive at an arbitrary time. For example, video conference applications use synchronous communication, while e-mail uses asynchronous communication.

With regard to the tasks they handle, interactive services are roughly classified in *conversation services* (e.g., video conferences), *messaging services* (e.g., e-mail), *query services* (e.g., digital libraries), and *tele-action services* (e.g., electronic banking). We will briefly describe these services below.

- *Conversation services*: A conversation service supports the dialog between remote users. It allows this over a bidirectional communication between the sender and the receiver, exchanging data streams synchronously. In this communication, it is important to minimize the transmission time to ensure that the natural flow of the dialog is not interrupted.

- *Messaging services*: A messaging service handles the exchange of messages between senders and receivers, where the users are humans. Messages exchanged in both directions asynchronously, and the time can be specified in advance. Users can send messages at any given time, so that it is not necessary to minimize the transmission time. These messages can contain all common types of digital media.

- *Query services*: A query service allows the exchange of messages between a sender and a receiver, where the sender — in this case called *client* — is a human user and the receiver — in this case called server — is a computer providing access to a database. The client requests information from a server, which stores the required information, and the server returns this information to the client.

  This is a bidirectional communication, being asynchronous from the client to the server, because this path does normally not define time limits. Communication from the server to the client can be either asynchronous or synchronous, depending on the requested media. If the client requests only textual information, then this communication can be asynchronous, i.e., it can be handled within a relatively unlimited time. In contrast, if the requested information includes continuous media, then that communication has to be synchronous, because it has to arrive "in-sync", i.e., the audio and video streams of a video film should arrive at the user machine concurrently. In the user's interest, the response times should generally be as short as possible.

- *Tele-action services*: Tele-action means "acting from a distance"; such actions are, for example, reading and writing information from/to a remote computer. Instead of dispatching a person to this distant location, the user can interact remotely with that computer. Tele-action services are used in many applications, including:

- Transactions in credit card management, ATMs, electronic banking.
- Business automation, e.g., access to medical and legal databases or real-estate databases.
- Monitoring and alarm systems, e.g., fire alarms, observation of risk patients, weather stations, or status and consumer meters for gas, water and electricity.
- Control of light systems, thermostats, industrial plants, hospital equipment.

9.4.2 Multimedia Distribution Services

These services are used to distribute information from one location to several remote locations. These services use unidirectional communication from the sending source to the receiving stations. Radio and television are popular examples for distribution services.

The technology enabling these services tends to move towards more interaction between the sender and the receivers, approximating interactive services. The reason is that the introduction of *video-on-demand* led to more control on the user side:

- *Pay-per-View*: Cable television customers can use a decoder to view different movies, where they pay for the movies they actually consumed. However, the user has no control over the broadcasted movie, except the decision to watch it.
- *Near Video-on-Demand*: This service broadcasts the same movie over several channels at slightly different times. The user can switch between channels and jump forward and backward within the movie.
- *True Video-on-Demand*: This service provides the ultimate flexibility in video services, allowing users to select any video program at any time, and to perform VCR-like user interactions.

The first two types of service do not require any adaptation of conventional cable TV networks. The third service requires special equipment to support the exchange of information in both directions.

9.5 Media Usage

Media usage means interacting or seeing, hearing and feeling multimedia information. Seeing and hearing are certainly the most common type of media usage, while feeling multimedia information could be experienced in a movement-controlled amusement park, using virtual reality technology.

This section concentrates on the visual consumption of multimedia information (e.g., presentations). A presentation of multimedia information is often created in authoring systems, but they could also be based on other applications. The main requirements of media usage, which actually have to be met by any multimedia application, are user *friendliness* and *easiness of use*. This means that the application used for the presentation should be easy to learn and operate. Particularly when introducing interfaces using new media, the user should be offered a familiar way of interaction, because most users prefer applications with interaction options equal or similar to familiar applications.

Multimedia documents are normally read in either of two different ways: superficially or in detail (e.g., in search sessions).

- *Superficial reading* means that a user browses through a document quickly in an attempt to find out what kind of information it contains. For example, many users read only the headlines in newspapers or the table of contents in a book or the abstract in a scientific article. This reading behavior can also be supported in multimedia document by using appropriate functions (e.g., tables of contents, graphical structures, different levels of detail, summaries, or short excerpts).
- *Detailed search* means that a user needs specific functions to access the entire content. This can be supported by displaying the full content and providing search functions, index lists, and cross references.

Chapter 6 includes a discussion of the design issues with regard to viewing multimedia documents. The following sections deal with typical multimedia applications in more detail, i.e., electronic books and magazines, kiosk systems, tele-shopping, and entertainment.

9.5.1 Electronic Books and Magazines

Books and magazines can be interactive multimedia documents delivered electronically to the user, who can then print this data on paper or view on a computer. Instead of distributing the same version of a magazine to all readers, the electronic access to that data can be linked to a *user profile*. This allows the creation of a special version adapted to the requirements of a user, thus saving paper and offering a more personalized choice. In addition, the user will always have access to the latest news, as data is constantly updated on the information server. Although these are important benefits, current experiments have shown that many readers are not interested in personalized adaptations of contents and still prefer paper copies.

9.5.2 Kiosks

A *kiosk* is a computer-based system designed for public access, allowing users to retrieve information and do transactions, where access is preferably anonymous [Hol97]. There are two fundamental requirements for these applications: the user interface should be simple and the response time to user requests should be short.

Most kiosk users are inexperienced computer users, so that it is important to allow fast, intuitive, and effective interaction. A major prerequisite is therefore a clear and simple user interface (see also Chapter 9 and Chapter 7).

The components of a kiosk system vary strongly, depending on the application. A basic system is composed of a multimedia computer, including loudspeakers and a touch-sensitive screen. An expanded configuration would include a keyboard, printer, and camera as well as devices for special applications, e.g., to read check cards or change currency.

Typical applications for information-providing kiosk systems include airport or railroad station kiosks with timetables, museum kiosks with information about current and future exhibitions, bank kiosks informing people about new financial services and savings plans, cinema kiosks with information about current movies, kiosks in department stores with information about new products and floor plans, and real-estate kiosks featuring catalogs or images and videos about real-estate offers.

Kiosk systems can be used as ticket booking systems to reserve transport or admission tickets, and banking systems for customers to control their financial transactions. Many modern kiosk systems are based on the World Wide Web, although this is not always desirable, e.g., for security reasons.

9.5.3 Tele-Shopping

Tele-shopping allows users to shop from the comfort of their homes. For example, a user with a computer and Internet access can connect to a database server to browse a multimedia catalog and order products. These products can be presented in the form of video and sound, or images with a descriptive text. The user can select, order, and pay for products electronically. Tele-shopping is frequently used in retail, ticket sale (e.g., theaters, cinemas, concerts, or travel bookings) and classified ads.

9.5.4 Entertainment

Entertainment is one of the most important applications for multimedia technology. Many users spend more money for computer games than for office applications, and the purchase and installation of special expansions, e.g., stereo sound cards and graphic accelerators, has become an important business, mainly because hardware requirements increase continually. The visualization effects enabled by multimedia result in a new application quality for computers, representing an important expansion of conventional entertainment media, such as cinema or television, because the user has additional interaction options. Virtual reality, interactive video/audio, and computer games have become the most important multimedia entertainment applications.

Virtual Reality   The term *virtual reality* (*VR*) promises more than current technology can offer. The term has been used in many different ways for a specific type of user interfaces: on the one hand for artificial environments presented over *head-mounted* *displays* (*HMD*) and, on the other hand, for traditional animated computer graphics on conventional screens and even for text-based multi-user games.

Computer-based virtual reality systems in the context of this book are three-dimensional, interactive (as opposed to passive), and use one or more devices (visual, acoustic or haptic) to give the user a feeling of presence. In addition, a *data glove* can be used to control head movements, video and audio, and haptic feedback by devices generating pressure and counter-pressure.

One of the major problems of current VR applications is that they require enormous computer power to calculate complex environments and their objects in realistic quality and speed. Another problem is that conventional display devices do not support the graphic resolution required to create a photo-realistic impression of virtual worlds.

Interactive Video   Research and development efforts in the field of interactive video concentrate on issues regarding *interactive television* and *video-on-demand*. Interactive television refers to cable and wireless television, while video-on-demand concerns television broadcasting on the computer.

Interactive television offers the user a much higher degree of influence, compared to the conventional TV technology. In the simplest case, users can "produce" the program they are interested in themselves. For example, a user could select the set of different camera positions of a broadcasted sports event and add information about the team or players. Or a user could define different levels of detail in a school TV program for lesions or degrees of difficulty for test questions. The implementation of interactive television requires several technical solutions, because wireless television utilizes the full bandwidth, so that there are no capacities available for additional channels. This means that special cable channels have to be provided and subscribed by the user, or data have to be ordered directly from a telecommunication service. In either case, a decoder and additional devices have to be used to decode the signal and communicate with the TV station or producer.

Video-on-Demand (*VoD*) is a service offering video information from one or more video servers. A user can select a movie from a catalog and has VCR-like control over the movie. The directness and speed of interaction are some of the most important quality criteria. The communication structure of a VoD connection is asymmetric, because the main stream from the server to the user requires much more bandwidth than the control information from the user to the server.

Interactive Audio   Similar to VoD, interactive audio is a service offering the user a choice of several titles stored on an audio server, normally including music clips and speech clips. The audio information is transmitted over a network to the user, who can play it back and control (start, stop, forward, backward). Similar to VoD, the connection is implemented by streaming technology. *Streaming* means that the audio and video data does not have to be fully received before it can be played. In fact, the data stream can be controlled while data is being sent, so that the user can skip forward and backward as if this data was available locally (see also Volume 2 Chapter 4 and 6).

Computer Games Modern computer games are programs with audiovisual output, and capable of managing dynamic system models. In contrast to normal applications, computer games often hide part of the information about internal states to increase the challenge for the player. Games are normally based on interactivity between the computer and the user (e.g., [HB01], [VM01], [PSW01]).

Computer games can be classified by the storage location, the degree in which the environment is represented, and the number of players. Some games are stored and executed on the local computer, while others are stored and executed on different computers (tele-games). With regard to how the environment is represented, there are interactive game environments using traditional audiovisual components, and games that integrate sophisticated VR technologies (VR helmets, data gloves, surround sound). With regard to the number of players, there are games for one single player and games where two players can use different input devices to control the computer concurrently. In addition, there are games that use networks for synchronous connection of many players, so that the players get a feeling that they are all acting jointly in an artificial world.

9.6 Case Study: i-LAND

i-LAND is an interactive cooperation environment for creative, innovative and multimedia work. This section introduces i-LAND as a case study representing the role and appearance of a multimedia computer in the working world of the future.

In 1997, the Institute for Integrated Publication and Information Systems (IPSI) at the Fraunhofer Gesellschaft in Darmstadt, Germany, initiated a workgroup for the development of innovative work environments that adapt dynamically to different work situations.

9.6.1 Motivation

Future side conditions of work (and cooperation) will be characterized by flexibility and dynamics far beyond the scope of current developments. "On-demand" and "ad-hoc" teams, virtual organizations, spatially distributed and mobile collaborators are a few examples for this trend. Contents and participants as well as contexts, processes, and structures of future cooperation will change in many different ways. These design developments and the flexibly and dynamically configurable work environments should be addressed from the technical view.

The introduction of information and communication technology has changed many work flows and contents. In contrast, the design of work worlds, particularly in the sense of practical work environments (e.g., offices, buildings) has remained almost unchanged, and very little has been oriented to the early integration of information and communication technologies. For the new forms of work to develop at high standards, we need task, user, and group-oriented designs of innovative information and communication technologies (hardware, software, networks), and a coordinated interplay based on high-performing spatial and physical structures. This integration of information and communication technologies into the physical environment is called *roomware* [SGH98].

The i-LAND cooperation environment is an example for a possible work world of the future. It is based on an integrated design of real environments and virtual information rooms, offering dynamically configurable and flexibly available resources for project teams (e.g., on-demand and ad-hoc teams). The system supports two main issues: Development of roomware components and specific software tools to support multimedia group work, particularly for creative teams. Figure 9-3 is a schematic view of the ideas of i-LAND in the conceptional planning phase.

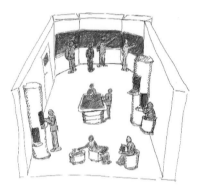

Figure 9-3 Example of the i-LAND environment with subgroups and single persons working in parallel.

One central idea is to support different phases of team work, e.g., presentation for the entire group, parallel work in subgroups, research conducted by single persons, and collating and discussing the results. To support such phases, the system uses modular elements, which can be used individually or combined dynamically. This is the responsibility of the roomware concept.

9.6.2 The Roomware Concept

Roomware means interior objects, such as furniture, doors or walls, equipped with integrated computers and optionally communicating over wireless networks. The current implementation of i-LAND includes an interactive electronic wall (*Dynawall*), an interactive table (*InteracTable*), and two chairs with integrated computers (*CommChairs*).

9.6.3   The DynaWall

The *DynaWall* is an interactive electronic wall based on a touch-sensitive representation surface in a size of 4.50 m wide and 1.10 m high (see Figure 9-4). The availability of large representation surfaces is very important in most visual tasks. DynaWall is an innovative way to let you visualize both complex information structures and several persons interacting with this information. Two or more persons can use the entire representation surface independently or concurrently. The size of the DynaWall adds a new dimension to human-computer interaction. For examples, information objects can be moved from one point of the wall to another, or shuffled from one side to another, where the users always see dialog windows.

Figure 9-4   Example with DynaWall and two CommChairs.

9.6.4   The InteracTable

The *InteracTable* is the first prototype of a series of computer-based components that dispose of an arbitrarily shaped representation and interaction surface with no defined orientation (see Figure 9-5).

Figure 9-5   Example with InteracTable.

The table was designed for discussions and annotations of electronic material, where people can stand around the table. Information objects displayed on the table surface can be rotated and moved. The participants can use gestures or hand movements to interact. A pen, an infrared keyboard or speech can be used to add annotations.

9.6.5 The CommChair

The *CommChair* represents a new type of seat. Two variants were available with the initial introduction of i-LAND: one with integrated computer and another one with connector to connect laptops in the form of an integrated docking station (see Figure 9-6).

Figure 9-6   Example with two variants of the CommChair.

To ensure maximum mobility, each chair has an interface for wireless networks and a self-contained power supply. The participants can use CommChairs to connect their jointly used work areas or connect to the DynaWall and the InteracTable. At the same time, they can write notes or annotations within their private work areas. Sensors are used to automatically position the CommChairs in a room, identify the participants through the chairs, and establish a network connection between CommChairs.

9.6.6 Software for Creativity and Innovation

While the functionality of roomware components can be adapted to different situations, a special application scenario was selected for the software. This scenario reflects the work of *creative teams* or small workgroups within an organization handling creative tasks, e.g., planning new products or marketing strategies. Several of these teams were interviewed within a study to define their requirements to the work environment and software [SRH98]. To meet the requirements identified in this study, the system's software tools were designed and developed to contain the desired functions (creativity techniques, project and time management, visualization and presentation options). The tools were developed on the basis of tools previously developed by GMD-IPSI, e.g., DOLPHIN [SGHH94]; they reflect the findings from empirical evaluations of various versions of DOLPHIN [MHS97, SRH97]. These tools are used in connection with new interaction techniques and visualization metaphors and the options offered by innovative roomware components. In addition, this software supports the use of knowledge bases, including the proprietary GMD product—*Organizational Group Memories*—and external databases.

9.6.7 Dynamic Offices

Earlier experimental studies regarding the support of group work in so-called *electronic conference rooms* [MHS97, SRH97] showed that a possibility for flexible change between individual work, subgroup work and plenum situations leads to better results in group work. It is therefore believed that this aspect should be supported both by the software functionality and the design or work environments.

The *dynamic offices* concept of i-LAND utilizes the modularity and mobility of the roomware components. This means that the components can be configured in a dynamic way within a room to support changing group situations of a team and different teams. This configuration is not limited to the combination of roomware components; it also supports "playing" with these components in the software to create different cooperation environments in line with the different sets of contents and team tasks. This means that a room can be used as a quasi-permanent project room for different teams and projects; at the same time, it is available for other purposes, e.g., as a multimedia presentation and information room for customers and visitors.

9.6.8 The Role of Computers in i-LAND

The i-LAND environment is based on an innovative approach, corresponding to the requirements of empirical studies. The computer functionality within the roomware concept is available over integrated information devices across the entire team work space (or across the building, as originally planned), i.e., i-LAND implements *ubiquitous computing*. At the same time, these computers are *invisible*, because they are integrated in the architecture of the room, *augmenting* the physical reality or adding functionality. The modularity and mobility (except DynaWall) of the components, combined with cooperative software communicating over wireless networks, offer flexible configurations that can be composed or modified depending on the phases or activities of team work.

This means that i-LAND offers an unprecedented amount of flexibility, combined with the characteristics of the roomware components, leading to innovative forms of human-computer interaction or a new quality of team-information interaction.

9.7   Closing Remarks

We can observe the following trends in current multimedia applications:

- In the future, multimedia applications will be more oriented to distributed multi-user environments.
- Current multimedia applications depend on the underlying platform and system. The trend is towards open solutions, so that applications can be ported to different platforms.
- In contrast to the current passive use, media will be used actively, where the user can increasingly decide which media they want to consume where, how and when.
- Media communication will shift from *unidirectional* to *bidirectional* information flows, e.g., games and interactive television.

And finally, multimedia research and development should bear in mind that even the best and most advanced system properties are appreciated by users only provided that there are useful and exciting applications. A look into the past discloses, for example, that when Alexander Graham Bell invented the telephone, its main application was originally to hear a concert. For this reason, this chapter merely discussed and categorized multimedia applications as representative examples, without expressing opinion of what makes a multimedia application the best.

Bibliography

[Abi97]   S. Abiteboul. Querying semi-structured data. *ICDT*, pages 1–18, 1997.

[AC91]   D. Anderson and P. Chan. Toolkit Support for Multiuser Audio/Video Applications. In R.G. Herrtwich, editor, *Proceedings from 2nd International Workshop on Network and Operating System Support for Digital Audio and Video*, pages 230–241, Heidelberg, Germany, November 1991. Springer-Verlag.

[AC97]   A. Analyti and S. Christodoulakis. *Multimedia Databases in Perspective*, chapter Content-Based Querying. Springer-Verlag, London, 1997.

[ACF+96]   M. Arya, W. Cody, C. Faloutsos, J. Richardson, and A. Toga. *Issues and Research Directions*, chapter The QBISM Medical Image DBMS MMDBMSs. Springer-Verlag, Berlin-Heidelberg, 1996.

[Adi96]   M. Adiba. *Design and Implementation Strategies*, chapter STORM: An Object-Oriented Multimedia DBMS, MMDBMSs. Kluwer Academic Publishers, Dortrecht/London, 1996.

[AG96]   I. Agi and L. Gong. An Empirical Study of Secure MPEG Video Transmissions. In *ISOC Symposium on Network and Distributed System Security*, San Diego, CA, 1996.

[AK94]   K. Aberer and K. Klas. Supporting temporal multimedia operations in object-oriented database systems. In *IEEE International Conference on Multimedia Computing Systems*, Boston, USA, May 1994.

[And93]   J. R. Anderson. *Rules of the Mind.* Lawrence Erlbaum, Hillsdale, NJ, 1993.

[App90]   W. Appelt. *Dokumentenaustausch in Offenen Systemen.* Springer-Verlag, Berlin, Heidelberg, New York, 1990.

[AT97]   F. Asnicar and C. Tasso. ifWeb: a Prototype of User Model-Based Intelligent Agent for Document Filtering and Navigation in the World Wide Web in Adaptive Systems and User Modeling on the World Wide Web. In *Workshop Proceedings, 6th International Conference on User Modeling,* Cagliari, Italien, June 1997.

[ATM97]   ATM_Forum. *Phase 1 ATM Security Specification (3rd Draft),.* ATM Forum, 1997. BTD-SEC-01.03.

[BA94]   K. Böhm and K. Aberer. An Object-Oriented Database Application for HyTime Document Structure. In *Proceedings of Third International Conference on Information and Knowledge Management,* Gaithersburg, MD, USA, Nov. 29 - Dec. 1 1994.

[BAK97]   K. Böhm, K. Aberer, and W. Klas. Building a hybrid database application for structured documents. *Multimedia - Tools and Applications,* 1997.

[BAN95]   K. Böhm, K. Aberer, and E.J. Neuhold. *Administering Structured Documents in Digital Libraries Advances in Digital Libraries,* volume 916 of *Lecture Notes in Computer Science.* Springer-Verlag, 1995.

[BANY97]   K. Böhm, K. Aberer, E.J. Neuhold, and X. Yang. Structured Document Storage and Refined Declarative and Navigational Access Mechanisms in HyperStorM. *VLDB Journal,* 6, 1997.

[BE98]   C. Boyle and A. O. Encarnacion. *Adaptive Hypertext and Hypermedia,* chapter Metadoc: An Adaptive Hypertext Reading System. Kluwer Academic Publishers, 1998.

[BHK+02]   A. P. Black, J. Huang, R. Koster, J. Walpole, and C. Pu. Infopipes: An abstraction for multimedia streaming. *ACM Springer Multimedia Systems,* 8(5):406–419, 2002.

[BHLM92]   P. Binstadt, W. Henhapl, J. Löffler, and U.A. Michelsen. *Informations- und kommunikationstechnische Grundbildung: Konzeptionen — Konkretionen — Gestaltungsvorschläge.* Leuchtturm, Alsbach/Bergstraße, 1992.

[BKC01]   B. Bailey, J. A. Konstan, and J. V. Carlis. DEMAIS: designing multimedia applications with interactive storyboards. In *Proceedings of the 9th ACM International Conference on Multimedia 2001*, pages 241–250, Ottawa, Canada, 2001.

[BKS97]   E. Benaki, V.A. Karkaletsis, and C.D. Spyropoulos. User Modeling in WWW: the UMIE Prototype in Adaptive Systems and User Modeling on the World Wide Web. In *Workshop Proceedings, 6th International Conference on User Modeling*, Cagliari, Italien, June 1997.

[BKV98]   P. Brusilovsky, A. Kobsa, and J. Vassileva. *Methods and Techniques of Adaptive Hypermedia*. Kluwer Academic Publishers, 1998.

[Bla91]   G. Blakowski. Concept of a Language for the Description of Transport and (Re-)presentation properties of Multimedia Objects. *(in German) Informatik Fachberichte*, 293:465–474, 1991. Springer-Verlag.

[BMBLY97] D. Benham, N. Memon, B.-L. Yeo B.-L., and M. Yeung. Fast Watermarking of DCT-based Compressed Images. In *CISST '97 International Conference*, 1997.

[Böh97]   K. Böhm. *Managing Multimedia Data: Using Metadata to Integrate and Apply Digital Data*, chapter Metadata Handling in HyperStorM. 1997.

[BR86]   S. Bly and J.K. Rosenberg. A comparison of tiled and overlapping windows. In *Proceedings CHI 1986*, pages 101–106, 1986.

[BR94]   K. Böhm and T. C. Rakow. Metadata for multimedia documents. *ACM SIGMOD Record Special Issue on Metadata for Digital Media*, 23(4):21 – 26, Dec 1994.

[Bra87]   S. Brand. *The Media Lab, Inventing the Future at MIT*. Viking Penguin, 1987.

[Bra96]   E. Brauer. Akzeptierbare Sicherheit. *UNIX open*, January 1996.

[BRD91]   BRD. Bundesdatenschutzgesetz, 1991.

[BSW95]   Beutelspacher, Schwenk, and Wolfenstetter. *Moderne Verfahren der Kryptographie*. Vieweg-Verlag, 1995.

[BTH96]   L. Boney, A. H. Tewfik, and K.N. Hamdy. Digital Watermarks for Audio Signals. In *Proc. of IEEE Multimedia* , pages 473–480, 1996.

[BWPSW98] J. Beck-Wilson, H.-R. Pfister, C. Schuckmann, and M. Wessner. Bridging the gap: Incorporating work and learning using cooperative learning environments. In *Proceedings of the BITE 98*, pages 443 – 450, Maastricht, Netherlands, March 25-27 1998.

[Car95]   G. Caronni. Assuring Ownership Rights for Digital Images. In *Verläßliche IT-Systeme, Proceedings der GI-Fachtagung VIS'95*, 1995.

[CB88]   J. Conklin and M. L. Begeman. gIBIS: A Hypertext Tool for Exploratory Policy Discussion. *ACM Transaction on Office Information Systems*, 6(4):303–331, October 1988.

[CB97]   R. Carey and G. Bell. *The annotated VRML 2.0 Reference Manual*. Addison-Wesley, 1997.

[CBM02]   G. Coulson, S. Baichoo, and O. Moonian. A retrospective on the design of the GOPI middleware platform. *ACM Springer Multimedia Systems*, 8(5):340–352, 2002.

[CC96]   H.J. Chang and S. K. Chang. *Multimedia Information Storage and Management*, chapter Temporal Modelling and Intermedia Synchronization for Presentation of Multimedia Streams. Kluwer Academic Publishers, 1996.

[CG87]   B. Campbell and M. Goodman. HAM: A General Purpose Hypertext Abstract Machine. In *Hypertext '87*, November 1987.

[Cha03]   Y. Chawathe. Scattercast: an adaptable broadcast distribution framework. *ACM Springer Multimedia Systems*, 9(1):104–118, 2003.

[Che95]   C.Y.R. Chen. Design of a Multimedia Object-Oriented DBMS. *Multimedia Systems*, 3(5-6):217– 227, 1995.

[Chi86]   D. Chin. User Modelling in UC: the UNIX Consultant. In *Proceedings of the CHI-86 Conference*, Boston, 1986.

[CHT86]   S. Christodoulakis, F. Ho, and M. Theodoridou. The Multimedia Object Presentation Manager of MINOS: A Symmetric Approach. In *Proc. Int. Conf. on Management of Data*, pages 295–310, Washington, 1986.

[CJT96]   S.-K. Chang, E. Jungert, and S.-K. Tortora. Intelligent image database systems. *World Scientific*, 1996.

[CKLS97]   I.J. Cox, J. Kilian, T. Leighton, and T. Shamoon. Secure Spread Spectrum Watermarking for Multimedia. *IEEE Trans. on Image Processing*, 6(12):1673–1687, 1997.

[CL97]   I.J. Cox and J-P Linnartz. Some general methods for tampering with watermarks. *IEEE Journal Selected Areas of Communications (JSAC)*, 1997.

[Com95]   D.E. Comer. *Internetworking with TCP/IP*. Prentice Hall, Englewood Cliffs, 1995.

[Con]   Hermes Consortium. Esprit long term research project no. 9141.

[Dan97]   R. L. Danielson. Work in Progress: Learning Styles, Media Preferences and Adaptive Education in Adaptive Systems and User Modeling on the World Wide Web. In *Workshop Proceedings, 6th International Conference on User Modeling*, Cagliari, Italien, June 1997.

[deC98]   L. deCarmo. A new architecture for multimedia. *PC Magazine*, 6, 98.

[DH95]   S. Deering and R. Hinden. *Internet Protocol, Version 6 (IPv6) Specification*, 1995. RFC 1883.

[DH98]   J. Dittmann and M. Haberhauer. working paper. Technical report, GMD, 1998.

[DJ91]   T.M. Duffy and D.H. Jonassen. Constructivism: New implications for instructional technology? *Educational Technology*, 31:7–12, 1991.

[DNSS98]   J. Dittmann, F. Nack, A. Steinmetz, and R. Steinmetz. Interactive Watermarking Environments. In *IEEE Multimedia Systems Conference (ICMS'98)*, Austin Texas, June/July 1998.

[DS97a]   J. Dittmann and A. Steinmetz. Konzeption von Sicherheitsmechanismen für das Projekt DiVidEd. *D-Studie Nr. 312*, 1997.

[DS97b]   J. Dittmann and A. Steinmetz. Sicherheitsproblematik in verteilten, digitalen Videoanwendungen und Präsentation eines technischen Lösungsansatzes zur transparenten Verschlüsselung von MPEG-2 Video. *Verläßliche IT-Systeme: Zwischen Key Escrow und elektronischem Geld, DuD Fachbeiträge, Vieweg-Verlag*, pages 157–170, 1997.

[DSS98]   J. Dittmann, M. Stabenau, and R. Steinmetz. Robust MPEG Video Copyright Protection Technology. In *submitted to the SEC'98 14th International Information Security Conference*, August-September 1998.

[EFSS]   KLaus-Peter Eckert, Marinko Festini, Peter Schoo, and Gerd Schürmann. TANGRAM: Development of object-oriented frameworks for TINA-C based multimedia telecommunication application. In *Proceedings of the 3rd Symposium on Autonomous Decentralized Systems (ISADS'97)*, Berlin, Germany, April 9–11.

[EK03]   S. Emmanuel and M. S. Kankanhalli. A digital rights management scheme for broadcast video. *ACM Springer Multimedia Systems*, 8(6):444–458, 2003.

[fGD95]   Frauenhofer-Institut für Graphische Datenverarbeitung. *Informationsblatt TIE*, 1995. http:// www.igd.fhg.de/www/igd-a8/projects/tie/tie.htm.

[FJP97]   E. Franz, A. Jerichow, and A. Pfitzmann. Systematisierung und Modellierung von Mixen. *Verläßliche IT-Systeme: Zwischen Key Escrow und elektronischem Geld, DuD Fachbeiträge, Vieweg-Verlag*, pages 171–190, 1997.

[FKS97]   J. Fink, A. Kobsa, and J. Schreck. Personalized Hypermedia Information Provision through Adaptive and Adaptable System Features: User Modeling, Privacy and Security Issues in Adaptive Systems and User Modeling on the World Wide Web. In *Workshop Proceedings, 6th International Conference on User Modeling*, Cagliari, Italien, June 1997.

[Flu95]   F. Fluckinger. *Understanding networked multimedia applications and technology.* Prentice Hall, 1995.

[FOS98]   F. Friedl, N. Ott, and B. Stein. *Typography - when who how.* Könemann, Köln, 1998.

[Fri93]   G. L. Friedmann. The Trustworthy Digital Camera: Restoring Credibility to the Photographic Image. *IEEE Transactions on Consumer Electronics*, 39(4):905 – 910, November 1993.

[Fri97]   J. Fridrich. Methods for data hiding. *Center for Intelligent Systems & Department for System Science and Industrial Engineering, SUNY Binghamton*, 1997.

[FSBS98]   S. Fischer, A. Steinacker, R. Bertram, and R. Steinmetz. *Open Security.* Springer-Verlag, Heidelberg, 1998.

[FT88]   E. Fiume and D. Tsichritzis. Multimedia Objects. In D. Tsichritzis, editor, *Active Object Environment*, pages 121–128. June 1988.

[FWC84]   J. D. Foley, V.L. Wallace, and P. Chan. The human factors of computer graphics interaction techniques. *IEEE Computer Graphics & Applications*, pages 13–48, November 1984.

[GBD+91]   S. Gibbs, Ch. Breiteneder, L. Dami, V. de May, and D. Tscichritzis. A Programming Environment for Multimedia Applications. In *2nd International Workshop on Network and Operating System Support for Digital Audio and Video*, Heidelberg, Germany, November 1991.

[GCD02]   R. Grigoras, V. Charvillat, and M. Douze. Optimizing hypervideo naviga-
            tion using a Markov decision process approach. In *Proceedings of the
            10th ACM International Conference on Multimedia 2002*, pages 39–48,
            Juan les Pins, France, 2002.

[GEE97]   W. Geyer, A. Eckert, and W. Effelsberg. Multimedia-Technologie zur
            Unterstützung der Lehre an Hochschulen: Das Projekt TeleTeaching der
            Universitäten Mannheim und Heidelberg. *Multimediales Lernen in der
            Beruflichen Bildung*, 1997.

[GELP99]   V. Goebel, I. Eini, K. Lund, and T. Plagemann. Design, implementation,
            and application of toomm: A temporal object-oriented multimedia data
            model. In *8th IFIP 2.6 Working Conference on Database Semantics (DS-
            8), Semantic Issues in Multimedia Systems*, Rotorua, New Zealand, Janu-
            ary 1999. Kluwer.

[GG02]   H. Guo and N. D. Georganas. Digital image watermarking for joint own-
            ership. In *Proceedings of the 10th ACM International Conference on Mul-
            timedia 2002*, pages 362–371, Juan les Pins, France, 2002.

[Gol84]   A. Goldberg. *Smalltalk-80. The Interactive Programming Environment*.
            Addison-Wesley, Reading, 1984.

[Gol91]   Ch. F. Goldfarb. HyTime: A Standard for Structured Hypermedia
            Exchange. *IEEE Computer*, 24(8):81–84, August 1991.

[Goo73]   N. Goodman. *Sprachen der Kunst. Ein Ansatz zu einer Symboltheorie*.
            Suhrkamp, Frankfurt am Main, 1973. Original: Languages of Art. An
            approach to a Theory of Symbols. The Bobbs-Merrill Company Inc.
            1968.

[GRG95]   M. Ghandi, E. Robertson, and D. Gucht. Modelling and querying primi-
            tives for digital media. In *IEEE Int. WS on MMDBMSs*, pages 82–89, Los
            Alamitos, CA, April 1995. IEEE Computer Society Press.

[Gro96]   Bloor Research Group. Illustra and Informix. Bloor Research Group,
            1996.

[Gru89]   J. Grudin. The case against user interface consistency. *Communications of
            the ACM*, 32(10):1164–1173, October 1989.

[GS90]   P. Gloor and N. Streitz. *Hypertext and Hypermedia*. Springer-Verlag,
            1990. Informatik Fachberichte 249.

[Gui86]   Apple Human Interface Guidelines. *The Apple Desktop Interface*. Read-
            ing, MA, 1986.

[GWJ91]   A. Gupta, T. Weymouth, and R. Jain. Semantic queries with pictures: the VIMSYS model. In G. M. Lohman, A. Sernadas, and R. Camps, editors, *Proceedings of Int. Conf. Very Large Data Bases*, pages 69–79, Barcelona, Spain, 1991. Morgan Kaufmann.

[Ham95]   V. Hammer. *Sicherheitsinfrastrukturen - Gestaltungsvorschläge für Technik, Organisation und Recht*. Springer-Verlag, Berlin Heidelberg, 1995.

[Har89]   L. Hardman. Evaluating the Usability of the Glasgow Online Hypertext. *Hypermedia*, 1(1):34–63, 1989.

[Har96]   R. L. Harris. *Information graphics: a comprehensive illustrated reference*. Management Graphics, Atlanta, 1996.

[Has95]   J. Hasebrook. *Multimedia-Psychologie*. Spektrum Akademischer Verlag, Heidelberg, Berlin, Oxford, 1995.

[HB01]   T. Henderson and S. N. Bhatti. Modelling user behaviour in networked games. In *Proceedings of the 9th ACM International Conference on Multimedia 2001*, pages 212–220, Ottawa, Canada, 2001.

[HBG98]   H. Hohl, H.-D. Böcker, and R. Gunzenhäuser. *Adaptive Hypertext and Hypermedia*, chapter Hypadapter: An Adaptive Hypertext System for Exploratory Learning and Programming . Kluwer Academic Publishers, 1998.

[HEG98]   F. Hartung, P. Eisert, and B. Girod. Digital Watermarking of MPEG-4 Facial Animation Parameters. *Computers & Graphics (Special issue on "Data Security in Image Communication and Networks")*, 22(3), 1998.

[Her90]   R. G. Herrtwich. Time Capsules: An Abstraction for Access to Continuous-Media Data. In *IEEE Real-Time Systems Symposium*, pages 11–20, Orlando, Florida, December 1990.

[HG97a]   F. Hartung and B. Girod. Digital Watermarking of MPEG-2 Coded Video in the Bitstream Domain. In *Proceedings ICASSP 97, Volume 4*, number April, pages 2621–2624, Munich, Germany, 1997.

[HG97b]   F. Hartung and B. Girod. Einbettung digitaler Wasserzeichen in MPEG-2 codierte Videosequenzen. In *Proceedings 7. Dortmunder Fernsehseminar*, Dortmund, Germany, October 1997.

[HGP98]   P. Halvorsen, V. Goebel, and T. Plagemann. Q-l/mrp: A buffer manage-
           ment mechanism for qos support in a multimedia dbms. In *Proceedings of
           1998 IEEE International Workshop on Multimedia Database Manage-
           ment Systems (IW-MMDBMS'98)*, pages 162–171, Dayton, Ohio, USA,
           August 1998.

[HHN86]   E.L. Hutchins, J.D. Hollan, and D.A. Norman. *User-Centered System
           Design: New Perspectives in Human-Machine Interaction* , chapter Direct
           manipulation interfaces, pages 87–124. Hillsdale: Lawrence Erlbaum,
           1986.

[Hoc87]   J. Hochuli. Das Detail in der Typografie. *Compugraphic*, 1987.

[Hof91]   M. Hoffman. *Benutzerunterstützung in Hypertextsystemen durch privated
           Kontexte*. PhD thesis, Naturwissenschaftliche Fakultät der Technischen
           Universität Carolo-Wilhelmina, Braunschweig, Germany, 1991.

[Hoh93]   S. Hohoff. Produkthaftung, Urheberrecht, Datenschutz in Industrie und
           EDV. Technical report, Roentgen Software GmbH, Freiburg im Breisgau,
           1993.

[Hol97]   W. Holfelder. Interactive remote recording and playback of multicast vid-
           eoconferences. In *Proceedings of 4th International Workshop on Interac-
           tive Distributed Multimedia Systems and Telecommunication Services
           (IDMS 1997)*, September 1997.

[HR89]   G. Rainer Hofmann and K. Reichenberger. Realismus als eine Kategorie
           technischer Bildqualität? In Manfred Paul, editor, *Proceedings des 19.
           Jahrestages der GI, Bd I*, pages 486–496, Heidelberg, 1989. Springer.

[HSDK+03] Stefan Hoermann, Cornelia Seeberg, Luka Divac-Krnic, Oliver Merkel,
           Andreas Faatz, and Ralf Steinmetz. Building Structures of Reusable Edu-
           cational Content Based on LOM. In *Proceedings of The 15th Conference
           On Advanced Information Systems Engineering workshop on Semantic
           Web for Web-based Learning*, June 2003.

[HSF97]   R. Housley, D. Solo, and W. Ford. *509 Certificate and CRL Profile, Inter-
           net Public Key Infrstructure Part I*. IETF PKI Working Group (PXIX),
           Jan 1997.

[IK97]   L. Issing and P. Klimsa. *Information und Lernen mit Multimedia*. Psy-
           chologie Verlags Union, Weinheim, 2nd edition, 1997.

[Joh95]   J.A. Johnson. A comparison of user interfaces for panning on a touch-
           controlled display. In *Proceedings CHI'95*, pages 218–225, 1995.

[Kam97]   T. Kamps. *A Constructive Theory of Diagram Design and its Algorithmic Implementation*. PhD thesis, Dissertation am Fachbereich Informatik der TU-Darmstadt, Darmstadt, Germany, 1997.

[Kap95]   V. Kaptelinin. A comparison of four navigation techniques in a 2d browsing task. In *Proceedings CHI'95*, pages 282–283, 1995.

[KdVB97]   W. Klas, A. de Vries, and C. Breiteneder. *Multimedia Databases in Perspective*, chapter Current and Emerging Applications. Springer-Verlag, London, 1997.

[KFC98]   C. Kaplan, J. Fenwick, and J. Chen. *Adaptive Hypertext and Hypermedia*, chapter Adaptive Hypertext Navigation Based On User Goals and Context . Kluwer Academic Publishers, 1998.

[KFK96]   M. Kuhn, F. Findeiß, and N. Klinnert. *Jugend und Neue Medien*, Formen des Lernens am Computer. A-L-F Verlag, Nürnberg, 1996.

[KJ97]   M. Kutter and F. Jordan. Digital Signatures of Color Images using Amplitude Modulation. In *SPIE-EI97 Proceedings*, 1997.

[KKS96]   V. Kashyap, K.Shah, and A. Sheth. *Issues and Research Directions*, chapter Metadata for Building the Multimedia Patch Quilt MMDBMSs. Springer-Verlag, Berlin-Heidelberg, 1996.

[Kos96]   T. Koschmann. *CSCL: Theory and practice of an emerging paradigm*. Lawrence Erlbaum, Mahwah, NJ, 1996.

[KR95]   T. Kamps and K. Reichenberger. *Designing Interfaces for Hypermedia*, chapter A Dialogue Approach to Graphical Information Access, pages 141–155. Springer-Verlag, Berlin, 1995.

[Kur94]   R. Kuron. Prototypische Implementierung eines wissensbasierten Systems zur Unterstützung der Dokumentgestaltung. In *FOGRA Forschungsbericht Nr. 64.004*, München, 1994.

[KVMW98]   T. Kunkelmann, H. Vogler, M.L. Moschgath, and L. Wolf. Scalable Security Mechanisms in Transport Systems for Enhanced Multimedia Services. In *Proc. 3rd European Conference on Multimedia Applications, Services and Techniques (ECMAST'98)*, Berlin, Germany, 1998.

[KZ95]   E. Koch and J. Zhao. Towards Robust and Hidden Image Copyright Labeling. In *Proceedings of 1995 IEEE Workshop on nonlinear signal and image processing* , pages 452–455, Neos Marmaras, Halkidiki, Greece, June 20-22 1995.

[Leu93]   O. Leu. *Kleine Stilkunde der Typographie* . Bruckmann, München, 1993.

[LG90]   T.D.C. Little and A. Ghafoor. Synchronization and storage models for multimedia objects. *IEEE J. on Selected Areas in Comm*, 8(3):413–427, 1990.

[LG92]   T.D.C. Little and A. Ghafoor. Scheduling of bandwidth constrained multimedia traffic. *Computer Communications*, 15(6):381–387, 1992.

[LKF+02] Q. Liu, D. Kimber, J. Foote, L. Wilcox, and J. S. Boreczk. FlySPEC: a multi-user video camera system with hybrid human and automatic control. In *Proceedings of the 10th ACM International Conference on Multimedia 2002*, pages 484–492, Juan les Pins, France, 2002.

[LM90]   V. Y. Lum and K. Meyer–Wegener. An Architecture for a Multimedia Database Management System Supporting Content Search. In *Proceedings of Conference on Computing and Information*, Niagara Falls, Ontario, Canada, May 1990.

[LN02]   C. L. Lisetti and F. Nasoz. MAUI: a multimodal affective user interface. In *Proceedings of the 10th ACM International Conference on Multimedia 2002*, pages 161–170, Juan les Pins, France, 2002.

[LÖD96]   J. Z. Li, M. T. Özsu, and D.Szafron. Spatial reasoning rules in multimedia management system. In *Proceedings of International Conference on Multimedia Modelling*, pages 119–133, Toulouse, France, November 1996.

[LOP94]   A. Laursen, J. Olkin, and M. Porter. Providing consumer based interactive access to multimedia data. In *Proc. ACM SIGMOD*, pages 470–477. Minneapolis, May 1994.

[LÖSO97] J. Z. Li, M. T. Özsu, D. Szafron, and V. Oria. MOQL: A Multimedia Object Query Language. In *Proceedings of Third International Workshop on Multimedia Information Systems*, Como, Italy, September 1997.

[LPC90]   L. Ludwig, N. Pincever, and M. Cohen. Extending the Notion of a Window System to Audio. *IEEE Computer*, 23(8):66–72, August 1990.

[LR95]   M. Löhr and T.C. Rakow. Audio support for an object-oriented database management system. *Multimedia Systems*, 3, 1995. Special Issue on MMDBMSs.

[Mas87]   Y. Masunaga. Multimedia databases: A formal framework. In *Proc. IEEE CS Office Automation Symp.*, pages 36–45, Los Alamitos, CA, April 1987. IEEE Computer Society Press.

[ME97]   M. Müller and A. Everts. Interactive image retrieval by means of abductive inference. In *Proceedings of the 5th Conference: Computer-Assisted Information Searching on Internet (RIAO 1997)*, pages 450–466, Montreal, Canada: McGill University, June 25-27 1997.

[Mey91]   K. Meyer-Wegener. *Multimedia Datenbanken*. B. G. Teubner, Stuttgart, 1991.

[Mey97]   B. Meyer. *Object-oriented software construction*. Prentice Hall, 2nd edition, 1997.

[MG94]   J. Meyer and F. Gadegast. Sicherheitsmechanismen für Multimediadaten am Beispiel MPEG-1 Video. Technical report, TU Berlin, 1994.

[MHE93]   MHEG. *Information Technology – Coded Representation of Multimedia and Hypermedia Information (MHEG), Part 1: Base notation (ASN.1)*. Committee draft ISO/IEC CD 13522-1, June 1993. ISO/IEC JTC1/SC29/ WG12.

[MHS97]   G. Mark, J. Haake, and N. Streitz. Hypermedia use in group work: Changing the product, process, and strategy. *Computer Supported Cooperative Work: The Journal of Collaborative Computing*, 6:327–368, 1997.

[MNO+96]   Cliff Martin, P. S. Narayanan, Banu Ozden, Rajeev Rastogi, and Avi Silberschatz. The Fellini Multimedia Storage Server. In *IEEE Multimedia Systems Conference*, pages 117–146, 1996.

[MR97]   U. Marder and G. Robbert. The KANGAROO Project. In *Proc. 3rd Int. Workshop on Multimedia Information Systems*, pages 54–57, Como, Italy, 1997.

[MS95]   T.B. Maples and G.A. Spanos. Performance Study of a Selective Encryption Scheme for the Security of Networked Real-time Video. In *Proc. 4th International Conference on Computer and Communications*, Las Vegas, NV, 1995.

[MS96]   S. Marcus and V.S. Subrahmanian. *MMDBMSs, Issues and Research Directions*, chapter Towards a Theory of MMDBMSs MMDBMSs. Springer- Verlag, Berlin-Heidelberg, 1996.

[MS97]   S. McCanne and B. Smith. Toward a common infrastructure for multimedia-networking middleware. In *Proceedings of NOSSDAV 97*, 1997.

[Mye90]   B. Myers. All the widgets. *ACM SIGGRAPH Video Review*, 57, 1990.

[Nar96]   A. Narasimhalu. Multimedia databases. *Multimedia Systems*, 5(4):226–249, Oct 1996.

[Nie90]   J. Nielsen. *Hypertext and Hypermedia*. Academic Press, 1990.

[NS95]   K. Nahrstedt and J. M. Smith. The QoS Broker. *IEEE Multimedia*, 2(1):53–67, Spring 1995.

[Nyk97]   O. Nykänen. Work in Progress: User modeling in WWW with prerequisite graph model in Adaptive Systems and User Modeling on the World Wide Web. In *Workshop Proceedings, 6th International Conference on User Modeling*, Cagliari, Italien, June 1997.

[ÖHK96]   G. Özsoyoglu, V. Hakkoymaz, and J. D. Kraft. Automating the assembly of presentations from multimedia databases. In *Proc. 12th IEEE Int. Conf. on Data Engineering*, pages 593–601, New Orleans, Lo, USA, 1996.

[ÖIS+97]   M. T. Özsu, P. Iglinski, D. Szafron, S. El-Medani, and M. Junghanns. An Object-Oriented SGML/HYTIME Compliant Multimedia Database Management System. In *Fifth ACM International Multimedia Conference (ACM Multimedia 1997*, pages 239–249, Seattle, WA, November 1997.

[OMA97]   R. Ohbuchi, H. Masuda, and M. Aono. Embedding Data in 3D Models. In *Interactive Distributed Multimedia Systems and Telecommunication Services, 4th International Workshop, IDMS'97*, Darmstadt, 1997. Springer-Verlag, Berlin-Heidelberg.

[OÖL+95]   V. Oria, M.T. Özsu, L. Liu, X. Li, J.Z. Li, Y. Niu, and P. Iglinski. Modelling Images for Content-Based Queries: The DISIMA Approach. In *Second International Conference on Visual Information Systems*, San Diego, CA, December 1995.

[Org86]   International Standard Organization. *Information Processing – Standard Generalized Markup Language*. ISO, Genf, 1986.

[Org92]   International Standard Organization. *Hypermedia/Time-based Document Structuring Language (HyTime)*. ISO/IEC, IS10744 edition, 1992.

[Org96]   International Standards Organization. Information technology- generic coding of moving pictures and associated audio information (mpeg2), part2: Video. International Standard ISO/IEC IS 13818, 1996. ISO IEC 1.

[OW98]   T. Oberle and M. Wessner. *Der Nürnberger Trichter — Computer machen Lernen leicht!?* . Leuchtturm, Alsbach/Bergstraße, 1998.

[PAK98]   F.A.P. Petitcolas, R. J. Anderson, and M. G. Kuhn. Attacks on copyright marking systems. In *Second Workshop on Information Hiding*, Portland, Oregon, USA, 14-17 April 1998.

[Pal81]   S. E. Palmer. *Computing and categorization* , chapter Aspects of Repre-
            sentation, pages 259–303. Hillsdale, New York: Earlbaum, 1981.

[PB97]   L. Pesin and P. Brusilovsky. SQL Web-Tutor in Adaptive Systems and
            User Modeling on the World Wide Web. In *Workshop Proceedings, 6th
            International Conference on User Modeling*, Cagliari, Italien, June 1997.

[PCS95]   C. Plaisant, D. Carr, and B. Shneiderman. Image browser taxonomy and
            guidelines for designers. *IEEE Software*, pages 21–31, March 1995.

[Per97]   J. Perl, editor. *Informatik im Sport*. Verlag Karl Hofmann, Schorndorf,
            1997.

[Pfi96]   B. Pfitzmann. Information Hiding Terminilogy. In *Proc. of Information
            Hiding, First International Workshop*, Cambridge, U.K, 1996.

[PHR97]   A. Perrig, A. Herrigel, and J. Ruanaidh. Copyright Protection Environ-
            ment for Digital Images. *Verläßliche IT-Systeme: Zwischen Key Escrow
            und elektronischem Geld, DuD Fachbeiträge, Vieweg-Verlag*, pages 1–16,
            1997.

[Pit96]   I. Pitas. A Method for Signature casting on Digital Images. In *Proc. of the
            IEEE Int. Conf. on Image Processing, ICIP-96*, Lausanne, Switzerland,
            1996.

[PSR93]   K. Patel, B.C. Smith, and L.A. Rowe. Performance of a Software MPEG
            Video Decoder. In *Proc. ACM Multimedia*, Anaheim, CA, 1993.

[PSW01]   C. Poellabauer, K. Schwan, and R. West. Coordinated CPU and event
            scheduling for distributed multimedia applications. In *Proceedings of the
            9th ACM International Conference on Multimedia 2001*, pages 231–240,
            Ottawa, Canada, 2001.

[PU03]   A. Pommer and A. Uhl. Selective encryption of wavelet-packet encoded
            image data: efficiency and security. *ACM Springer Multimedia Systems*,
            9(3):279–287, 2003.

[PWP90]   B. Pfitzmann, M. Waidner, and A. Pfitzmann. Rechtssicherheit trotz Ano-
            nymität in offenen digitalen Systemen. Technical report, Fakultät für
            Informatik der Universität Karlsruhe, Institut für Rechnerentwurf und
            Fehlertoleranz, 1990.

[QN97]   L. Qiao and K. Nahrstedt. A New Algorithm for MPEG Video Encryp-
            tion. In *Proc. 1st International Conference on Imaging Science, Systems
            and Technology*, Las Vegas, NV, 1997.

[RBCD91]   L. Ruston, G. Blair, G. Coulson, and N. Davies. A Tale of Two Architectures. In *2nd International Workshop on Network and Operating System Support for Digital Audio and Video*, Heidelberg, Germany, November 1991.

[RDF97]   K. Rothermel, G. Dermler, and W. Fiederer. QoS Negotiation and Resource Reservation for Distributed Multimedia Applications. In *Proc. 4th IEEE Int. Conf. on Multimedia Computing and Systems*, IEEE Computer Society Press, pages 319–325. Ottawa, Ontario, Canada, 1997.

[Rei95]   U. Reimers. *Digitale Fernsehtechnik: Datenkompression und Übertragung für DVB*. Springer-Verlag, Heidelberg, 1995.

[RHGL02]   Y. Rui, L. He, A. Gupta, and Q. Liu. Building an intelligent camera management system. In *Proceedings of the 9th ACM International Conference on Multimedia 2001*, pages 2–11, Ottawa, Canada, 2002.

[RK95]   J.A. Rody and A. Karmouch. A remote presentation agent for multimedia datbases. In *Proc. of the IEEE Int. Conference on Multimedia Computing Systems 1995*, pages 223–230, Washington DC, VA, USA, 1995.

[RK97]   K. Reichenberger and J. Kleinz. APALO - Ein Modell typographischer Gestaltung und seine Implementierung. In K. Eickemeyer, editor, *Technische Information in Elektronischen Medien, Proceedings der Fachtagung 1997*, pages 239–250, Lübeck, 1997. Schmidt-Römhild.

[RKKB98]   K. Reichenberger, T. Kamps, J. Kleinz, and J. Bateman. Communicative goal-driven NL generation and data-driven graphics generation: an architectural synthesis for multimedia page generation. In *submitted to International Workshop on Natural Language Generation*, 1998.

[RKN96]   T.C. Rakow, W. Klas, and E. J. Neuhold. Research on MMDBMSs at GMD-IPSI. *IEEE Multimedia Newsletter*, 4(1):40–45, 1996.

[RM93]   T. C. Rakow and P. Muth. The v3 video server-managing analog and digital video clips. In *Proceedings ACM SIGMOD'93*, pages 556–557, Washington DC, 1993.

[RP97]   J. J.K. O Ruanaidh and Th. Pun. Rotation, Scale and Translation Invariant Digital Image Watermarking. *Signal Processing*, January 1997.

[RS92]   L.A. Rowe and B.C. Smith. A continuous media player. In *Proc. of the Third Int. Workshop on Network and Operating System Support for Digital Audio and Video*, pages 237–249, La Jolla, CA, USA, 1992. LNCS 712, Springer.

[RVT96]   S. Roa, H. Vin, and A. Tarafdar. Comparative evaluation of server-push and client-pull architectures for multimedia servers. In *Proc. of the Fifth International Workshop on Network and Operating System Support of Digital Audio and Video (NOSSDAV'96)*, pages 45– 48. Springer-Verlag, 1996.

[SC96]   Schneider and S.-F. Chang. A Robust Content Based Digital Signature For Image Authentication. In *Proc. of International Conference on Image Processing*, pages 1–4, June 1996.

[SCF96]   H. Schulzrinne, S. Casner, and R. Frederick. *RTP: A Transport Protocol for Real-Time Applications* , 1996. Request for Comments: 1889.

[Sch94]   J. Schwenk. Sicherheit von Pay-TV-Systemen. Technical report, Deutsche Telekom AG, Highlights aus der Forschung, 1994.

[Sch96]   B. Schneier. *Angewandte Kryptography: Protokolle, Algorithmen und Sourcecode in C*. Addison-Wesley, Bonn, 1996.

[Sch97]   R. Schulmeister. *Grundlagen hypermedialer Lernsysteme*. Oldenbourg Verlag, München Wien, 1997.

[Sch03]   Markus Schumacher. *Security Engineering with Patterns - Origins, Background and New Applications*. Lecture Notes in Computer Science (LNCS), LNCS 2754. Springer Verlag, August 2003. PhD thesis.

[SF92]   R. Steinmetz and Ch. Fritsche. Abstractions for Continuous Media Programming. *Computer Communication*, 15(4), July 1992.

[SGH98]   N. Streitz, J. Geißler, and T. Holmer. Roomware for cooperative buildings: Integrated design of architectural spaces and information spaces. In *Proceedings of the First International Workshop on Cooperative Buildings (CoBuild'98)*, pages 4–21, Darmstadt, Germany, February 1998.

[SGHH94]   N.A. Streitz, J. Geißler, J. M. Haake, and J. Hol. Dolphin: Integrated meeting support across liveboards, local and remote desktop environments. In *Proceedings of the 1994 ACM Conference on Computer Supported Cooperative Work (CSCW '94)*, pages 345–358, Chapel Hill, N.C., October 1994.

[Shn97]   B. Shneiderman. *Designing the User Interface*. Addison Wesley, 3 edition, 1997.

[SHRS90]   Ralf Steinmetz, Reinhard Heite, Johannes Rückert, and Bernd Schöner. Compound Multimedia Objects - Integration into Network and Operating Systems. In *International Workshop on Network and Operating System Support for Digital Audio and Video, International Computer Science Institute, Berkeley, CA, USA*, November 1990.

[SIK+82]   D.C. Smith, C. Irby, R. Kimball, B. Verplank, and E. Harslem. Designing the star user interface. *BYTE*, pages 242–282, April 1982.

[SM92]   R. Steinmetz and T. Meyer. Multimedia Synchronization Techniques: Experiences based on Different System Structures. In *Proceedings of 4th IEEE ComSoc International Workshop on Multimedia Communications*, pages 305 –314, Monterey, CA, April 1992.

[SMW95]   R. Staehli, D. Maier, and J. Walpole. Device and data independence for multimedia presentations. *ACM Computing Surveys, Special Issue on Multimedia Systems - Symposium on Multimedia*, 27(4):640–642, 1995.

[SN95]   R. Steinmetz and K. Nahrstedt. Resource management in networked multimedia systems. *IEEE Computer*, pages 52–63, 1995.

[SRH97]   N. Streitz, P. Rexroth, and T. Holmer. Does roomware matter? Investigating the role of personal and public information devices and their combination in meeting room collaboration. In *Proceedings of the European Conference on Computer-Supported Cooperative Work (E-CSCW'97).*, pages 297 – 312, Lancaster, UK, September 1997.

[SRH98]   N. Streitz, P. Rexroth, and T. Holmer. *Groupware und organisatorische Innovation (D-CSCW'98).* , chapter Anforderungen an interaktive Kooperationslandschaften für kreatives Arbeiten und erste Realisierungen. Teubner, Stuttgart, 1998.

[SSFS99]   Achim Steinacker, Cornelia Seeberg, Stephan Fischer, and Ralf Steinmetz. Multibook: Metadata for the Web. In *2nd International Conference on New Learning Technologies, Bern, Switzerland*, pages 16–24, August 99.

[Sta95]   W. Stallings. *Sicherheit im Datennetz* . Prentice Hall Verlag GmbH, 1995.

[Ste02]   Achim Steinacker. *Medienbausteine für web-basierte Lernsysteme*. PhD thesis, Darmstadt University of Technology, Darmstadt, 2002.

[Sto96]   D. Storck. A new approach to integrity of digital images. In *Proc. of IFIP 1996 World Conference - Mobile Communication*, Canberra, 1996.

[Str97]   T. H. Strömer. *Gesetz zur digitalen Signatur (Signaturgesetz - SigG)*, 1997. http://www.netlaw.de/gesetze/sigg.htm, Gesetzessammlung Online-Recht netlaw.de .

[SU97]   J. . Schwenk and J. Ueberberg. Tracing traitors using finite geometries. Technical report, Deutsche Telekom AG, 1997.

[Sut63]   I.E. Sutherland. Sketchpad: a man-machine graphical communication system. Technical Report 296, MIT Technical Report, 1963.

[SW96]   M. Specht and G. Weber. Episodic adaptation in learning environments. In *Proceedings of the European Conference on Artificial Intelligence in Education*, Lisbon, Portugal, September 1996.

[Tan96]   L. Tang. Methods for Encrypting and Decrypting MPEG Video Data Efficiently. In *Proc. 4th ACM International Multimedia Conference*, Boston, MA, 1996.

[TK96a]   H. Thimm and W. Klas. ?-sets for optimized reactive adaptive playout management in distributed MMDBMSs. In *Proc. 12th IEEE Int. Conf. on Data Engineering*, pages 584–592, New Orleans, LO, USA, 1996.

[TK96b]   H. Thimm and W. Klas. *MMDBMSs, Design and Implementation Strategies*, chapter Playout Management in MMDBMSs. Kluwer Academic Publishers, Dortrecht/London, 1996.

[TK96c]   H. Thimm and W. Klas. *Playout Management in MMDBMSs MMDBMSs, Design and Implementation Strategies*. Kluwer Academic Publishers, Boston/Dortrecht/London, 1996.

[TKW+96]   H. Thimm, W. Klas, J. Walpole, C. Pu, and C. Cowan. Managing adaptive presentation executions in distributed MMDBMSs. In *Proc. IEEE Int. WS on MMDBMSs*, pages 152–159, Blue Mountain Lake, NY, USA, 1996. IEEE Computer Society Press.

[VB96]   M. Vazirgiannis and S. Boll. Events in interactive multimedia applications: Modelling and implementation design. In *IEEE International Conference on Multimedia Computing and Systems*, Ottawa, Ontario, Canada, June 3-6 1996.

[VKBG95]   A. Vogel, B. Kerherve, G. Bochmann, and J. Gecsei. Distributed multimedia and QOS: A survey. *IEEE Multimedia Systems Journal*, pages 10–19, 1995.

[VM01]   J. Vogel and M. Mauve. Consistency control for distributed interactive media. In *Proceedings of the 9th ACM International Conference on Multimedia 2001*, pages 221–230, Ottawa, Canada, 2001.

[VR96]   H. Vin and V. Rangan. *Multimedia Systems and Techniques*, chapter Multimedia Storage Systems. Kluwer Academic Publishers, 1996.

[VVVV96]   N. G. Venkat, Raghavan V. Vijay, and K. Vanapipat. *Applications MMDBMSs*, chapter A Unified Approach to Data Modelling and Retrieval for a Class of Image Database. Springer-Verlag, Berlin- Heidelberg, 1996.

[Wat87]   H. Watanabe. Integrated Office Systems: 1995 and Beyond. *IEEE Communication Magazine*, 25(12):74–80, December 1987.

[WF97]   Wilberg and Forsmann. *Lesetypographie*. Mainzer Presse, 1997.

[WGN02]   D. Wichadakul, X. Gu, and K. Nahrstedt. A programming framework for quality-aware ubiquitous multimedia applications. In *Proceedings of the 10th ACM International Conference on Multimedia 2002*, pages 631–640, Juan les Pins, France, 2002.

[WK87]   D. Woelk and W. Kim. Multimedia information management in an object oriented database system. In *Proc. of the 13th VLDB Conference*, pages 319–329, 1987.

[XF02]   C. Xu and D. D. Feng. Robust and efficient content-based digital audio watermarking. *ACM Springer Multimedia Systems*, 8(5):353–368, 2002.

[YLTC96]   Z. Chen Y. Li, S. Tan, and R.H. Campbell. Security Enhanced MPEG Player. In *Proc. IEEE 1st International Workshop on Multimedia Software Development (MMSD'96)*, Berlin, Germany, 1996.

[ZC97]   D. Zhong and S.-F. Chang. Video Object Model and Segmentation for Content-Based Video Indexing. In *IEEE International Conf. on Circuits and Systems*, Hong Kong, June 1997.

[ZF88]   J.E. Ziegler and K.P. Fähnrich. *Handbook of Human-Computer Interaction*, chapter Direct manipulation, pages 123–133. Amsterdam: North-Holland, 1988.

[ZK95]   J. Zhao and E. Koch. Embedding Robust Labels Into Images For Copyright Protection. In *Proc. of the International Congress on Intellectual Property Rights for Specialized Information, Knowledge and New Technologies*, pages 242–251, Vienna, Munich, 1995. R. Oldenbourg.

Index

Numerics

Printing and Binding: Stürtz AG, Würzburg